"A love story. Yes: this is a love story.
It's about passion, sensual pleasure, deep pulls, lust, fears, yearning hungers. It's about needs so strong they're crippling. It's about saying good-bye to something you can't fathom living without.

I loved the way drink made me feel, and I loved its special power of deflection, its ability to shift my focus away from my own awareness of self and onto something else, something less painful than my own feelings. I loved the sounds of drink: the slide of a cork as it eased out of a wine bottle, the distinct glug-glug of booze pouring into a glass, the clatter of ice cubes in a tumbler. I loved the rituals, the camaraderie of drinking with others, the warming, melting feelings of ease and courage it gave me.

When you love somebody, or something, it's amazing how willing you are to overlook the flaws...I started to notice that tiny blood vessels had burst all along my nose and cheeks. I started to dry-heave in the mornings, driving to work in my car. A tremor in my hands developed, then grew worse, then persisted for longer periods, all day sometimes.

I did my best to ignore all this. I struggled to ignore it, the way a woman hears coldness in a lover's voice and struggles, mightily and knowingly, to misread it."

CAROLINE KNAPP

DRINK-ING

a love story

QUARTET BOOKS

Author's Note

The names and other identifying details of some major and minor characters have been changed to protect individual privacy and anonymity.

First published in Great Britain by Quartet Books Limited in 1996
A member of the Namara Group
27 Goodge Street
London W1P 2LD

Published by arrangement with the Dial Press, an imprint of Dell Publishing, a division of Bantam Doubleday Dell Publishing Group Inc. New York, New York, USA.

A catalogue record for this book is available from the British Library

ISBN 0 7043 8033 1

Printed and bound in Finland by WSOY

For my parents, Jean and Peter Knapp, with love
For Rebecca and Morelli, with gratitude

Acknowledgements

I am indebted beyond words to my agent, Colleen Mohyde of the Doe Coover Agency, and my editor, Susan Kamil of the Dial Press, for bringing this book into being with so much wisdom, enthusiasm, and support.

To Kathleen Jayes and Susan Schwartz of Dial Press, for moral and technical support.

To dear friends, lifelines through this project: Susan Birmingham, Sandra Shea, Beth Wolfensberger, Brucie Harvey, Maureen Dezell, Jane Bambery, Bill Regan, Mary Stavrakas, Glee Garard, Robbyn Issner, and Cary Barbor.

To my guide, David Herzog.

Contents

1   Love   3

2   Double Life I   12

3   Destiny   27

4   Hunger   52

5   In Vodka Veritas   59

6   Sex   71

7   Drinking Alone   94

8   Addiction   111

9   Substitution   122

10   Denial   136

11   Giving Over   152

12   A Glimpse   171

13   Double Life II   175

14   Hitting Bottom   193

15   Help   219

16   Healing   233

Appendix A
Source Notes   255

Appendix B
Where to Get Help   257

About the Author   259

Prologue

I₁ HAPPENED THIS way: I fell in love and then, because the love was ruining everything I cared about, I had to fall out.

This didn't happen easily, or simply, but if I had to pinpoint it, I'd say the relationship started to fall apart the night I nearly killed my oldest friend's two daughters.

I'd been visiting my friend Jennifer over Thanksgiving weekend a few years ago, and we'd all gone for a walk after dinner, she and her husband and the two daughters and me. The kids were five and nine years old, beautiful little blue-eyed girls with freckles and wide grins, and I'd been playing Rambunctious Friend of Mom's. I chased them around, and hoisted them into the air, and then, in a blur of supremely bad judgment, I dreamed up the Double Marsupial Hold.

I put the older girl, Elizabeth, on my back, piggyback, and then I picked up the younger one, Julia, and held her facing me, so that her arms were around my neck and her legs around my waist. I was sandwiched between them, holding 130 pounds of kid. Then I started running across the street, shouting like a sportscaster: "It's the Double Marsupial Hold! They've accomplished the Double Marsupial Hold!" And then I lost my balance.

I flew forward and came crashing down and I still believe it's a miracle that Julia's tiny, five-year-old skull wasn't the first thing to hit the pavement. Somehow, I kept her in my arms and allowed my right leg to take the fall, and I remember hitting the ground and feeling something like a minor explosion in my knee. The kids were okay, but I ended up in the emergency room with a gash on my knee so deep the nurses could see my kneecap.

This is the truth: I was extremely drunk that night and I put those kids in serious jeopardy.

Three months later I quit drinking, beginning the long, slow process of disentangling myself from a deeply passionate, profoundly complex, twenty-year relationship with alcohol.

1 *Love*

I DRANK.

I drank Fumé Blanc at the Ritz-Carlton Hotel, and I drank double shots of Johnnie Walker Black on the rocks at a dingy Chinese restaurant across the street from my office, and I drank at home. For a long time I drank expensive red wine, and I learned to appreciate the subtle differences between a silky Merlot and a tart Cabernet Sauvignon and a soft, earthy Beaucastel from the south of France, but I never really cared about those nuances because, honestly, they were beside the point. Toward the end I kept two bottles of Cognac in my house: the bottle for show, which I kept on the counter, and the real bottle, which I kept in the back of a cupboard beside an old toaster. The level of liquid in the show bottle was fairly consistent, decreasing by an inch or so, perhaps less, each week. The liquid in the real bottle disappeared quickly, sometimes within days. I was living alone at the time, when I did this, but I did it anyway and it didn't occur to me not to: it was always important to maintain appearances.

I drank when I was happy and I drank when I was anxious and I drank when I was bored and I drank when I was depressed, which was often. I started to raid my parents' liquor cabinet the year my father was dying. He'd be in the back of their house in Cambridge, lying in the hospital bed in their bedroom, and I'd steal into the front hall bathroom and pull out a bottle of Old Grand-dad that I'd hidden behind the toilet. It tasted vile—the bottle must have been fifteen years old—but my father was dying, dying very slowly and gradually from a brain tumor, so I drank it anyway and it helped.

My mother found that bottle, empty, that April, the day of my father's funeral. I'd thrown most of the others away but I must have forgotten that one, and she'd discovered it stashed behind the toilet as she was cleaning the front bathroom for guests. I was sitting at the dining-room table and as she walked through the room, the bottle in her hand, she glared at me, a look of profound disappointment. So I lied.

"That was *before*," I said, referring to a promise I'd made her six months before my father died. "Two drinks a day," I'd said. "No more than that. I promise I'll cut down."

I'd made the promise on a Sunday the previous July, in the midst of a pounding hangover. I'd been visiting my parents at their summerhouse on Martha's Vineyard and I'd gotten so drunk the night before, I almost passed out on the sofa, sitting right there next to my mother. I'd done the drinking in secret, of course, stealing off to my bedroom every thirty minutes or so to take a slug off a bottle of Scotch I'd stashed in my bag, and I vaguely remember the end of the night, my words slurring when I tried to talk, my eyelids so droopy I had to strain to keep them open. I was usually more careful than that, careful to walk the line between being drunk enough and too drunk, careful to do most of the serious drinking at the very end of the night, after everyone else had gone to bed. But I slipped up that time and my mother caught me. The next day she asked me to take a walk with her on the beach, an unusual move for my mother, who requested a private audience only when she had something very serious to say. I remember it was a sunny morning, mid-July, with a stiff breeze and hot light, and I remember a feeling of dread and contrition; I was hoping she wouldn't be mad at me.

We made our way down the dirt path that led from our house

to Menemsha Pond, a blue arc of water at the bottom of the hill, and then we walked for a while in silence. Finally she said, "I need to talk to you. I'm very worried about your drinking."

I said, "I know." I walked beside her, keeping my eyes on my feet in the sand, afraid that if I looked up I'd bump too abruptly into a truth I didn't really want to see. I added, softly, "I am too." I could tell from her tone that she wasn't angry, just worried, and I had to admit to her: I was too. Sort of.

We walked some more. She said, "This is very serious. It's more serious than smoking."

My mother was the sort of person who chose her words with the utmost care, and I understood that a wealth of meanings ran beneath that simple phrase: *more serious than smoking.* Smoking caused cancer, a disease that was killing my father, that had killed several women in her family, that would kill her just a few years later. She understood that drinking was more dangerous and she understood why: smoking could ruin my body; drinking could ruin my mind and my future. It could eat its way through my life in exactly the same way a physical cancer eats its way through bones and blood and tissue, destroying everything.

"It *really is* serious," she said.

I kept my head lowered. "I know."

And I meant it, at least just then. There are moments as an active alcoholic where you *do* know, where in a flash of clarity you grasp that alcohol is the central problem, a kind of liquid glue that gums up all the internal gears and keeps you stuck. The pond was beautiful that day, rippled and sparkling, turning the sand a deep sienna where it lapped against the shore, and for an instant, I did know, I could see it: I was thirty-three and I was drinking way too much and I was miserable, and there had to be a connection.

My mother was such a gentle woman. She said, "What can I do to help you? I'll do anything I can," and that's when I made the promise.

I looked out across the pond, not wanting to look her in the eyes. "I don't know," I said. "I know I have to deal with it." I told her I'd look into Alcoholics Anonymous. I said, "In the meantime I'll cut down. Two drinks a day. No more than that. I promise."

I'd meant it. That afternoon I took the ferry from Martha's Vineyard to Woods Hole, en route back to Boston where I lived, and I remember sitting there on the boat, vaguely nauseated, my head still aching from the night before. I wanted a beer, just one beer to help ease the headache, and I debated with myself about that for several long minutes: Shouldn't I prove to myself that I could go a day—just one simple day—without a drink? Shouldn't I? The ninety-minute ride to Boston loomed ahead. The sky was clear, with the sharp light of late afternoon, and people wearing windbreakers and sweatshirts and sunglasses lolled on the deck in canvas chairs, sipping Budweiser and Michelob Light from tall plastic cups.

I had the beer. And then, when I got back to my apartment, I had a little wine with dinner. Just a little: two glasses, but they were small ones, so I considered them half-glasses and counted them as one. From that point on, though, I was always very careful around my mother—careful not to drink more than two glasses of anything in front of her, careful never to call her when I was drunk—but I didn't keep the promise.

And that's how it works. Active alcoholics try and active alcoholics fail. We make the promises and we really do try to stick with them and we keep ignoring the fact that we can't do it, keep rationalizing the third drink, or the fourth or fifth. *Just today. Bad day. I deserve a reward. I'll deal with it tomorrow.*

A few weeks after the walk with my mother, I read a book that mentioned a test people could take in order to determine whether or not they're alcoholics. The test involved setting limits: three drinks a day for six months, no more, no less, and no variation no matter what the circumstances. Someone dies, you still don't have more than three. You get fired from your job, just three. Weddings, funerals, celebrations, disasters—it doesn't matter. I can't even remember how many times I took that test—dozens of times. I also can't remember consciously deciding to stray from the rule or to cheat, to have the fourth glass of wine, or to pour the three glasses in such enormous goblets that I might as well have had six.

I just couldn't do it. Alcohol had become too important. By the end it was the single most important relationship in my life.

A love story. Yes: this is a love story.

It's about passion, sensual pleasure, deep pulls, lust, fears, yearning hungers. It's about needs so strong they're crippling. It's about saying good-bye to something you can't fathom living without.

I loved the way drink made me feel, and I loved its special power of deflection, its ability to shift my focus away from my own awareness of self and onto something else, something less painful than my own feelings. I loved the sounds of drink: the slide of a cork as it eased out of a wine bottle, the distinct glug-glug of booze pouring into a glass, the clatter of ice cubes in a tumbler. I loved the rituals, the camaraderie of drinking with others, the warming, melting feelings of ease and courage it gave me.

Our introduction was not dramatic; it wasn't love at first sight, I don't even remember my first taste of alcohol. The relationship developed gradually, over many years, time punctuated by separations and reunions. Anyone who's ever shifted from general affection and enthusiasm for a lover to outright obsession knows what I mean: the relationship is just there, occupying a small corner of your heart, and then you wake up one morning and some indefinable tide has turned forever and you can't go back. You *need* it; it's a central part of who you are.

I used to drink with a woman named Elaine, a next-door neighbor of mine. I was in my twenties when we met and she was in her late forties, divorced and involved with a married man whom she could not give up. Elaine drank a lot, more than I did, and she drank especially hard when the relationship with the married man got rocky, which was often. She drank beer and vodka, and she'd call me up on bad nights and ask me to come over. The beer made her overweight and the vodka made her sloppy, and she'd sit on her sofa with a bottle and cry, her face stained with tears and mascara. I used to sit there and think, *Whoa*. I'd sympathize and listen and say all the things girlfriends are supposed to say, but inside I'd be shaking my head, knowing she was a wreck and knowing on some level that the booze made her that way, that the liquor fueled her obsession for the married man, fueled her tears, fueled her hopelessness and inability to change.

But some small part of me (it got larger over the years) was always secretly relieved to see Elaine that way: a messy drunk's an ugly thing, particularly when the messy drunk's a woman, and I could compare myself to her and feel superiority and relief. I wasn't *that* bad; no way I was *that* bad.

And I wasn't that bad. I had lots of rules. I never drank in the morning and I never drank at work, and except for an occasional mimosa or Bloody Mary at a weekend brunch, except for a glass of white wine (maybe two) with lunch on days when I didn't have to do too much in the afternoon, except for an occasional zip across the street from work to the Chinese restaurant with a colleague, I always abided by them.

For a long time I didn't even need rules. The drink was there, always just there, the way food's in the refrigerator and ice is in the freezer. In high school the beer just appeared at parties, lugged over in cases by boys in denim jackets and Levi's corduroys. In my parents' house the Scotch and the gin sat in a liquor cabinet, to the left of the fireplace in the living room, and it just emerged, every evening at cocktail hour. I never saw it run out and I never saw it replenished either: it was just there. In college, of course, it was there all the time—in small, squat refrigerators in dorm rooms, in kegs at parties, in chilled draft glasses on tavern table-tops—and by the time I graduated, by the time I was free to buy alcohol and consume it where and when I wanted, drinking seemed as natural as breathing, an ordinary part of social convention, a simple prop.

Still, I look in the mirror sometimes and think, What happened? I have the CV of a model citizen or a gifted child, not a common drunk. Hometown: Cambridge, Massachusetts, backyard of Harvard University. Education: Brown University, class of '81, magna cum laude. Parents: esteemed psychoanalyst (dad) and artist (mom), both devoted and insightful and keenly intelligent.

In other words, nice person, from a good, upper-middle-class family. I look and I think, What *happened?*

Of course, there is no simple answer. Trying to describe the process of becoming an alcoholic is like trying to describe air. It's too big and mysterious and pervasive to be defined. Alcohol is everywhere in your life, omnipresent, and you're both aware and unaware of it almost all the time; all you know is you'd die without it, and there is no simple reason why this happens, no single moment, no physiological event that pushes a heavy drinker across a concrete line into alcoholism. It's a slow, gradual, insidious, elusive *becoming.*

My parents' house on Martha's Vineyard is in the town of Gay Head, on the westernmost side of the island, in a dry town, a forty-minute drive from the nearest liquor store or bar. When I was a teenager, our lack of proximity to alcohol was fine, a fact, something I didn't notice. Then, in my twenties, it became slightly questionable. I'd come for a weekend to visit my parents, and I'd assume my father would have gin for martinis and wine for dinner, and he would, and I'd be somewhat relieved, without really knowing it. And then, after I turned thirty, it became more than questionable; it became a problem, this dry town on Martha's Vineyard, a forty-minute drive from the nearest liquor store.

Somewhere inside I acknowledged that this made me nervous.

Somewhere inside I'd become desperately aware that the last time I was at the house, there was only one bottle of wine for dinner—one bottle to share between four or five people—and that the level of liquid in the gin bottle was dangerously low by the end of the weekend. I'd remember, very clearly, that I'd had to compensate for the lack of wine by returning to that gin bottle several times, surreptitiously, sneaking into the kitchen to top off my drink while the rest of the family sat outside on the porch. In some dark place an anxiety about this festered: I didn't want to be trapped there again with an insufficient supply, but I didn't want to let on that I was anxious about the supply either.

So I'd debate, without even noticing the arguments and counterarguments circling in the back of my mind. Should I show up for the weekend with a case of wine, on the pretext that I'd brought it there "just to have it in the house"? Should I forget about the whole thing and just hope someone else had restocked the liquor cabinet? Should I borrow the car and drive the forty minutes to the liquor store, pretending to be off for a solo trek at the beach? In a back corner of my mind I'd notice that this question of what there was to drink in the house had become a big deal, and that fact would nag at me just a little bit, raising a tiny flag, a question about how much I seemed to need the alcohol. The questions would continue: what to do, how to do it, who'd notice, why didn't anyone else drink the way I did? And after a while these voices would start to feel too big and too confusing and too overwhelming, and in the briefest instant I'd just do it: I'd mentally wash my hands of the whole business, and I'd pick up a bottle of Scotch the day before the trip, and I'd stash it in my weekend bag.

There. Problem solved.

That, of course, is how an alcoholic starts *not* to notice it. *Just this one time.* That's how you put it to yourself: I'll just do it this one time, the same way a jealous woman might pick up the phone at midnight to see if her lover is home, or cruise slowly past his house to check his lights, promising herself that this is the last

time. *I know this is insane, but I'll only do it this once.* I'll just bring
the Scotch this one time because I'm particularly stressed out this
week and I just want to be able to have a Scotch where and when
I want it, okay? It's no big deal: just a little glass in my room
before dinner so I don't have to steal into the kitchen and sneak
one there. Just a little glass so I don't drink up any more of Dad's
liquor. No big deal; it makes *sense*.

And it *would* make sense, in a certain perverse way. There I'd
be, out on the porch on Martha's Vineyard with my family, and
I'd excuse myself for just a minute—just a minute, to go to the
bathroom. Then, on the way to the bathroom, I'd make a quick
detour to my bedroom, and I'd pull the Scotch out from the bag,
and unscrew the cap and take a long slug off the bottle and
swallow. The liquor would burn going down, and the burn would
feel good: it would feel warming and protective; it would feel like
insurance.

Yes: insurance: the Scotch in my bag gave me a measure of
safety. It let me sit at the table during dinner and not obsess
through the whole meal about whether there was enough wine,
whether anyone would notice how fast I slammed down my first
glass, whether or how I could reach for the bottle to refill my glass
without calling too much attention to myself. It let me know I'd
be taken care of when the need became too strong.

When you love somebody, or something, it's amazing how willing
you are to overlook the flaws. Around that same time, in my
thirties, I started to notice that tiny blood vessels had burst all
along my nose and cheeks. I started to dry-heave in the mornings,
driving to work in my car. A tremor in my hands developed, then
grew worse, then persisted for longer periods, all day sometimes.

I did my best to ignore all this. I struggled to ignore it, the way
a woman hears coldness in a lover's voice and struggles, mightily
and knowingly, to misread it.

2 Double Life I

I HOBBLED INTO the newspaper where I worked the Monday after Thanksgiving weekend, my knee swathed in a large white bandage. Marsha, the managing editor, saw me first. She said, "What happened to *you?*" I just rolled my eyes. "Oh. Really *stupid*," I said, and told her about racing around with the kids. I didn't mention that I was drunk and she wouldn't have thought to ask.

The phrase is *high-functioning alcoholic*. Smooth and ordered on the outside; roiling and chaotic and desperately secretive underneath, but not noticeably so, never noticeably so. I remember sitting down in my cubicle that morning, my leg propped up on a chair, and thinking: *I wonder if she knows. I wonder if anyone can tell by looking at me that something is wrong.* I used to wonder that a lot, that last year or two of drinking—*Something is different about me,* I'd think, sitting in an editorial meeting and looking around at everyone else, at their clear eyes and well-rested expressions. *Can anybody see it?* The wondering itself made me anxious, chipping away at the edges of denial.

The fact is, nobody would have known from looking. An outsider walking past my cubicle that morning would have seen a petite woman of thirty-four with long, light brown hair pulled back in a barrette, neat and orderly-looking. Closer inspection would have suggested a perfectionistic, polished exterior, a careful attention to detail: a young woman with well-manicured nails and black leggings and Italian shoes; a daily list of things to do sitting on the desk, written in perfect print, several items already neatly ticked off; a workspace so compulsively tidy that one of my staff writers used to say you could fly a plane over my desk and it would look like a map of the Midwest, everything at perfect right angles. Colleagues saw me as smart and introspective, a little reserved maybe, and a paragon of efficiency at work: organized, professional, productive.

I ran and edited the lifestyle section of *The Boston Phoenix*, a large alternative weekly newspaper, and I wrote a weekly column, one of the paper's most popular features, and I never missed a deadline, not once, not even when my parents were dying. When I finally went into rehab, I told everyone at work I was going off to a spa, two weeks of rest and relaxation and Swedish massage, and no one had any reason not to believe me. I hid it that well. Most high-functioning alcoholics do.

Most are in very good company, too, and lots of it. Functioning alcoholics are everywhere: plugging away at jobs and raising families and standing alongside you in the grocery store. We're often professionals—doctors and lawyers, teachers and politicians, artists and therapists and stockbrokers and architects—and part of what keeps us going, part of what *allows* us to ignore the fact that we're drunk every night and hung over every morning, is that we're so very different from the popular definition of a "real" drunk.

Alcoholic is a nasty word, several decades of education about the disease notwithstanding. Say it out loud and chances are you still get the classic image of the falling-down booze-hound: an older person, usually male, staggering down the street and clutching a brown paper bag. A pathetic image, hopeless and depraved. Or a ludicrous image, a man made funny and stupid by drink: think of Dick Martin, slurring his words on *Laugh-In*, or Otis, the happy drunk on *The Andy Griffith Show*, a precursor to Dudley

Moore's character in the *Arthur* movies. In fact, the low-bottom, skid-row bum is the exception, representing only three to five percent of the alcoholic population, a mere fraction. The vast majority of us are in far earlier stages of the disease: we're early- and midstage alcoholics, and we function remarkably well in most aspects of our lives for many, many years.

My friend Helena completed her Ph.D. in biology while she was actively drinking. My friend Ginny rose up the ranks of a very competitive law firm. My friend Sarah founded and ran a well-known environmental advocacy group. Sometimes, as a way of reminding myself how hidden the symptoms and effects of alcoholism can be, I'll look around an AA meeting and tick off our collective accomplishments: that one was a vice-president at a large financial institution when he bottomed out. That one was the head nurse in a cardiac intensive-care unit. That one had his own architecture firm. That one, his own economics-research company.

These are utterly typical examples: strong, smart, capable people who kept drinking—who put off looking at the dozens of intangible ways alcohol was affecting their lives—precisely because they *were* strong, smart, and capable. In retrospect, a lot of the alcoholics I know are amazed at how much they accomplished in spite of themselves, how effectively they constructed and then hid behind facades of good health and productivity. At the time, they just got through. Just hunkered down and worked and got through the days.

Me too. I wrote a book during my last, most active year of alcoholism. I wrote several award-winning columns. I spent my days in a bustle of focused, highly concentrated activity—editing stories, working with designers, meeting with writers and editors —and only a very particular sort of person (probably another alcoholic) could have peered into that cubicle and realized that, in fact, I was clicking away at my computer with a pounding hangover, or sitting there at the end of the day, my body screaming for a drink.

Or, more to the point, that my life was actually in shambles. By the time I hit bottom, I'd lost both my parents, my father to a brain tumor and my mother to metastatic breast cancer. I was involved with two men—unable to extricate myself from an enormously destructive relationship with an old boyfriend, Julian, and unable to fully involve myself in a more positive relationship with a new boyfriend, Michael. I was living with Michael, still seeing Julian, lying to both men about the other. I was drinking every night, drinking to get drunk, to obliterate.

Perception versus reality. Outside versus inside. I never missed a day of work because of drinking, never called in sick, never called it quits and went home early because of a hangover. But inside I was falling apart. The discrepancy was huge.

On the outside, remarkably, I created an impression of searing honesty. Regular readers of my column had a sense of me as someone who was brutally direct about life's struggles: I wrote long, vivid columns about dealing with my parents' deaths, and I wrote eloquently about the long struggle with anorexia I'd gone through in my twenties, and I channeled boatloads of baggage into humor, into bemused and ironic columns about the young, single life, about the perils of living alone and obsessions with bad men and confusion over what it meant to be a grown-up. My alter ego, the frequent subject of my column, was a tortured and hapless young woman in her thirties named Alice K., who lay in bed at the start of each story literally writhing with anxiety, obsessing about men, chronically stuck in a rut. People at work were forever coming up to me on Thursdays, the day the paper came out, and saying things like "I can't believe how self-revealing you are in your writing," and "How does it feel to spill your guts like that every week?" It was always clear to friends and colleagues that the line between me and Alice K. was very thin, that I, too, felt stuck in a rut, that this character's angst was tied very closely to my own.

What wasn't clear—to colleagues, to me—was how closely linked alcohol was to all that angst, how much I clung to both of them. Once, a reader wrote me and said, "Let's hope you never settle down and get happy. What would you have to *write* about? Would your columns get all warm and fuzzy?"

I chuckled at that, but also took the questions fairly seriously: I think I knew on some level that the drinking and the depression were connected, but I also believed that the undercurrents of despair were somehow central to my work, that drink was an occupational hazard, part of the writer's territory. Tennessee Williams said that he never wrote without first drinking wine. William Styron used liquor, and often, not to help him write but to help him think, a means, he writes, of letting his mind "conceive visions that the unaltered, sober brain has no access to."

I identified with that. I identified with legions of drinking writers: Carson McCullers, Dylan Thomas, Dorothy Parker, and Thomas Wolfe; Eugene O'Neill, William Faulkner, and F. Scott Fitzgerald; Ernest Hemingway, Theodore Roethke, and Jack London. Drinking seemed like part of the turf to me, and there was a hard-edged glamour to writers like that I found deeply attractive. These were dark and tortured souls, artists, people who lived life on a deeper plane than the rest of us, and drinking seemed like a natural outgrowth of their lives and work, both a product of and an antidote to creative angst.

Plus, with rare exceptions, I never expressed the full extent of my own depression. I made jokes out of it, described Alice K. staring at the ceiling in despair, poked fun at her obsessive, overly introspective, fearful nature. When people asked me how it felt to be so "revealing," I'd usually shrug and say something inconsequential, but the honest answer would have been: Well, it feels . . . *incomplete*. Humor, after all, is a classic defense, a foil that allowed me to create an impression of distance and self-irony while keeping the real depths of those feelings carefully tucked away, hidden in the deepest corners of my heart. That's where the truly secretive nature of the high-functioning alcoholic exists, in those deep corners. It's not so much that people like me hide the truth about our drinking from others (which most of us do, and quite effectively); it's that we hide from others (and often from ourselves) the truth about our real selves, about who we really are when we sit in our offices dashing off memos and producing papers and preparing presentations, about what is really churning beneath the surface.

Beneath my own witty, professional façade were oceans of fear, whole rivers of self-doubt. I once heard alcoholism described in an AA meeting, with eminent simplicity, as "fear of life," and that seemed to sum up the condition quite nicely. I, for example, had spent half my professional life as a reporter who lived in secret terror of the most basic aspects of the job, of picking up the phone and calling up strangers to ask questions. Inside, I harbored a long list of qualities that made my own skin crawl: a basic fragility; a feeling of hypersensitivity to other peoples' reactions, as though some piece of my soul might crumble if you looked at me the wrong way; a sense of being essentially inferior and unprotected and scared. Feelings of fraudulence are familiar to scores of people in and out of the working world—the highly effective, well-defended exterior cloaking the small, insecure person inside —but they're epidemic among alcoholics. You hide behind the professional persona all day; then you leave the office and hide behind the drink.

Sometimes, in small flashes, I'd be aware of this. One night after work, on my way to a bar to meet a friend for drinks, a sentence popped into my head. I thought: *This is the real me, this person driving in the car.* I was anxious. My teeth were clenched, partly from spending a long day hunched over the computer and partly from the physical sensation of wanting a drink badly, and I was aware of an undercurrent of fear deep in my gut, a barely definable sensation that the ground beneath my feet wasn't solid or real. I think I understood in that instant that I'd created two versions of myself: the working version, who sat at the desk and pounded away at the keyboard, and the restaurant version, who sat at a table and pounded away at white wine. In between, for five or ten minutes at a stretch, the real version would emerge:

the fearful version, tense and dishonest and uncertain. I rarely allowed her to emerge for long. Work—all that productive, effective, focused work—kept her distracted and submerged during the day. And drink—anesthetizing and constant—kept her too numb to feel at night.

You wouldn't have known that version either. Even if you'd seen me at a party, or drinking my fifth glass of wine in a bar, the only real difference you would have noted was a slight crack in the reserve, a general loosening up. My closest friends used to say they could see it in my eyes, my drunkenness. They could see my eyelids grow heavy and they'd notice a slight retreat, a sense that I'd shut down on some key level. But even if they saw me stagger a bit, or heard me start talking in a voice just a shade louder than normal, most people wouldn't have looked at me and said: *Drunk.* Mostly I got loaded quietly, politely. It was something that took place in my own head.

Superficially, I also amassed plenty of evidence to suggest I was safe, way over on the nonalcoholic side of the population. If you knew me well enough, you could spot a little addictive behavior around the edges—too many cigarettes; too much coffee; a rather obsessive attitude toward *The New York Times* crossword puzzle—but nothing out of line, nothing problematic. Most of the time the public persona was healthy and sociable. I exercised madly. I sat at my desk and ate healthy, low-fat foods for lunch. I had friends and admiring colleagues, a classy little apartment downtown, a casual-chic wardrobe, a good shrink. So there you go: no problem.

Most of the time, that's how I saw it too. Alcoholism, after all, is a progressive illness; it sneaks up on you so subtly, so insidiously, that you honestly don't know you're falling into its grip until long after the fact. If you'd charted my drinking on a graph, you would have seen it creep up very gradually over a long period of years, and you would have seen a host of social factors supporting its rise. Conveniently enough, my twenties coincided with the 1980s, the decade of excess: if the line on my drinking graph began to creep upward, intake and frequency rising, it did so culturally, as well: I had plenty of company. I moved to Boston in the mid-eighties, when I was twenty-five, right around the time fancy restaurants with elaborate wine lists began cropping up all over the city. Everyone drank, or so it seemed, and it seemed utterly normal—utterly normal—to pass a whole evening in a restaurant or a bar, ordering a third or fourth or fifth bottle of Merlot for the table. "Let's go get a drink." "Wanna meet for a drink?" "Let's talk about it over drinks." Those were standard phrases in my circle.

The line on my graph probably took a sharp rise around my thirtieth birthday, right around the time it dipped everywhere else: the early nineties, when everyone quit smoking and turned abstemious. The culture swung in a new direction and I didn't swing with it, and I remember being conscious of that, aware that all of a sudden it was getting chic to stand around at a party and drink Perrier. *Perrier?* I'd stand there clutching my wineglass, trying to scope out the two or three other people in the room who might be sneaking a cigarette in a corner, and regard this new restraint with a cynical eye. *What a stupid trend. What fun is this?*

But alcoholics are masters of denial, and I managed to keep whatever worries I harbored about my own drinking nicely compartmentalized, stashed away on the same shelf in my cubicle where I kept my growing collection of books about addiction. *So, I drink a little too much; it's not really a problem.* I said that to myself often, and I meant it. Real alcoholics drank themselves straight out of jobs: they got loaded at lunch and never came back to the office; they were so hung over they couldn't get to work in the first place; they stashed gin in their desks and received repeated warnings about their failing job performance, and they were finally fired. I wasn't like that, not in the least.

I also had a long list of reasons to drink, a growing list. No one would have begrudged me that. Two major losses in the space of two years. A stressful job: deadlines and responsibilities. A messy romantic life: ambivalent and confused. *So I drink a little too much; it's situational. I deserve it.* I said that to myself, too, with increasing conviction. Stress. Depression. An exceptionally bad day, or week, or month. Too much going on. Need a little relief. *Deserve* it.

That's classic logic among functioning alcoholics: Over time the drink itself becomes the reward, the great compensation for our ability to keep it all together during the day, and to keep it all together so well.

A drinker I know named Mitch says he developed an amazing tolerance for pain during his drinking days. He's a software designer and he could sit in his office and work for ten, twelve, fourteen, sixteen hours in a row without a break, just work and work and work, as long as he knew he could have that drink at the end, as long as he knew the reward was waiting. Me too. I could sit at that computer and crank out words from dawn to dusk, and I always liked drinking best after a really hard, solid day at the desk, a day of blood and sweat on the pages. I'd *earned* it. Times like that, the tension and anxiety I'd feel at the end of the day, the feeling that every one of my cells was crying out for a glass of wine, seemed justifiable and easily explained, a direct result of the daily expenditure of energy. And so the drink seemed justifiable too. *God, I need a drink.* Lots of people say that at the end of a long hard day. Even in the abstemious nineties they say it.

High-level functioning stands in the alcoholic's path like a huge road sign, flashing the message that everything is under control. You're cranking away at work and getting promotions and making money and never missing a deadline. No alcoholics here! It's not possible. Toward the end of my drinking it would occur to me that my professional life managed to move forward precisely *because* it was the one area in my life where I never got drunk. Even with an occasional hangover I was able to grow, able to see my mistakes and learn from them, able to gauge my own limits and to hone my understanding of where further work needed to be done. My vision didn't get muddied in the office in quite the same way it did in my personal life, and it was the one rule I held fast to: no drinking on the job. That's not uncommon among high-functioning alcoholics: drinkers like me tend to expend vast amounts of energy protecting our professional lives, maintaining the illusion that everything is, in fact, just fine. It's part of what keeps us going.

But I began to worry. In the last six months of my drinking I began to see myself plotting more, planning my schedule around drinking in more deliberate ways. I wrote a weekly column and I'd think to myself: *Okay, Wednesday won't be too busy, so I can write all day Wednesday, which means I can't get too drunk on Tuesday*. I had the feeling that I was working my most creative efforts into the margins of things, struggling to make time for them, and that scared me. A month or so before I finally quit, I heard Pete Hamill interviewed on National Public Radio. His memoir, *A Drinking Life*, had just come out and the interviewer asked if his drinking had ever affected his work. Hamill thought for a minute, then said that after a while he got the feeling that he was squeezing his talent through a tube of toothpaste, that his focus and concentration and feeling of literacy all seemed more strained and constricted. I shuddered, hearing that, because I was beginning to feel the same way.

One day (I don't remember exactly when; this sort of thing happened all the time), I went into the ladies' room at work at five or six o'clock and looked at myself in the mirror. I'd been hung over all day, but had worked through it all morning and when the headache hadn't gone away by noon, I left the office and went to get some exercise. That's a pretty common strategy among alcoholic drinkers—sweat away the hangover—and I exercised a lot. I'd taken up sculling on the Charles River, and I went out that day and rowed hard for an hour, six miles. Toward the end the wind picked up and the water got choppy and I flailed along in my little boat—a long, precarious thing, about twelve inches wide and twenty-one feet long—thinking, *I must be nuts*. There I was, sweaty and hung over and literally trying to muscle my body into a different state. It felt like self-punishment and in a way I guess it was.

I'd returned to work that afternoon, gotten some writing done, then started to get ready to leave. My reflection in the mirror looked awful: my skin was pale and my face was drawn and I had large dark circles under my eyes. I had on a scoop-necked sweater and I could see little burst blood vessels all over my chest, red marks that looked like the beginnings of a rash. My twin sister Becca, a doctor, would see those periodically and tell me she thought they were alcohol related, and I always thought, *Nonsense: they're from too much sun, back when I was younger*. In any event, I looked like hell, and somewhere inside I understood that if I kept this up, kept drinking and working and flailing around like this, I'd die, slowly, but literally kill myself.

The truth gnaws at you. In periodic flashes like that I'd be painfully aware that I was living badly, just plain living wrong. But I refused to completely acknowledge or act on that awareness, so the feeling just festered inside like a tumor, gradually eating away at my sense of dignity. You know and you don't know. You know and you *won't* know, and as long as the outsides of your life remain intact—your job and your professional persona—it's very hard to accept that the insides, the pieces of you that have to do with integrity and self-esteem, are slowly rotting away.

That was such a typical day, and such a typical moment of insight, a feeling that surfaces in a second, then gets buried just as fast. I splashed some water on my face, put on some lipstick and some blush, and went back out to the newsroom. "Hey," I said to a reporter named Mark. "Wanna grab a drink across the street?"

"Across the street" meant the Aku-Aku Lounge, which was my favorite bar at the end: exactly twenty-seven steps away from the office, twenty-two if you crossed the street really fast.

The Aku was actually a Chinese restaurant, but the right half of the space was occupied by a bar, and everybody from work drank there, hunkered over tables on pink vinyl-covered chairs. The room was dark, the primary light coming from votive candles in dark red, bowl-shaped glass candleholders, and it was tacky beyond belief: we'd sit at a table and make fun of the neon murals that decorated two sides of the room: neon Polynesian themes, depicting active volcanoes and rivers with bamboo rafts. Ridiculous. Some people drank beer at the Aku, but the real drinkers ordered Johnnie Walker Black on the rocks, which they served in glasses as big as goblets—a hefty two shots for $2.25, one of the best bargains in town.

Some professions seem to invite a lot of drinking, at least in the public mind: along with the angst-ridden artist or writer there's the hard-drinking cop or detective who nearly lost the battle with booze—Captain Furillo on *Hill Street Blues*; or the protagonists in mystery novels by James Lee Burke and Lawrence Block. There's the gin-guzzling salesman, like Jack Lemmon in *Days of Wine and Roses*; and the over-the-top, high-stakes gambler of high finance, like the Michael Keaton character in *Clean and Sober*. These are men's men (and with rare exceptions they're always men), and drink always seemed to me like part of their tough-guy territory, their world, their personae.

And, of course, there are journalists. Pete Hamill epitomized the hard-drinking reporter, and reading his memoir, you can see how naturally and easily he was drawn to drink. You can see him covering fires and murders for the *New York Post*, hunched over a bar with a source, hoisting a cold beer before returning to his typewriter to pound off a good, clean story. You can understand the good times, the role alcohol played: Hamill getting blasted in a beer hall in Brussels, drinking with American paratroopers, and Hamill interviewing John Wayne over glasses of rum in Barcelona Bay, and Hamill drinking beer with the mariachis in the Plaza Garibaldi. You can *feel* it, the heady, exuberant camaraderie of men drinking with men.

None of my colleagues were as tough or hard boiled as Pete Hamill, and neither was the kind of drinking we did at the Aku, but it felt *earned* in the same way. It had a Lou Grant feel: the group of us trooping in after a long day in the office, a handful of us gathering at a table, carping about our jobs and smoking ciga-rettes, letting the tension of the day ease out of our bones. The place was an exercise in sensory overload: a jukebox blared, and a Pac-Man table beeped and hummed, and a giant video screen suspended over one side of the bar showed movies, usually with the volume up way too loud.

For some reason I liked all the competing noises. After a while someone would usually force the bartender to turn down the vol-ume on the movie, or turn it off altogether, and we'd turn our attention to the TV on the other side. I liked that, too, the routine of it. You could sit back and watch the news, or *Wheel of Fortune* or *Jeopardy* after the news, and that way you could float in and out of whatever conversation happened to be going on at the table. The atmosphere was easy and collegial and you could order six drinks in a row there without raising an eyebrow. "You wan one moe?" The waitress was a small-boned Asian woman who didn't speak English very well, and that was pretty much the only question she ever asked. "Wan one moe? Okay." They loved us at the Aku, the waitress and the bartenders, because we'd sit for hours and we always left big tips.

Seeing me in the Aku, nobody would have known this was the place I merely warmed up. Most of the time I'd only stay there for a drink or two and then off I'd go. "Gotta run," I'd say, or "I'm out of here." Then I'd grab my bag and my coat and scoot off into the night, off to my busy life, or so it seemed. At the end I'd become so good at compartmentalizing my drinking that nobody had a clear sense of my true intake, including me half the time. A drink or two at the Aku with work friends. Then dinner at a restaurant with someone else, three or four glasses of wine with a meal, perhaps a glass of brandy afterward. Then home, where the bottle of Cognac lurked beneath the counter, and a bottle of white wine always stood in the refrigerator, cold and dewy and waiting.

I was rarely conscious of this, rarely conscious of how much planning went into the whens and wheres and with-whoms of all that drinking. It was just a drink here and a drink there: so available, so very easy.

The year my father was dying, I'd go to the Aku after work almost every day and have two Johnnie Walker Blacks before going over to the house to see him. The bar was a retreat, a place to hide and fuel up for something difficult. But I started noticing that year that it was getting harder to find a regular group stationed at the Aku, a reliable drinking crew. Several of my drinking companions had gotten married or had kids so they went straight home after work; others had moved on to other jobs; the daily trek across the street began to seem like a less absolute occurrence, as though it had slipped a notch or two on the office priority list. This is a fairly common experience for drinkers: you look up one day and realize you're the only one left in the bar.

So sometimes I'd go to the Aku by myself, sit at the bar, and have a drink alone. I usually tried to look busy and goal-oriented at those times—I'd bring a notebook and make a list of things to do, or I'd check my watch every five minutes, as though I were waiting for someone who was late—but in fact I'd be totally focussed on the drink, melting into the feeling of the Scotch going down, and I'd feel relieved at the solitude, perched there out in the open and hiding at the same time.

Another woman, someone I didn't know, used to sit alone at the bar too. According to the bartender she came in every evening at about five, and she sat at the same barstool, and she drank gin and watched TV. She was always there, and I gather she always stayed until closing. I spoke to her only once, in the ladies' room, on a day when she'd apparently quit her job. She kind of reeled in there, very drunk, and slurred something about quitting that "fucking place, those fucking losers." I was washing my hands and I just looked at her. She stared back at me and said, "Do you know what I *mean?* Am I making myself *clear?*" I had no idea what she was talking about so I just smiled and said, "Oh, yes. Absolutely," then sidled out of the ladies' room and went back to my table.

She was a very reassuring presence to me, this strange woman at the Aku, so obviously a drunk. When a group of us sat at a table near her barstool, we'd glance over at her once in a while and whistle softly: *What a life, huh?* She was far worse than my friend Elaine and far, far worse than me, and so she was very helpful to me for a very long time, symbolizing not what I feared I might become but what, for the moment, I wasn't. My drinking was so social by comparison, so normal. Wasn't it?

I can't say for sure when the drinking shifted from normal to necessary: maybe the year my father got sick, maybe before that. At some point I began to notice how edgy I'd start to get every afternoon around four or five o'clock, and a small part of me began to observe the way I responded. I'd get up from my desk and wander around the office until I found someone who looked about ready to wrap up for the day. I forced a tone of nonchalance. "Any interest in a quick drink at Aku?" "How 'bout a quick drink?" It was always a "quick drink," as if I had things to do, places to rush off to afterward.

I was conscious of this, conscious of the feeling of need behind the words, but I managed to ignore this for a long time. I suppose a part of me meant it—just a quick drink: no big deal. The need, and its intensity, was a secret I kept from everybody, myself included.

3 *Destiny*

ALCOHOL TRAVELS THROUGH families like water over a landscape, sometimes in torrents, sometimes in trickles, always shaping the ground it covers in inexorable ways.

In some families alcohol washes across whole generations, a liquid plague. My friend Abby comes from so many generations of alcoholics she can't count them. An Irish family; the drinking goes all the way back to the potato fields, hundreds of years. Her mother is an alcoholic, and so are five of her mother's six brothers and sisters. Every one of those siblings married an alcoholic except for Abby's mother. Almost every one of Abby's twenty-eight first cousins is an alcoholic as well. Needless to say, Abby is an alcoholic herself.

Growing up, I heard stories about other families like that too. Not many, but a few, and all of them told in hushed tones by people who witnessed the effects. My friend Lauren's father drank. Lauren knew that, and so did all of her best friends, and we all knew that something was wrong about it, the way he'd sit in the living room for hours with a drink in his hand, the way you'd never know what to expect from him. Sometimes he'd seem jovial and cheery, sometimes he'd get sour and disapproving and mean. Lauren was scared of him, so we were too. This was when we were ten and twelve and fourteen: if we went to Lauren's after school or spent the night at her house, we kept our distance from her father and managed to avoid being alone with him in the same room.

Lauren told dark stories about her father's past: he'd been married to a crazy woman who also drank; they'd had a daughter and she'd gone crazy too—we didn't quite know how or why, but something had happened and we knew that alcohol was part of the equation, that it had to be.

In the last years of my drinking I developed a routine of meeting another friend, Eliza, for dinner once or twice a month at a restaurant called Davio's. Eliza's mother is an alcoholic, so sometimes we'd talk about what it was like for her to grow up in an alcoholic household, how crazy and unpredictable it had been. She'd talk about her mother sitting at the dinner table, working on her fifth or sixth or seventh bourbon, her eyes glazed, her head drooping, drooping, drooping toward the plate; she'd describe her mom calling her on the phone late at night and slurring her words, making no sense, remembering none of it the following day. Eliza's house sounded like a place of chaos and storm, where people lost their tempers then staggered up the stairs, slamming doors behind them.

Craziness, dark secrets, alcoholic furies: *that's* how you become an alcoholic, right? It's encoded in your DNA, embedded in your history, the product of some wild familial aberration. There was always an undercurrent of moral failing in the stories I heard about alcoholics: they were unstable, unwell, irresponsible, and if they were parents, they tore through the lives of their children like tornadoes, drinking and divorcing, screaming and raging. Alcoholics from households like that made sense. When Eliza told me that her brother was an alcoholic, too, I nodded. Of *course* he was. Who wouldn't be, with a family like that?

Of course, active alcoholics love hearing about the worst cases; we cling to stories about them. Those are the *true* alcoholics: the unstable and the lunatic; the bum in the subway drinking from the bottle; the red-faced salesman slugging it down in a cheap hotel. Those alcoholics are always a good ten or twenty steps farther down the line than we are, and no matter how many private pangs of worry we harbor about our own drinking, they always serve to remind us that we're okay, safe, in sufficient control. Growing up, whatever vague definition of alcoholism I had centered around the crazy ones—Eliza's mother, Lauren's father's ex-wife, the occasional drunken parent of a friend. Alcoholics like that make you feel so much better: you can look at them and think, *But my family wasn't crazy; I'm not like that; I must be safe.* When you're drinking, the dividing line between you and real trouble always manages to fall just past where you stand.

I met Abby toward the end of my first year of sobriety. She showed up at an AA meeting on her third day without a drink, a small woman of thirty-eight, rather fragile in appearance, with high cheekbones and wide eyes, and she looked as shell shocked as a Vietnam vet, blank and vacant and exhausted. We became friendly early on and started hanging out together a couple of times a week at a little café in Cambridge called the 1369 Coffee House.

We'd hook up there before meetings and sit in the back, where smoking is allowed, drinking sixteen-ounce lattes in tall glasses. The more sober Abby got, the more her own background and history came into focus, and over the first few months of our meetings, she'd let little details of her life drop, one by one, little bombshells on the square wooden tabletop. She'd mention one day that her older brother was schizophrenic. Then, another, that he'd committed suicide. Then, the next, that he'd come on to her sexually two nights before the suicide, climbing into her bed in the middle of the night; she'd fended off the advance and he'd killed himself two days later, carbon-monoxide poisoning. Abby had discovered his body in the garage. She was fifteen.

She told me about the suicide one afternoon in March. Abby cried all the time back then. We'd sit in the back of the 1369 and she'd weep and later on we'd joke that everyone in the café must have thought the two of us were having a huge, complicated love relationship, breaking up back there two, three times a week. That day she was smoking a Marlboro Light and struggling not to cry, but you could see the pain cross her face in waves, washing up from some dark place inside.

I didn't know what to say. I rarely knew what to say when Abby talked about her family, so I'd just sit there and look at her intently and murmur things: *Oh, God*, or *Ugh*. Part of this was the sheer horror of the details; there aren't words for stories about schizophrenia and suicide. But part of it was something else too. I could always feel some part of me using Abby's story to call my own alcoholism into question, to compare, to look back and say: *Me? No way*. She came from the kind of household you'd expect an alcoholic to come from, and my own family was so different from that, so much more stable and quiet in its confrontations with pain.

We joked about this the day she told me about her brother's suicide. "I should be writing *your* story," I said. "It's so much more dramatic than mine."

She arched an eyebrow and looked at me. "Oh, you've got your own shit."

I nodded and we talked about the difference: her story was a miniseries, an epic drama spanning generations, something that would star Brad Pitt and Julia Ormond. Mine was more along the lines of a John Updike novel, or a short story by John Cheever.

"You're the nice, quiet alcoholic," Abby said. "The good, intellectual alcoholic."

She was right, of course. The nice, quiet alcoholic. I smiled. "You never would have known," I said, and then I told her about the very first time I got drunk in secret. I was sixteen, a senior in high school, and I'd realized over the course of a phone call that the boy I'd been dating was losing interest in me. I forget the phone call, but I remember the feeling: pending rejection; the sense I'd done something wrong. *I didn't kiss well; was that it? I wasn't pretty enough.*

I was in my bedroom, on the second floor of our house, and I stole downstairs and snuck a bottle of wine out of an open case in my parents' kitchen. Then I took a corkscrew from the kitchen drawer and went upstairs and drank the whole thing, straight from the bottle. I hid the empty bottle in my closet. This was not the first time I'd ever gotten smashed—I don't remember the details, but I probably had my first drink at age twelve or thirteen, and I know I was getting drunk at least periodically by my freshman year of high school, age fourteen. Nor was this an alcoholic frenzy, a question of physical craving, the way it would be later on. The drinking felt more like an experiment, an act based on some vague hypothesis I'd begun to form about the connection between liquor and anxiety, liquor and sadness, how one corrected the other.

"Drink as remedy," I told Abby. "A little equation I picked up at home."

My father drank. He was a tall, distinguished man of bracing intelligence and insight and I grew up scared of him, not because he was mean or violent but because he was anxious and sad himself and because he had a kind of intensity that made you feel he could see right through you.

I was his favorite, and I grew up suspecting that his partiality had to do with some core kinship between the two of us, something he sensed early on. I guess I sensed it too. As far back as I can recall, I had the feeling that my father was equipped with a mysterious power, a kind of X-ray vision, as though he could turn his psychic laser on me and see a shared darkness, a seed of sadness he wanted to watch over as I grew.

"Your mother and I made an agreement." He announced this to me one day the year he was dying. We were sitting outside on my parents' deck and he just blurted it out. "It was so much work, taking care of twins, that we decided she'd take care of Becca and I'd take care of you. We sort of divided you up."

I reported this to my mother several months after he died and she was so mad she practically spit. "That is *bull*shit," she said. "We did nothing of the kind." She dismissed it as one of his fantasies, of which, it appeared, there were many.

But most fantasies can be bound with a thread of reality; all it takes is a certain willingness to believe. Whether he wished it were true or deluded himself into believing it, the agreement was real to him: my father had always seen me as *his* child, separate from the others, aligned with him at the core. Both of us had always understood that, without acknowledging it openly, and the understanding had entangled us in ways that would shape me all my life: our sympathy had the feel of a pact.

That link was hard to live with, hard for a child to understand. My father had a probing manner, an analytic intensity tempered by a vague detachment, and whenever I sensed him turn his attention to me, the feeling on my part was instinctual and claustrophobic: *Don't yield. Let this man in too deeply and he'll consume you.*

A few times, when I was small, he'd come up to my room before I went to sleep and ask me to draw pictures on a white pad, a form of free association for children. I didn't know what he was after, but I knew he was after something, so I drew obvious things: scary monsters, storms in the night. I could sense, even at age eight or nine, that he was on an expedition, probing for something that may have had more to do with him than with me, so I neither fought him nor gave him any answers. Let him think I'm afraid of the dark.

Later, the probing became more direct. We didn't talk much, at least not in the easy, familial ways I imagined other fathers talked to their daughters, but when we did he always wanted to *know* something, always wanted something I couldn't give him. When I was thirteen, my best friend was a girl named Nina, who lived about twenty minutes west of Boston by car, and my father would sometimes drive me out to her house on a Saturday and come back to pick me up the next day. We'd be alone in the car for twenty minutes at a stretch and this terrified me.

"How *are* you?" he'd ask.

I'd stare out the window and say, "Fine," trying for a casual tone.

A moment would pass and he'd try again: "How are you *feeling?*" Then he'd shift his eyes from the road and look at me. My father was a big man, six feet tall and 165 pounds, with a high, distinguished forehead and a grave, thoughtful expression. When he questioned me like that, I could see a glint of yearning in his eyes, not a physical yearning but a deeply emotional one, edged with discomfort, as though he understood that his efforts to reach me were failing, that I couldn't answer him fully and wouldn't if I could.

I'd look at him, then quickly look away. I felt small and exposed in his presence, as though my body was transparent and fragile as air, as though I might evaporate at any moment, or blow away. I'd say, "I'm feeling okay," and a leaden silence would follow.

The older I got, the more powerful my father seemed—probably because I figured out over time that his influence extended well beyond me. He was revered in his profession: adored by students at Boston University Medical School, where he taught for forty-nine years; universally respected by colleagues (he directed the medical school's department of psychosomatic medicine); considered a national leader in psychosomatic research.

When he died, I was charged with writing his obituary. In it I used weighty words—*distinguished; esteemed*—and I used fifteen-syllable phrases—*training analyst at the Boston Psychoanalytic Institute; past president of the American Psychosomatic Society; a member of dozens of national and international psychiatric associations and the author of scores of articles and monographs*—and I regretted that I didn't have the room to communicate how devoted he was to his work, how he'd cried in the hospital after his diagnosis when it came time to write letters to his analytic patients explaining that he'd have to terminate their therapy, how deeply engaged he was his whole life in that particular world of ideas. At his funeral colleague after esteemed colleague stood up and talked about him: what a fascinating mind he had; how accessible and generous he was with his time; what a rich, enthusiastic presence he'd been.

None of the accolades surprised me. I'd always known my father was a brilliant man, but I suppose his intellect fed the sense of hunger I felt around him as a teenager, my feeling that he had this secret store of wisdom that I could only tap into periodically, through subtle glances of understanding or flashes of humor. Humor was the one connection we had that felt simple and unambiguous: despite his weighty presence my father had a droll, witty side, all charm and charisma, and I loved that version of him. He made the best speeches and toasts. At large family gatherings or dinner parties he was the person everybody depended on to stand up at just the right moment and say something perfect, something eloquent and wry and thoughtful, words that filled the whole room with a sense of meaning. He had one of the all-time great smiles too: when you said something he found amusing, his whole face would twist into a grin, all teeth and crinkled eyes, as if you'd just slayed him with humor. He could make you feel really special that way, singularly special, as though you were a bright light in his life and he had some key to that light, a way of accessing the things about you that were real and true.

In a sense, even his dark questioning could make you feel that way: there was genuine interest behind it, as though he really wanted to get in there and *know* you, guide you, share something central. But he was such an odd combination of articulate and awkward, so complex and pensive and remote, and his oblique, psychiatric manner often gave me the weird sensation of being attended to and invisible at the same time, deeply connected and yet misunderstood. Mostly, though, he left me sad, this present, unreachable man. I think my father genuinely wanted to be close to me, to be a loving and helpful parent. The problem was that he got in too deep, and that left me with the feeling of being a specimen instead of a daughter, something to be investigated and shaped instead of just loved, just simply loved.

Aside from his intensity I don't have that many memories of my father from childhood. I can recall minor things: the way he used to carry my sister and me upstairs to bed at night and scare us, tipping back, back, back as he ascended the steps, pretending he was about to fall. We'd cling to his neck and squeal. Sometimes, if we couldn't sleep at night, he'd set a chair in the hall outside our bedroom and count out loud. We'd listen to the counting and drift off and in the morning he'd tell us the precise number at which we'd fallen asleep. It never occurred to me that he'd have no way of knowing this: I just assumed my dad knew everything about me, he seemed that big and that all-knowing, like the Wizard of Oz.

One morning, when I was sixteen, I came downstairs to breakfast and found him at the kitchen table with his black coffee and English muffin. He was reading *The New York Times* and he set aside the paper when I sat down and peered at me over his reading glasses. I'd been out on a date the night before, making out in a car with some boy and feeling all scared and tingly. As I recall, I was hungover that morning too. He continued to look at me.

He said, "What's *new?*" The question wasn't casual: his delivery—deliberate, penetrating—always made me feel like I was supposed to produce some piercing insight, or hand him some deeply held secret, right there at the table. Sitting in front of him felt like sitting before God. I felt like he could peer straight into my skull and see a thousand things, see me drinking beer and kissing a boy, see the outlines of sexual feeling rising up in my skinny adolescent body, and times like that I felt so overwhelmed I wanted to curl up under the table and die.

I reached for a glass of orange juice and muttered something noncommittal: "Nothing much."

He peered some more, as if searching for the right way in, words that would tap into whatever it was we shared. "So," he said. "Do you have any new thoughts or feelings?"

I sat there, absolutely mute. Communication with my father could feel so stunted that way, aborted: his questions were so big, so personal and all-encompassing, they left you with only two choices: confess all or clam up entirely. That morning, like most mornings, I chose the latter, choked out a single, guilty, self-protective "No."

Alcohol offered another kind of protection, a much more effective, liquid kind that lightened things, diluted some of the distance and confusion and reserve. I learned that early on, just from watching him. My father had a particular fondness for martinis. He'd come home late after seeing patients—seven o'clock, seven-thirty—and he'd take a bath, change out of his jacket and tie, then go into the living room and make up a pitcher. My mother set up the cocktail tray every night—a small bowl of raw carrots, a small bowl of unsalted peanuts, a tiny glass dish with his twists of lemon—and they'd sit together on the sofa and he'd drink the first one. He never got ugly, not even once; he never even seemed to get drunk until later in his life, when he'd sometimes fall asleep on the couch after dinner. But you could tell, watching him sip those martinis year after year after year, that there was something central about the ritual, something deeply soothing and needful about it.

I liked that ritual long before I started to drink myself. Without realizing it I learned to look forward to it. My parents were normally so quiet: they'd sit on the sofa, my mother knitting and my father staring out the window, and a tension would hang over the room like fog, a preoccupied silence that always made me feel wary, as though something bad were about to happen. My mother would say something about her day—how she'd ordered some new curtains, say, or taken the dog to the vet—and even though my father didn't ignore her in any obvious way, you'd get the sense that he wasn't listening, that his thoughts were about six blocks down the street. Five minutes would pass like that, or ten. Then he'd drink his martini, perhaps pour the second one. He'd begin to loosen up, and within a few minutes it would feel as though all the molecules in the room had risen up and then rearranged themselves, settling down into a more comfortable pattern.

The difference was subtle but real, a sense that he'd shifted from slightly disengaged to slightly more available. He might tell a joke after that first drink, or shift his gaze from the window and meet your eyes, or respond to my mother in a more present way. "What kind of curtains?" he'd say, or "What's wrong with the dog?" The martini seemed to take some core stiffness out of him, to ease a deep sadness, and sitting there watching them, I'd feel like I'd been holding my breath for a long time and finally I could let it out.

My father introduced me to martinis and Spanish sherry and single-malt Scotch. More relief, a more complete protection. The summer after my senior year in high school, he took me to dinner at a Greek restaurant in downtown Boston. It was the first time we'd ever gone out to dinner alone and he ordered a martini for himself and wine for me. We sat in a red leather booth with paneled walls and when we sat down the waiter addressed my father by name. "Good evening, Dr. Knapp," he said, and my father nodded in his brusque, formal way and ordered the drinks.

I sat on my hands. I remember feeling that particularly acute brand of teenage awkwardness, unable to think of a word to say, and I remember a thick, interminable silence. I also remember an empty feeling, a wariness, something I often felt in my father's presence—looking for some nod of encouragement or approval from him, hoping for something to fill the gap between us.

But then the wine came, one glass and then a second glass. And somewhere during that second drink, the switch was flipped. The wine gave me a melting feeling, a warm light sensation in my head, and I felt like safety itself had arrived in that glass, poured out from the bottle and allowed to spill out between us. I don't remember what we talked about that night, but I do know that the discomfort was diminished, replaced by something that felt like a kind of love.

Like drinking stars. That's how Mary Karr describes it in her memoir, *The Liar's Club*, a line she picked up from her mother. She drank red wine and 7-Up one night from a bone-china cup when she was a kid and she felt that slow warmth, almost like a light. "Something like a big sunflower was opening at the very center of my being," she writes, and when I read that, I knew exactly what she meant. The wine just eased through me in that Greek restaurant, all the way through to my bones, illuminating some calm and gentler piece of my soul.

Drinking with my father always made me feel like that. It wasn't so much that he got any less God-like when we drank; it was that I'd feel more God-worthy, less intimidated with a few drinks in me, more self-assured. I could plop down next to him on the sofa and talk. I could evoke those wide grins from him, punch him in the shoulder, create a version of a father-daughter rapport that felt more natural and ordinary. I took to calling him by his name when I drank—"Hey, Pete," I'd say—and calling him that felt good, like we were a pair of regular folks, special in our attachment but human too.

What a relief it was, what release: the drink turned that weird bond of ours into something I could hold in my hand, like a treasure, instead of something that just glinted in the air between us; it allowed me to respond to my father in a new way, to align myself with him without fear, to seal our pact.

Over the years I've come to think of memories as tiny living things, microorganisms that swim through the brain until they've found the right compartment in which to settle down and rest. If the compartment isn't available, if there's no proper label for the memory, it takes up residence somewhere else, gets lodged in a corner and gnaws at you periodically, cropping up at odd times, or in dreams.

All through my adolescence I dreamed that the kitchen floor in our house was about to collapse, that the wood beneath the linoleum had rotted out and at any moment the whole family would fall through. I dreamed about getting lost and not being able to find my way back home, and about picking up the telephone and not being able to punch in the right numbers. These are anxious images: false surfaces, false maps, an inability to connect, impending danger.

At the time I couldn't explain those feelings, the anxiety and the sense of disconnection; they certainly didn't stem from anything you could see by looking. On the outside my parents' lives appeared eminently calm and controlled, nothing alcoholic about them. No jail sentences, no crashed cars, no messy divorces: those things happened in other families, other classes, and we seemed insulated from all that, equipped with all the elements of protection. We had money and health and intelligence. We had a big, modern house in Cambridge and a summer home on Martha's Vineyard, and we went to Puerto Rico for spring vacations every year, or rented beach homes in Florida.

"It's a very small world at the top." My father would repeat that regularly, reminding me that I was one of the lucky ones, with access to education and opportunity. That world was shaped in distinct ways by place and time, by Cambridge in the 1960s and 1970s—our politics were liberal, our fibers natural, our schools Ivy League—but for the most part it was quiet and gently rarified, the kind of home where issues of *The New Yorker* and *Harvard Magazine* eased through the mail slot and landed in the front hall with a quiet *thwack*.

There were certain givens, fixed rules, which simplified our lives as kids: my brother and sister and I could ask for things that might enrich us (music lessons, books, summer camp) but not for things that would merely indulge (frivolous clothing, junk food); we were disciplined with words—"spoken to"—but never hit; we were expected to do well in school, and to value education not as a means to an end but because learning was noble and would make us better people. It was a well-ordered household. An Updike family, a Cheever clan: calm, educated, cocktails at seven. If you sat down to dinner with us at seven-thirty, you would have been struck by the sense of reserve: the white twelve-inch candles flickering in the center of the table, the silence punctuated by the periodic clatter of a knife or fork against a plate, the actual sound of people swallowing. Our parents were generous and consistent in their own quiet way, but they were markedly undemonstrative. When you went to kiss my mother or father good-night, they'd lift their chins a little, heads turned up and away, and present one cheek to you, then the other, a family adaptation of the European air-kiss. You rarely got kissed back.

Instead, you got calm and ritual and clear priorities. The main living spaces in our house—kitchen, dining and living rooms— were modern additions, built onto the original structure in 1959, the year I was born. The living room had soaring ceilings. Tall picture windows lined one whole wall, and a fireplace and chimney, painted white, stretched up to the ceiling at the far end, dividing the living room from the dining area. The whole space had a spare, elegant quality—furniture covered in muted fabrics; my mother's abstract oils forming sporadic squares of color on the walls; a sense of graceful hush. There was nothing identifiably wrong in there, nothing but a lingering suspicion of anxiety and sadness, something so subtle it seemed to exist only in the farthest reaches of the rooms, under the gray rug on the floor, or whispering behind the curtains.

Yet somewhere along the line—through small moments in other people's homes, small observations about their families—I became aware that the lack of storminess in our household spoke to its own set of problems, to a quality of subterfuge, as though difficult and dangerous things lay beneath the surface, too difficult and dangerous to speak of or even acknowledge.

I remember being at a friend's house in second grade and seeing her father scoop her up when he came in from work, scoop her up and give her a big hug. I was startled and envious and also a little put off by that—it seemed so odd. We didn't hug in my family. I remember snooping through the bathroom of a friend's mother when I was in fourth or fifth grade, and being struck by the array of *stuff* in there, the lotions and powders, the tubes and compacts that opened and closed with a satisfying click, *thock*. My mother didn't go in for comforts like that—except for lipstick and a tiny bit of powder, she wore no makeup, and except for a stock of Pears glycerine soap, which she special-ordered from a catalogue, she didn't indulge in fancy beauty products.

These were tiny realizations, perceived as the little oddities of others, but they spoke to a quality of spareness in our house, a shying away from things sensual, a certain difficulty with indulgence. I snooped through that bathroom with a combination of longing and disdain, sensing that my family was different and that I wasn't supposed to want such things at home as a result, that we were above them somehow.

Growing up, I never heard my parents say "I love you," not to us and not to each other. I never heard them fight either. That's something else I picked up as a kid: adults didn't have conflicts, or, if they did, they kept them to themselves, closeting any hints of distress behind closed doors. I remember that my mother had a lot of headaches when I was a teenager. She'd say, "I have a headache," and then she'd shut herself up in her bedroom to take a rest before dinner. Sometimes she'd stay in there for several hours and I'd creep past the door and try to be quiet. I had a sense that the pain she felt was more than merely physical, but it was such a veiled feeling, so disconnected from anything you could see, that I never pursued it, never asked her about it.

I also remember one of my father's odder pronouncements. I was about eighteen and he and I were standing in my grandmother's apartment before a family dinner. He looked out the window and said, "Anger and sex: the two great human impulses." He was famous for making statements like that, one-line truths that seemed to zing out from some deep part of his brain, a neurological file labeled INSIGHT. I didn't really know what he was talking about at the time, but something about the sound of his voice and the look in his eye indicated that his comment was far more personal than it was intellectual, that he was reflecting on his own anger, his own intensely sexual drives. We were both holding glasses of Chardonnay, staring out the window. I nodded soberly and gulped down the rest of my wine.

I often seemed to be the subject of my father's statements. We'd be sitting in the living room alone before dinner and he'd look at me, then pierce the silence between us with a summary phrase.

"You feel like an outsider in the family," he announced once, out of the blue.

"I do?"

I was fourteen or fifteen and I just looked at him sideways, then stared at my feet.

He was right, of course: the human X ray. He touched on my moodiness a lot, my tendency toward depression. He commented on how much time I spent away from home as a teenager, sleeping at girlfriends' houses, getting away. After a while I couldn't tell if these things were statements of fact or allusions that became fact because he prompted them. And not once did it occur to me that these were the very issues that preoccupied *him*: depression, anger, a need to flee. At the time he just unnerved me.

The thing is, hints of distress are like air: you can't see them, can't hold them in your hand and subject them to proper examination. There was no tangible evidence of anger between my parents, and no outward expression of lust or sexual drive either. Sometimes I'd wake up late at night and hear them arguing in their bedroom. My room was directly above theirs and although I couldn't make out any words, I could hear raised voices, and long angry pauses. But I tried not to make too much of that. My parents always had a strong intellectual bond and they were both deeply passionate about books and music and art; for all I knew, they were down there arguing about Proust. Like I said, there was no tangible evidence of trouble. When they sat down to cocktails in the living room every evening, my parents were a picture of staid sophistication. The bowl of unsalted peanuts; the tiny glass dish of lemon twists. My mother would knit; my father would hold his martini and gaze out across the room, rage and sexuality simmering so far beneath the surface they barely caused a ripple.

The quiet control of our household complicated matters for me, and still does. There's so little to point to: *My father singled me out in this weird way and I became an alcoholic. I grew up in a quiet and controlled setting, and I became an alcoholic.* Somehow it doesn't have quite the same ring to it as Abby's story: *I come from generations of alcoholics and I, too, became an alcoholic.*

A lot of AA meetings begin with what's called a "qualification," which means someone stands or sits in the front of the room and tells their story to the rest of the group—what happened when they drank, how they changed after they stopped. It's not uncommon to hear very dramatic qualifications, stories that start with the words "There was a lot of abuse in my household" and go on to catalogue the full range of modern American trauma: sexual abuse, physical abuse, psychological abuse. I sometimes feel a little out of place by comparison, a little guilty that my own narrative is so spare, and I often wish I had a story that would lay it all out in clearer, more vivid detail. *Here's the setup; here's precisely what happened.* But there's rarely a single defining event and even people from the most chaotic alcoholic backgrounds struggle with that knowledge, even people like Abby. For all the concrete reasons she had to drink, she still can't look back and say, with certainty, *It's because of this,* or *It's because of that.* None of us can.

I can say that alcohol traveled in my family, but it did so with characteristic subtlety, in the quiet, winding manner of a hidden stream, and only from one direction, my father's side.

My mother's family didn't drink at all to speak of, at least not alcoholically. Her parents, descendants of Russian Jews who emigrated to the U.S. in the 1890s and early 1900s, lived in Brookline, Massachusetts, outside of Boston; her father was a successful businessman who rose up the ranks of the Converse Rubber Company and became quite wealthy; they created a genteel household and when we went to visit them for Sunday dinner, which we did every week when I was a kid, the adults would gather in the living room before dinner and sip their drinks in a quiet, noncompulsive way that suggested a pleasant ritual, nothing more. Top-shelf vodka on the rocks for my grandmother; expensive gin for the men. I never saw my mother have more than two drinks—almost always a very watered-down Scotch—and I never saw any member of her family drunk. When I went to rehab many years later, an uncle from that side of the family would take me aside and say, "You'll be okay. Your Jewish blood will carry you through."

For good or ill I seemed to have inherited more blood from my father's side. I looked like him: same high forehead, same hands and feet, same constitution. I also drank like him, and took to liquor in much the same way. Not long ago I found a journal he'd kept when he was nineteen, during a summer he'd spent on a ranch in the Southwest. Every third page had a drinking story: drinking in small-town bars, drinking with dinner, repeated references to "demon alcohol." He grew up in a prominent Protestant family in upstate New York, the son of wealth on his mother's side, and although he never talked about it this way, drinking was a natural and significant part of his milieu, as much a part of the landscape he grew up in as old money and Ivy League educations. Rarified living: there are great photographs of my father and his brother Bob during their early twenties, sitting on the patio outside their family's grand estate in upstate New York, dressed in tennis whites and sipping martinis. *Marts*, they called them. *Let's have a mart.*

My father showed up for his Harvard Medical School interview with a raging hangover. He'd tell me that story in a bemused way, an example of youthful indiscretion, but he didn't tell it often and he rarely told other stories like it. I don't know if my father's parents drank, or how much, or in what ways. If drinking wreaked havoc on his side of the family, it did so privately, and the details were never shared with outsiders.

There were clues, though, scattered bits of evidence that alcohol caused problems, but they seemed distant and played out, safely tucked away in the past. Years before I was born, my father had been arrested for drunk driving, twice I gather. Back then, before he met my mother, he'd also been married to an alcoholic, a woman named Shelby.

We used to hear about Shelby in ugly bits and pieces when I was growing up—she'd call on the phone, drunk and yelling, making unreasonable demands—and an unspoken mythology grew up around her: *she* was a drunk, a sick woman, bad news, and the polar opposite of my mother, who was beautiful and graceful and controlled. We never talked about alcoholism, though, and we spoke about Shelby only in code: *She* called. *She's* having a fit about money, or about one of their three kids. We all believed, I think, that my father had left chaos and illness behind when he left Shelby, exchanging those qualities for my mother's goodness. And we all did our best to ignore our feelings about Wicky, the truest legacy of that marriage, and the one piece that followed him, inescapably, into his union with my mother and into my own early childhood.

Wicky was my father's third child from his marriage to Shelby. He was blind from birth, emotionally disturbed, and severely retarded, although no one used that word, *retarded*. I didn't see him much when I was kid, but he was always there in the background, an issue that wouldn't go away, a source of strain—and the only obvious one—between my parents.

Wicky lived with them from 1956 to 1958, the first two years of their marriage. As the story I grew up with went, they'd been in Italy on their honeymoon and Shelby, also in Italy at the time, had approached my father and said, essentially, "Here. He's yours. I can't deal with him anymore. *You* take him." My father couldn't say no, so they brought him home with them, to live.

Wicky was ten years old then, a blind, angry, uncontrollable kid who resented my mother and let her know it. He had tantrums, got into things, broke favorite possessions. An antique

Chinese jewelry box, a vase. My mother described those years as a nightmare: my father would go off to work in the morning and leave her there with Wicky, leave her to entertain and feed him, to haul him off to appointments with this specialist and that one.

Once, while she was taking him in a taxicab to see his therapist, Wicky lost control and tried to choke her, put his hands around her neck and just squeezed. After a while I don't think my mother felt even a shred of pity or sorrow for Wicky, just a resentment that grew to match his own. My father kept promising they'd get extra help, find the right person to come in and tend to him, find the right program or psychiatrist or group home to help him. The truth was, he couldn't admit how far beyond help Wicky really was.

My mother understood the truth but felt helpless to use it. For her the situation seemed hopeless and frustrating and, in its own way, humiliating. Her own family had been skeptical of my father from the start—a divorced, Protestant psychoanalyst, eleven years her senior, he seemed like an unorthodox choice at best. She'd told her parents that he had children, but she hadn't mentioned anything specific about Wicky, and she certainly hadn't been prepared to have the child living with them. But my father promised he'd be there for only a short time—a few months, just until they found the right situation—and she put up with it. She didn't feel she had a choice.

She also couldn't quite believe it. My father had wooed my mother with an intensity that seemed indissoluble. They'd met at a cocktail party and he'd seen her across the room—a dark-haired, naturally beautiful woman who radiated quiet intelligence and reserve—and as he told it, he'd fallen in love almost immediately. He pursued her in the most classical sense: wrote her love letters and sent her poems, focused on her like salvation. Shortly before they got married, he'd been smoking a cigarette in a restaurant and my mother looked at him and said, "If you keep that up, you're going to die on me."

My father had smoked two packs a day for more than twenty-five years. He put the cigarette out and never had another one. Wicky's presence was the first real sign that my father's devotion to her might be more complex, more qualified, than she'd felt it to be before; he was the first tangible sign of trouble from my father's past, of baggage brought and left, like the abandoned child, at her feet.

A few months with Wicky turned into six months, then a year. My parents renovated their house, my mother got pregnant with Andrew, my older brother; Wicky was still there.

When Andrew was an infant, my mother would find Wicky creeping blindly into his room and it terrified her. Later, when Andrew was about eighteen months old, Wicky turned a wheelbarrow over on him in the front yard and trapped him underneath. My mother was pregnant with my sister and me at the time. Wicky left shortly after that, went to a series of residential programs and schools for the blind and continued, essentially, not to improve.

He came back only occasionally from then on. Weekends here and there. Christmas, Easter, Thanksgiving. I found him upsetting and physically repulsive and I used to cringe when I heard he was coming to stay. Wicky was overweight and badly dressed and he had a pale, doughy face with a broad, flat nose and slitty eyes that seemed to roll back into his head without warning. He was spasmodic: my father would steer him to a chair in the living room and he'd sit there and rock back and forth, back and forth constantly. Periodically, he'd stop, just freeze, his head tilted up and to the side, as if he were listening for a bird in the distance. Then his hand might jerk up to his face or his head; he'd put his finger in his nose, or scratch his hair, or tug at his ears.

My father would often look absent and stressed and sad when Wicky was around, and he'd seem to get lost in his own thoughts. Wicky would be in the middle of a long monologue and then he'd interrupt himself and try to ascertain whether my father was listening, whether he was still, in fact, in the room. "Dad?" he'd say, looking up, looking perplexed. "Dad?" I hated that: it was like an exaggerated version of the way I so often felt, trying to gauge the depth of my father's presence.

I also hated watching Wicky eat, which he did with the undiscriminating hunger of a dog, stuffing too much food into his mouth at once, using his hands when he should have used a fork, sometimes picking his plate up at the end of a meal and licking it clean. My father would ignore this until my mother, appalled, glared at him with sufficient force. Wicky's hands would be searching the plate, groping at it for morsels, and you could see my mother freeze with tension, watching him. *"Pete,"* she'd say to my father, glaring, nodding toward Wicky, and my father would look up from his own plate, reach over, and place a fork in Wicky's hand. "Use this," he'd say, and Wicky would use the fork for a few minutes, then abandon it, and the whole cycle would start again.

After dinner Wicky would go up to his room, listen to music on a tape recorder, and talk to himself. He was always rehashing some event from a day or a week ago, obsessing over the details, repeating bits of conversation. You could hear him up there, muttering. My parents would sit in the living room, silently. They rarely fought openly about Wicky, or even talked about him, but you could feel his presence in the room like a great fatigue. My mother would stare down at her knitting, a tightness in her expression. My father would read, looking up periodically to stare out across the room at something the rest of us couldn't see.

Wicky explained that quiet sense of sadness in our house better than anything else and I learned to see him as the central problem, a cancer in my parents' marriage. It made perfect sense. The ill will he generated during his visits seemed entirely specific to him. My mother's tension and headaches, that freezing at the table; my father's preoccupied sadness in Wicky's presence; the weight of silence the rest of us felt at the table—it was Wicky, wasn't it? It was Wicky.

When I was twenty-nine, Wicky died suddenly, of a grand mal seizure. He was forty-two. A few months after his funeral my half-sister Penny, Wicky's oldest sister, sent me a letter about what it was like to grow up with him, breaking the silence about the role alcohol had played. "Nobody ever talked about it," she wrote, "but it's completely obvious to me now that he suffered from fetal alcohol syndrome."

Fetal alcohol syndrome? A life ruined by alcohol, just like that? The news was jarring, one of those facts that seems to come out of nowhere but also makes sense, a piece of some larger puzzle that was there all along, lurking but not identified.

I was drinking a glass of wine in my apartment when I opened Penny's letter. I'd read a little about fetal alcohol syndrome and, thinking about it, I could see that Wicky did have a lot of the characteristic features: elongated folds in his eyelids; a flat, low nasal bridge; a narrow upper lip. On some level I could also see by then that I was drinking too much, and I remember putting the letter back in its envelope and thinking I wouldn't be able to have children if I kept it up. If I ever got pregnant, I thought, the baby would turn out like Wicky. I couldn't do it.

The thought startled me, but only for a minute: the main feeling about his death was relief.

My father died four years later, on a Monday in April. I was thirty-two and unprepared.

The morning before he died, a hospice nurse named Carla came to the house to examine him and said he'd probably live for another few days, possibly even a week. He'd fallen into a coma three days earlier, but his vital signs were strong, his breathing even, his heart rate normal.

So we waited, which is what we'd done for the past eleven months.

I'd already been drinking daily for the previous five years, maybe more, but when my father's brain tumor was diagnosed, all bets were off. His illness opened a well of fear in my chest that felt bottomless and I drank to fill it, to escape it, to numb it. I drank because I felt I had no choice and because I didn't know what else to do. I drank without thinking.

For the two nights prior to Carla's visit I'd slept in the twin bed set up next to my father's hospital bed, in my parents' bedroom. The idea was to give my mother some relief: she was exhausted, waking up every time he stirred in the bed beside her, expecting him to die any second, so my sister and I sent her upstairs to my old bedroom for a couple of nights and I took over the vigil.

I was terrified that he might die alone, and I think I was sufficiently conscious of reality at the time, of the fact that he really was about to die, that I managed not to drink too much on those two nights. I could be lying about that: I don't remember what I was drinking, or how much, but I do remember standing by his bedside each evening before I went to sleep, and putting my hand on his hand.

"I love you, Dad," I'd whisper. "We're all here. Everything will be okay." These were not the kinds of things we said in my family —"I love you"; "We're all here"—but I forced myself to say them. And then I'd get into bed and try to listen to his breathing. I don't remember if I passed out those nights or not.

But when Carla came, when she told us the vigil would go on for several more days, I decided I'd leave the house and spend the night with Michael, my boyfriend, take a little break. He and I would have dinner at the house with my mother and Becca and her husband Andy and then we'd leave, drive the mile or so across Cambridge to his apartment.

I drank Cognac that night. I'd bought the bottle over the weekend, a $48 bottle of Ragnaud, which was my favorite, and I'd stashed it in my bag, and every half hour or so I'd go upstairs to my bedroom on the pretense of wanting to go smoke a cigarette, and I'd take the bottle out of the bag and I'd smoke and I'd slug the Cognac, huge gulps of it. I went through more than half the bottle that evening, plus wine with dinner, plus a few beers before dinner, and I don't even remember getting to Michael's house. I passed out within minutes, and I was so far gone, so deep in the fog, that he had to shake me awake at one-thirty in the morning when the phone rang, when Andy called to tell us that something had changed, something was different about my father's breathing and we'd better get over there, now.

Maybe we would have gotten there faster if I hadn't been drinking, if I'd been more alert, better able to throw on my clothes and jump into the car. I can't say. But my father died before we got to the house. Andy met us at the door. He looked at me and said, "About two minutes ago." I was still drunk.

4 *Hunger*

Around the time that Wicky died, I started taking those little quizzes about drug and alcohol abuse that you sometimes find in women's magazines or pamphlets at the doctor's office, and I started answering a lot of the questions positively. Do you find yourself having a drink or two before you go to a party where you know alcohol will be served, just to "get yourself in the mood"? Yes. Do you find yourself gulping drinks? Um . . . check. Do you drink more when you're under stress? Sure. But some of the questions seemed a little obvious, even kind of stupid. Do you drink alone? Well, of course I drink alone; I *live* alone. What kind of a question is that?

The real questions, the questions I would have asked myself if I'd been willing to look more closely, might have been more pointed: Are you driven by a feeling of hunger and need? When someone sets a bottle of wine on the dinner table, do you find yourself glancing at it subversively, possessively, the way you might look at a lover you long for but don't quite trust? When someone pours you a glass from that bottle, do you take careful note of the level of liquid in the glass, and measure it secretly against the level of liquid in the other glasses, and hold your breath for just a second until you're assured you have enough? Do you establish an edgy feeling of relationship with that glass, that wine bottle; do you worry over it, care about it, covet it, want all of it for yourself? Can you bear the thought that it might run out, that you'll be left sitting there without it, alone and unprotected?

In some ways I felt that way about drinking from the very start: conscious and needful and aware. It always seemed pointless to me to pour a drink and not finish it, or to hold back if someone offered me another one, and although I couldn't articulate it, I remember being vaguely aware that I drank differently from the way other people did. I can't remember ever turning down a drink, not even once; it would have been like a puppy turning down a proffered treat. Why not? Sure, I'll have another. Drinking is fun. It *feels* good.

My mother didn't drink that way. Neither did my sister. They'd have a glass of wine at dinner—a single glass—and if you tried to pour more, they'd cover the glass with a hand and say, "No, thanks. I've had enough."

Enough? That's a foreign word to an alcoholic, absolutely unknown. There is never enough, no such thing. You're always after that insurance, always mindful of it, always so relieved to drink that first drink and feel the warming buzz in the back of your head, always so intent on maintaining the feeling, reinforcing the buzz, adding to it, *not losing it*. A woman I know named Liz calls alcoholism "the disease of more," a reference to the greediness so many of us tend to feel around liquor, the grabbiness, the sense of impending deprivation and the certainty that we'll never have enough. More is always better to an alcoholic; more is necessary. Why have two drinks if you can have three? Three if you can have four? Why stop?

Why and *how*? Toward the end of my drinking I'd go to a party and promise Michael I wouldn't drink too much. He'd plead: "Just take it easy, okay? Watch yourself," and I'd swear: "I won't. I don't want to get too drunk." I'd mean that, of course, and I'd start out by measuring myself: one glass of wine the first half hour, one glass the second, and so on. But then something would snap, some uncontrollable process would kick in, and all of a sudden it would be two or three hours later and I'd be on my sixth or tenth or God knows what glass of wine, and I'd be plastered. I couldn't account for it, couldn't explain it, couldn't even rationalize it, although I struggled mightily to. I seemed to get drunk, blind drunk, against my will.

The knowledge that some people can have enough while you never can is the single most compelling piece of evidence for a drinker to suggest that alcoholism is, in fact, a disease, that it has powerful physiological roots, that the alcoholic's body simply responds differently to liquor than a nonalcoholic's. Once I started to drink, I simply did not know how or when to stop: the feeling of need kicked in, so pervasively that stopping didn't feel like an option. My friend Bill explains it this way to his mother, who has a hard time wrapping her mind around the disease concept of alcoholism and who holds fast to the belief that he could have controlled his drinking if only he'd exerted enough will. He says, "Mom, next time you have diarrhea, try controlling *that*." Crude, perhaps, but he gets the point across.

The need is more than merely physical: it's psychic and visceral and multilayered. There's a dark fear to the feeling of wanting that wine, that vodka, that bourbon: a hungry, abiding fear of being without, being exposed, without your armor. In meetings you often hear people say that, by definition, an addict is someone who seeks physical solutions to emotional or spiritual problems. I suppose that's an intellectual way of describing that brand of fear, and the instinctive response that accompanies it: there's a sense of deep need, and the response is a grabbiness, a compulsion to latch on to something outside yourself in order to assuage some deep discomfort.

About six months after my father died, Michael's parents came up to visit from Connecticut and the four of us went out to dinner. His parents don't drink much, so we ordered only one bottle of wine for the whole table, a single bottle, which poured out to about a glass and a half each. I remember feeling awkward in front of Michael's parents, whom I didn't know very well, and depressed about not having a father of my own, and generally apprehensive. Times like that, that fearful, grabby hunger would creep up on me in a way that felt so strong I couldn't concentrate on anything else.

We sat and picked at an appetizer of tomatoes and fresh mozzarella and Michael and his parents chatted idly about this and that—his sister and niece, a new car his parents had leased—and I felt so distracted by the hunger, so uncomfortable in my own skin, I thought I might explode. The feeling was unambiguous: *Nothing is going to do the trick here except wine. Nothing is going to make me feel less awkward or less depressed or less anxious except more wine. Nothing.*

"Could you excuse me for a minute?" I stood up and said something about looking for the ladies' room. The main part of the restaurant, where we were seated, was separated from the bar by a wooden partition that ran the length of the room. I made my way out of the dining area and then, instead of turning down the hall to the bathroom, I took a left and slid onto a seat at the bar. I ordered a glass of red wine and drank it in about two minutes, chugged it, really. I thought about doing it again, after dinner, but I was afraid of being caught. So later that night, back at Michael's and sitting around his living room chatting with his parents, I found an excuse to go out to my car. I think I told Michael's mom I had a book out there I wanted to lend her. In fact, I had a bottle of Scotch stashed under the front seat, and when I got to the car, I grabbed it and I sat there in the dark and drank a good two or three inches of it straight out of the bottle. I just remember the hunger, the *need*.

I need this. I might have actually said it aloud; I can't remember, but it wouldn't surprise me, it felt as strong as words.

Most alcoholics I know experience that hunger long before they pick up the first drink, that yearning for *something*, something outside the self that will provide relief and solace and well-being.

You hear echoes of it all the time in AA meetings, that sense that there's a well of emptiness inside and that the trick in sobriety is to find new ways to fill it, spiritual ways instead of physical ones. People talk about their fixations with *things*—a new house they're looking to buy, or a job they're desperate for, or a relationship—as though these things have genuinely transformative powers, powers to heal and save and change their lives. Searching, searching: the need cuts across all backgrounds, all socioeconomic lines, all ages and sexes and races.

Part of this, of course, is culturally determined or, at least, culturally reinforced. The search for a fix, for a ready solution to what ails, has become a uniquely American undertaking, an ingrained part of consumer culture, as prevalent as the nearest diet workshop or plastic surgeon. In some ways alcoholism is the perfect late twentieth-century expression of that particular brand of searching, an extreme expression of the way so many of us are taught to confront deep yearnings. *Fill it up, fill it up, fill it up. Fill up the emptiness; fill up what feels like a pit of loneliness and terror and rage; please, just take it away, now.* Our society has become marvelously adept at presenting easy—or seemingly easy—solutions to that impulse; all you have to do is watch enough TV and the answers come, one by one: the right body weight will do the trick. The right house. A couple of beers.

I sometimes think of alcoholics as people who've elevated that search to an art form or a religion, filling the emptiness with drink, chasing drink after drink, sometimes killing themselves in the effort. They may give up liquor, but the chase is harder to stop. This is why you hear people in AA meetings talk about thinking or acting alcoholically long after they've put down their last drink. The search for an external solution goes on: I want something. I need something. "My husband is acting like an idiot," a woman said at a meeting not long ago. "I have to remember that the solution is not 'Get a new husband.'"

This way of thinking is utterly familiar to me. When I was a kid, it was always something, some external fixation. I wanted a pair of patent-leather party shoes. I wanted horseback-riding lessons and along with them, knee-high riding boots and exactly the right kind of black velvet riding hat. I wanted the tallest Christmas tree in the lot. I obsessed about these things, railed about them, and when I couldn't have them, I felt misunderstood and bereft.

This was a constant feeling—I can't remember a time when there wasn't *something* hanging out there, some spiritual carrot on a stick promising comfort and relief—and it's important for me to remember that: for years it was party shoes and riding boots; later it would be alcohol. Same intent, same motivation; different substance.

I still don't know, today, if that hunger originated within the family or if it was something I was simply born with. In the end I don't suppose it matters. You get your comfort where you can.

As soon as I could sit up in my mother's lap, I started rocking, rocking myself back and forth, and I did this for years. When I was a child, my parents had to put a mattress against the wall in my bedroom because I'd sit against the wall during nap time and rock back and forth and bang my head into it. Later, I developed a more elaborate system: I'd get on my knees and elbows and curl up in a ball on the bed, facedown like a turtle in its shell, and rock away, for hours sometimes. In pictures of me at age five and six and seven, my hair is a matted mess, rings of knots framing my face. It got all tangled when I rocked on my head like that and the tangles became so hopelessly knotted after a while that my mother gave up trying to comb them out. I looked like a tiny blond Rastafarian.

I can see the rocking now as a first addiction of sorts. It calmed me, took me out of myself, gave me a sense of relief. I don't know what I needed relief from at that time—age five? age six?—but I clearly needed relief from something and the rocking worked. I did it daily, sometimes several times a day. I also did it for a long,

long time, although when I got old enough to feel self-conscious about it, I kept it secret from everyone: my parents, my sister, my friends. I'd sometimes go up to my room and rock for an hour or so before dinner, closing the door, turning on the radio, climbing onto the bed and rocking myself into a kind of alpha state. I almost always rocked that way before I went into sleep, rocking, rocking away for thirty minutes or an hour. I was deeply embarrassed that I did this, ashamed of it, really, but I needed it. I needed it and it worked.

The truth: I did this until I was sixteen.

The rocking was just like drinking.

5 *In Vodka Veritas*

B~UT DRINKING WAS~ so much more effective, its comfort so much more reliable. Over time, over many, many drinks, that knowledge is incorporated, the lessons folded into the soul: Liquor eases. Liquor soothes and protects, a psychic balm. Did that set me on the road to alcoholism? I wouldn't have thought so as a teenager or a young adult, not from looking around me. Reading books, watching TV and movies, I made connections between drinking and camaraderie, drinking and machismo, drinking and sophistication. Simple images: the boys slugging down beer at the end of a workday; Nick and Nora clinking cocktail glasses in the *Thin Man* movies. I knew people got into trouble with liquor, but those cases seemed isolated and largely foreign, the result of circumstances that had little to do with me. Betty Ford—well, she was a president's wife; imagine the stress of that. Celebrity addicts —Marilyn Monroe, Judy Garland, Liza Minnelli, Elizabeth Taylor, you name it: they crashed in direct response to the pressures of fame, their extraordinary careers and lifestyles; who wouldn't?

As for the rest of us, drinking looked entirely normal and, for the most part, entirely social: it was something that brought you out of yourself and into the world: into bars and parties and elegant restaurants. The idea that alcohol might play a more complicated internal role, that it might function on a much deeper emotional plane, was lost on me.

Once, though, I saw a hint, a tiny clue, written in a single sentence in the back pages of a book called *Getting Better*, by *New York Times* reporter Nan Robertson, a review copy of which arrived on my desk at work in 1988. The bulk of the book is about Alcoholics Anonymous: how it started; how it works; how it fits into current thinking about alcoholism. I flipped through it in my cubicle, thinking, *Ho hum. AA. Who cares?* But then I started reading the final chapter, called "Nan's Story," and came across a description of the way she used to drink. She said she was a boring drunk: she never got weepy or maudlin, never threw up on people at parties, never made embarrassing scenes. Drunk at a party, she might wander off to the guest bedroom and pass out for an hour or so ("a refreshing hour's nap," as she saw it), and then return, wondering why the rest of the guests were looking at her strangely. She wrote, "I withdrew in other, more subtle ways. My husband used to say, 'When Nan gets bombed, she goes off into some little room in her mind, and pulls down the shade.' "

That line stuck with me for many years. It was quite unlike anything I'd ever read about drinking or drunks, quite contrary to the images of alcohol I'd encountered in the past: the manly and tough drinker, or the smooth and elegant drinker. *She goes off into some little room in her mind and pulls down the shade.* Without stating so explicitly, that image had to do with the places alcohol can take you. It had to do with transportation, with the very real —and, to alcoholics, enormously seductive—phenomenon of taking psychic flight, ingesting a simple substance and leaving yourself behind.

I read it over and over and over.

Many of us drink in order to take that flight, in order to pour ourselves, literally, into new personalities: uncap the bottle, pop the cork, slide into someone else's skin. A liquid makeover, from the inside out.

Everywhere we look, we are told that this is possible; the

knowledge creeps inside us and settles in dark corners, places where fantasies lie. We see it on billboards, in glossy magazine ads, in movies and on TV: we see couples huddled together by fires, sipping brandy, flames reflecting in the gleam of glass snifters; we see elegant groups raising celebratory glasses of wine in restaurants; we see friendships cemented over barstools and dark bottles of beer. We see secrets shared, problems solved, romances bloom. We watch, we know, and together the wine, beer, and liquor industries spend more than $1 billion each year reinforcing this knowledge: drinking will transform us.

And it does, at least for a little while. It melts down the pieces of us that hurt or feel distress; it makes room for some other self to emerge, a version that's new and improved and decidedly less conflicted. And after a while it becomes central to the development of that version, as integral to forward motion as the accelerator on a car. Without the drink you are version A. With the drink, version B. And you can't get from A to B without the right equipment.

A man I know named Alex describes himself as a gregarious introvert: he can't stand being alone, can't stand sitting quietly with his own thoughts, and yet he is terribly shy. So when he discovered drink, in high school, he thought: *Ah, the elixir.* He could talk to anyone after a beer or two or three. The deep *thing* inside that made him grimace and squirm, the part that felt like a dry, steady itch of discomfort, just washed away. His whole being seemed to fall into place.

When Alex describes this in an AA meeting, the whole room nods. *Right. Absolutely.* It's the equation we all lived by, every single alcoholic I know: Discomfort + Drink = No Discomfort. The mathematics of self-transformation.

"It turned me into someone I *liked.*" A woman named Louise said that at a meeting during my first month's sobriety. She was teary when she spoke, a trace of grief in her voice, as though she was reduced to nothing without that special math, unlikable to herself and others. She said, "All this *shit* I feel—when I drank, it just went away."

For a long time, when it's working, the drink feels like a path to a kind of self-enlightenment, something that turns us into the person we wish to be, or the person we think we really are. In some ways the dynamic is this simple: alcohol makes everything better until it makes everything worse. And when drinking makes things better, it does so with such easy perfection, lifting you, shifting you—just like that—into another self.

I can trace that feeling back to early adolescence, age fourteen, age fifteen: I was that age the first time I took a sip from one of my father's martinis, and I felt the gin on my tongue, simultaneously cold and warming, the slightest tinge of citrus from the single spare twist of lemon. I was that age, fourteen, the first time I drank beer at a bar, the first time I heard the waitress setting down a pitcher on a hard linoleum table—*thunk*—then watched her pour the amber liquid into tall frosted glasses, then felt that glass in my hand, solid and cool and reassuring as a kind of currency.

I suppose that marked the start of what would become a cumulative process, a Pavlovian phenomenon of persistent reinforcement: this *feels* good, the way this glass of white wine flows from bottle to glass to throat to brain, the way it tingles and warms and lightens. This feels good, the way a group of us gather around a table, elbow to elbow, united in the camaraderie of drink and laughter and reward. Later, the sensations would grow more specific: *this* feels good, this snifter of Cognac warming in the palm, and this flute of Champagne, cool and delicate to the touch as mother of pearl, and this tumbler of gin, clear and icy and laced with lime: it feels like me; it feels *right*.

This is such a common sensation to a drinker. My friend Meg says she felt like the "real" her was trapped somewhere inside, locked up in a cage beneath her ribs. When she drank, that version was freed. "For years," she says, "it felt like the road to truth." She smiles and adds, *"In vodka veritas."*

* * *

About a year after I quit drinking, I heard some tinkly cocktail music on the radio in my car, part of the background of a commentary on National Public Radio. It sounded like the kind of music you'd hear in a fancy piano bar, and I flashed for an instant onto a period in my twenties, when I used to spend a lot of time drinking at the bar at the Ritz Hotel in Boston with my friend Sam.

Sam was great to drink with because he had a huge tolerance for alcohol but didn't drink alcoholically: he could match you drink for drink, and he'd never say no if you wanted to stick around for one more (or two or three more), but he'd never get too drunk: you could always count on Sam to be sane enough at the end of the night to figure out the tip or get you home. He was also great to drink with because he was always late; that meant when we'd meet in the bar after work, I'd get to sit there for at least a glass or two before he arrived. I'd sip the wine and I'd feel the tension ease and drain away, and I'd begin to feel elegant and calm and enveloped, a pretty young woman waiting at a table by the window, picking cashews out of the nut dish and waiting for her date.

When we drank together, my sense of time would shift. Sam would get there, and there'd be a slightly self-conscious twenty minutes or half hour until we'd eased our way into the drinks and conversation, and the next thing you knew, it would be two or three hours later and we'd be in the middle of some deep talk about family, or therapy, or work, and I'd feel *right there*, genuinely united, as though we'd really spoken to and heard one another.

I loved those moments, that sense that the world had boiled down to such simple elements: me and Sam and the two glasses on the table; everything else—the clink of waiters clearing tables, the low buzz of talk from others around us—just background music. Drinking was the best way I knew, the fastest and simplest, to let my feelings out and to connect, just sit there and connect, with another human being. The comfort was enormous: I was an easier, stronger version of myself, as though I'd been coated from the inside out with a warm liquid armor.

It's true—it's a statement of fact—that alcohol was key to that feeling. I'd learned that years earlier, watching my father mix his secret potion in martini pitchers, and in places like the Ritz I learned to tap into the same mystery myself, pouring myself over bars, pouring my emotions over people, pouring out all the stuff I kept bottled up. The amazing thing was how effective the drink was, how easily you could uncork a sense of well-being, how magical it was—magical! You could open a bottle and build yourself a liquid bridge.

That may be one of liquor's most profound and universal appeals to the alcoholic: the way it generates a sense of connection to others, the way it numbs social anxiety and dilutes feelings of isolation, gives you a sense of access to the world. You're trapped in your own skin and thoughts; you drink; you are released, just like that. One drink, and the bridge—so elusive in the cold, nerve-jangled sensitivity of sobriety—appears, waiting only to be crossed.

In many ways alcoholism has the feel of a psychological safety net, something a drinker constructs over a period of many years by making connections between feelings, like an emotional game of connect-the-dots. Take a difficult, sober feeling—shyness, fear —and connect it to its easier, drunken counterpart—disinhibition, courage. The net gets woven beneath you, a tight set of strings that promises to cushion you when you fall against a hard emotion. That's exactly what happened when I drank with Sam: dot A, *tension*; dot B, *relief*. In my head, out of my head. Disconnected, connected.

There were so many transformations like that, so many strings in the net: self-consciousness to less self-consciousness; inhibition to ease. I was painfully shy as a kid, shyer than my twin sister, and I hid behind her for many years, allowing her to speak for both of us when visitors bent over us and cooed questions. "How old are you girls? What grade are you in?" When I couldn't hide behind her any longer, when we began the process of separation that twins inevitably undergo, I turned to drink. There it was in high school, there it was at parties and in the backseats of boys' cars. When the feeling of shyness washed away my voice, there it was, the liquid solution, and there I was beside it, ready to reach for another one. Connect the dots: shy to less shy.

Growing up, I had an unsafe feeling. Because my parents weren't cuddly types, I didn't have access to comforting nooks, like laps, when we visited places where I felt scared. I remember being with my mother's family one Sunday and sitting at the table after dinner with the grown-ups. My grandparents lived in a big, formal house, with crystal chandeliers, and an honest-to-goodness powder room that actually smelled like powder, and a grand staircase that spiraled upstairs from the front hall. I was six or so, sitting silently as the adults talked, eating an Eskimo pie. My uncle Joel caught my eye and said, "What are *you* doing over there?" Everybody looked at me, and I felt like I'd been caught doing something wrong and I blushed. There was a great silence. Joel finally said, "I guess she's looking for the Eskimo who made that pie," and I felt so exposed I wanted to jump into my mother's lap and hide my head but I couldn't.

That unsafe feeling would stick with me for years, settling deep in my bones, but alcohol drove it out, replaced it with a feeling of courage. Drinking wine at age nineteen, age twenty, age twenty-five, I could sit at Sunday dinner with my mother's family and simply not care about who was watching me across the table, not care what they thought, not feel so tiny and vulnerable. Drinking wine, I could be the person I thought I was supposed to be, a more grown-up person who could appreciate the nuances of a fine Merlot, and comment on how beautifully it went with the roast. I could fit in, and when I sat there at the table with my aunts and uncles and parents, when I lifted the glass to my lips and watched the people around me swirl the liquid in their glasses, it felt right. I felt as though I'd made the right transition and that gave me a feeling of relief. Fear + Drink = Bravery; there you go.

Drinking always worked that way, at least it did until the end. There was a logic to it, an easy liquid logic that resolved some deep puzzle of need and wanting. *Ah! That's how it feels. Ah! Here it is; I've found the way.* Tennessee Williams describes this feeling in *Cat on a Hot Tin Roof*, when Big Daddy asks Brick why he drinks. His answer: "I do it for the click." Click: it's *right*, it's *me*. To a drinker the sensation is real and pure and akin to something spiritual: you seek; in the bottle, you find.

Once, when I was about thirteen, I dropped a bottle of milk on the floor before dinner and it crashed, shards of glass and pools of milk all over the linoleum. My father, sitting in the dining room, glared at me after I'd cleaned it up. "That was hostile," he said. He told me I was "expressing hostility" toward my mother; he told me Freud always said there was no such thing as an accident.

For years I trotted out that anecdote every time I wanted to explain the perils of growing up in a household headed by a Freudian analyst. *Trouble*. I'd laugh, rolling my eyes. *I knew from that day forward that having a shrink for a father was going to be trouble*. In fact, I knew no such thing. My parents were intensely private people, with a profound respect for what went on below the surface, and I didn't question their analytic orientation until I was well into my twenties. My mother once suggested that I make a list of all the things I hated about my parents, all the things that made my blood boil. I must have been about ten at the time and I remember standing there in her bedroom, blinking. Hated? About my *parents*? I never made the list, and it took me years to understand why the suggestion made me so deeply uncomfortable: if I hated things about them, did it mean they hated things about me?

Drinking, in a general sense, gave me a way to rewrite such

pieces of history, a way to address whatever lingering confusion I had about the person I'd been brought up to be. Again, simple math: I grew up in a confusing home and the drink made the confusion go away; it provided the easiest way out, an escape from my internal life.

The first time I told my friend Elaine that my father was an analyst, she burst out laughing. We were at a bar with another friend, James, and we were all a little drunk, and they both just shrieked with laughter.

"Oh, my God," James said. "Did he *analyze* you?"

"Oh, sort of," I said. They were fascinated and amused by this, so I continued, and told them the story about dropping the milk bottle, my early hostile gesture. James kind of squealed with glee, which pleased me. I was shy and James and Elaine both seemed much more worldly and sophisticated, and I liked being able to make them laugh. So I told them more stories. I told them about a time when I was twelve, and became morbidly depressed because our au pair had left and moved back to Denmark. I moped around the house for days, and cried at night in my room, and my parents finally sent me to a shrink. James and Elaine howled at this.

"Oh, my God," Elaine said. "Depressed over the au pair? How Cambridge can you get!"

I rolled my eyes, and said, "Incredible, huh?"

I laughed with them: ha, ha. Let's have another drink.

In fact, those were rather sad stories, painful reminders of the way I'd been taught to externalize feelings like sadness and rage. *Take them to a psychiatrist. Write them down on a pad.* But sitting there drunk, I felt none of that; instead, I had a sense of something that felt new and exciting, something like rebellion, as though the door to a new version of me, a nonintellectual, nonanalytical version, was opening before me.

The path, the liquid equation. I remember looking down at my drink and thinking about Elaine and James, about how different they were from the people I'd grown up around. Elaine and James didn't analyze their emotions, or engage in serious dialogues about hostility or anger; they drank, and when they drank whatever feelings bubbled and roiled beneath the surface just spilled out of them, spilled out and onto the table where you could see them.

I liked that. I liked belonging to crowds of people who dealt with emotion the same way, who simply *spewed* like that, who harbored a certain disdain for insight and analytic thinking. I liked being able to laugh with them, to sit on barstools and let my own emotions spill out the very same way, the sense of disinhibited high amusement. And I liked the way the drink helped turn me into that kind of person, someone more hardened and rebellious and cynical than the person I was raised to be, someone who could scoff and tell stories and make other people laugh. It was something I'd been looking for all my life.

Certainly I'd been looking for it since adolescence: a way out, a style that felt less constricted and cerebral than the one I grew up with. As a teenager I had a sense that appetites were to be reined in, kept in check. When my sister and I started bringing boyfriends over for dinner, we became aware that there was never enough food at the table. There was no financial reason for this, but it wasn't something we questioned. Dinner was simply served the same way every night and even when we had company, the family seemed to adhere to some unspoken rule about portion control: my mother would stack the plates in front of my father and he'd put a dollop of food on each one and the boyfriends would sort of blink down at the plate, as if to say, "That's *all?*" A chicken breast, a tiny dollop of rice. A piece of fish, a pile of green beans so small you could count them. I learned the acronym F-H-B from an early age: it stood for "Family Hold Back," and it was the rule we employed when we had company for dinner. There might not be enough to go around, so my mother would set the food on the table and whisper to us, or mouth the letters: "F-H-B."

Drinking released me from the compulsion to hold back, gave freer rein to appetites. In high school one of my favorite books was Virginia Woolf's *To the Lighthouse*, and one of my favorite characters was Mrs. Ramsey, the mother, who had an almost mystical ability to gather her flock of children and houseguests at the dinner table and *unite* them: awareness of the self would lift in her presence, rising like a dense fog, and the odd collection of characters around her would seem to meld and fuse, their sense of time and separateness yielding to a feeling of utter belonging. Woolf's descriptions of that phenomenon seemed to resonate deep in my bones, tapping something unfamiliar and desperately coveted. I wanted that feeling, and I couldn't seem to generate it on my own, and the amazing thing—the truly amazing and seductive thing—was that the drink could generate some version of it for me, a most convincing replica of ease and connection and relief, at least for a little while.

And there it was again, the connection: Repression + Drink = Openness. At heart alcoholism feels like the accumulation of dozens of such connections, dozens of tiny fears and hungers and rages, dozens of experiences and memories that collect in the bottom of your soul, coalescing over many many many drinks into a single liquid solution.

Of course, the problem with self-transformation is that after a while, you don't know which version of yourself to believe in, which one is true. I was the hardened, cynical version of me when I was with James and Elaine, and I was the connected, intimate version of me when I was with Sam, and I was the genteel, sophisticated version of me when I was with my relatives, and honestly, after a while I didn't know which was which, where one began or ended, whether the versions existed authentically within me or whether they needed outside people and circumstances to kick them into gear. For years my therapist said to me, "Sit with the feelings. What happens when you just sit still, by yourself? What happens when you just sit with the feelings?" I suppose he was trying to get at those very questions: What kind of person was I, really? What was I afraid of, angry about? Who was I when I didn't have other people to cue into? I couldn't answer, of course, because I couldn't do it. I couldn't sit still for ten minutes without a drink, without the anesthesia; I really couldn't.

One of the first things you hear in AA—one of the first things that makes core, gut-level sense—is that in some deep and important personal respects you stop growing when you start drinking alcoholically. The drink stunts you, prevents you from walking through the kinds of fearful life experiences that bring you from point A to point B on the maturity scale. When you drink in order to transform yourself, when you drink and become someone you're not, when you do this over and over and over, your relationship to the world becomes muddied and unclear. You lose your bearings, the ground underneath you begins to feel shaky. After a while you don't know even the most basic things about yourself—what you're afraid of, what feels good and bad, what you need in order to feel comforted and calm—because you've never given yourself a chance, a clear, sober chance, to find out.

Alcohol offers protection from all that, protection from the pain of self-discovery, a wonderful, cocooning protection that's enormously insidious because it's utterly false but it feels so real, so real and necessary.

And then, tragically, the protection stops working. The mathematics of transformation change. This is inevitable. You drink long and hard enough and your life gets messy. Your relationships (with nondrinkers, with yourself) become strained. Your work suffers. You run into financial trouble, or legal trouble, or trouble with the police. Rack up enough pain and the old math—Discomfort + Drink = No Discomfort—ceases to suffice; feeling "comfortable" isn't good enough anymore. You're after something deeper than a respite from shyness, or a break from private fears and anger. So after a while you alter the equation, make it stronger and more complete. Pain + Drink = Self-Obliteration.

6 *Sex*

ONE MORNING YOU wake up and open your eyes. Your head feels like it weighs way too much, so much it hurts to move: you feel a throbbing behind one of your eyes, or in your temple. A sharp pain, a steady ache. Your brain hurts, as though the fluid between your brain and skull is thick and inflamed. You feel mildly nauseated and you can't tell if you need to eat or if eating would make you sick. Inside, everything feels jittery and loose, like a car with bad wiring.

Next to you in the bed is a man. Perhaps you know him, perhaps you don't.

You experience a moment of disoriented panic—what happened? exactly what happened?—and you take a quick inventory. Are you naked? Clothed? Is there any evidence of birth control? An empty condom wrapper, your diaphragm case lying on the floor? You close your eyes: you want to pretend to be sleeping in case he stirs; mostly, though, you want to collect your thoughts, try to patch the evening back together.

Bits and pieces come back to you. You remember the early part of the evening clearly, the first few drinks, the way you started to loosen up. Perhaps you remember dancing, or sitting in a corner with this man, somewhere dark—a bar, a restaurant, a quiet room away from the main party. Then things start to get a little blurred.

You remember laughing: you were making jokes, or laughing at his jokes. You felt giddy and light and you had a sense of freedom, as though some secret part of you were rising up, a part you rarely have access to when you're not drinking. This felt like a kind of relief: sober is dry and uptight; drunk is fluid and liquid and loose.

There are more drinks; things get blurrier. At some point there was touch: he put his hand on your arm, or you put your hand on his arm. You looked at each other, smiling, and you felt *attractive*, and that feeling gave you a sense of power and possibility.

Your head pounds; you lie still in bed. The clear memories stop there and all you have is snippets. You were telling him things: things that felt important, *deep* things. What were they? Something about your mother. Some elaborate theory about human nature you had one day on the bus. Some . . . some story, some detail. You strain to remember and lying there in bed this makes you cringe, this wondering what you said, how intimate it might have been.

Other snippets: you remember leaning against him, or walking down the street with your arm around him, trying semiconsciously not to stumble on the sidewalk. You have a dim sense that that powerful feeling merged with a needy feeling, a wish for reciprocation. Does he find you attractive? How attractive? *Are* you attractive?

The sex, if you remember it, was disconnected and surreal. Your body did what it was supposed to do, or at least you think it did: all you have are tiny, discrete images—legs moving apart, legs wrapped around his hips, arms around his back. You remember sliding into sexuality in an almost instinctive way, mimicking what seemed like the appropriate behaviors: kissing him, holding on to him, throwing your head back in pleasure even though you didn't really feel pleasure, even though you didn't really feel much at all. And then your mind goes blank. You don't remember the rest.

You just have questions, and they gnaw at you.

Was he as drunk as you were? Did he notice how drunk you were? How much will *he* remember?

Were you a lunatic? *Are* you a lunatic?

You lie there with your eyes closed. All you want to do is get out, just get out and go home and take a shower and get all of this out of your mind, shove it straight back into history.

In 1993 Katie Roiphe's book *The Morning After: Sex, Fear, and Feminism* came out, and for a few weeks the radio talk shows and the op-ed pages were filled with commentary about the word *no*. Was there a serious date-rape crisis on college campuses? Roiphe said the issue was contrived, that it represented overhyped feminist paranoia and a misguided attempt to regulate the rules of sexual conduct, that today's women are strong and capable, that we are masters of our own "sexual agency." Roiphe's critics charged her with antifeminist rhetoric, with participating in a backlash against attempts to address the realities of women's lives, with deliberately ignoring the fact that women always have been, and continue to be, victims of sexual violence.

I remember listening to the arguments and counterarguments and thinking: *They're all missing the boat. No one here is really talking about booze.* Alcohol was trotted out now and then as a complicating factor—Roiphe herself writes about "thinking back on complicated nights, on too many glasses of wine, on strange and familiar beds." But by and large, excessive drinking was discussed as an accessory to the fact, something with tangible consequences: drinking impairs judgment; drinking wreaks havoc on your communication skills. The deeper connections between alcohol and self-worth and sexuality, the way women (at least women like me) use alcohol to deaden a wide range of conflicted feelings—longing for intimacy and terror of it; a wish to merge with others and a fear of being consumed; profound uncertainty about how and when to maintain boundaries and how and when to let them down—weren't addressed with much texture or depth.

No is an extraordinarily complicated word when you're drunk. This isn't just because drinking impairs your judgment in specific situations, like parties or dates (which it certainly may); it's because drinking interferes with the larger, murkier business of *identity*, of forming a sense of the self as strong and capable and aware. This is a difficult task for all human beings, but it's particularly difficult for women and it's close to impossible for women who drink.

My friend Meg used to go out to bars and get drunk and go home with men. The sex was anonymous—she usually didn't remember their names in the morning—and the consummation of the act was in many ways beside the point. There was something deep and compulsive about the behavior, some part of her that felt driven.

When she describes this, Meg talks about a component of anger and rebellion: she was in her late twenties and early thirties at the time, and she'd spent the better part of her young adult life responding to her fears about intimacy and sex by shutting men out, steering clear of relationships. There was something about drinking, something about getting drunk and sleeping with men she didn't know, that gave free rein to a host of buried feelings, to an undercurrent of neediness and longing she'd kept compressed in the darkest corner of her soul for years.

The drink released this current, let it stream up and out. There was a fuck-you element to it: a feeling of *fuck you, I am going to get what I want, even if I don't believe I deserve it*. Frustration and shame and fear and self-loathing and release, all rolled into one, all liquified and drained away by drink. She drank and she just did it, just said fuck you to her own complicated mix of feelings and *did it*. In some ways this worked: drunken, anonymous sex gave her the illusion of intimacy with none of the attendant risks, none of the aching vulnerability of sober sex.

If you both long for intimacy and fear it, if you feel unworthy of it and ill equipped to receive it and ashamed of yourself for wanting it, alcohol becomes a most useful tool, a way of literally drowning the conflict. It's a way of giving license to the part of you that wants to say yes. Yes to life and yes to deep connection and yes to touch and comfort and love. The sad thing is, whatever sense of affirmation you get from anonymous, drunken sex is usually metabolized away with the booze in your system. Meg would wake up in the morning and feel like an idiot. She'd feel shame and regret and confusion.

Oh, shit. Head pounds, hands shake, mind races. *Oh, shit: what have I done?*

She'd wish she'd said no.

Boundaries get so fucked up when you drink, so blurred. My sophomore year of college, some friends took over a lounge in one of the dorms on campus and threw me a birthday party, kegs of beer and bottles of vodka and trash cans full of ice everywhere. I wore a little black dress, one in a series of little black dresses I'd get plastered in over the years, and I got drunk and danced, something I never did sober. I danced with a guy named Bruce who had dark curly hair and blue eyes and seemed sweet in a shy way.

I remember getting drunk. I remember how the drink mixed with the rhythm of the music and gave me a sense of connection to my own body, gave it permission to move, and as the music shifted from fast to slow I found myself leaning against Bruce, my face against his neck, his arms around my waist and back. There was a sense of surrender, a melting into the shape of his body and a sense of myself as pretty and giddy and free.

Years later I would be reminded of this watching Meg Ryan in *When a Man Loves a Woman,* in a scene early in the movie when she and Andy Garcia are out at dinner on their anniversary and she's drunk and dancing with him that same way, draped all over him, laughing, just a tiny bit out of control. That's how I felt dancing at the party, as though the alcohol flipped some switch and—*click!*—worked its familiar magic, turned me into someone who laughed and danced and felt sexual.

Flash forward an hour or two later. No memory of what happened. None at all. Somehow, we ended up in bed in his dorm room, his roommate in the next bed. I had only the most dazed sense of this—a narrow twin bed; a fuzzy drifting in and out of consciousness; the briefest shock of recognition when it hit me that a penis, this man's penis, was pressing into me. After that I guess I passed out. In the morning I gathered up my clothes while Bruce was still asleep, put my black dress back on, and wobbled up the street toward my own dorm. It was seven o'clock on a Sunday. The campus was deserted. I had a feeling of shame.

Yes, no, maybe. Yes on one level, no on another, yes-and-no on yet another. Truman Capote once wrote that he saw in Elizabeth Taylor an "emotional extremism, a dangerously greater need to be loved than to love." Me, I was too cautious and inhibited and scared to give in to extremism of any kind in sobriety, emotional or otherwise. But when I drank, it happened. When I drank, the part that felt dangerous and needy grew bright and strong and real. The part that coveted love kicked into gear. The yes grew louder than the no.

The first time Meg had sex, her best friend advised her: "Just get drunk. It'll be easy." So that's exactly what she did. She got drunk then, and she got drunk the next time and the time after that, and after a while the idea of having sex with a man without getting drunk first seemed pretty much impossible.

Meg grew up the same time I did, coming of age in the late 1960s and early 1970s, long before people talked about things like safe sex, or even contraception, and many years before women's health organizations and magazines began encouraging women to "take charge" of their sexuality, to learn about sex and enjoy their bodies. The picture of female sexuality she acquired came from movies and TV, a little Marilyn Monroe here, a little Mary Tyler Moore there. Sex bomb; good girl. Those were really the only two options and even if you strove to emulate one of those, no one really told you how: how to be a sex bomb, how to be a good girl. How did these ideals translate into practical behavior?

Meg was scared of her own body, and she was scared of men's bodies, and so most of the time she'd just lie there with her drunkenness and her doubts. She felt as though she'd missed some key set of instructions, as though she was supposed to know instinctively how to move her body in ways that would be pleasing to herself and her partner, as though her lack of information on this subject signaled some fundamental weakness or failure on her part.

So she drank and the drink loosened her up enough to act sexual. Way inside, being female seemed like a painful thing—Meg felt mute, objectified, frightened—and alcohol took all of that away, just washed it away like the sea against sand.

Meg often slept with men she didn't want to sleep with: she didn't know how to say no. More precisely, she didn't know she was *allowed* to say no. She figured that flirting was a slippery slope: once you've given a man the signal that you're available, you're not allowed to go back, not allowed to change your mind.

Meg is a beautiful woman in her late thirties, with olive skin and dark eyes. She's also a wonderfully direct person who's taught herself in four years of sobriety to say exactly what's on her mind, so it's very hard to imagine her in that position, unable to make her own desires and limits clear, incapable of acting in a way that would preserve her own dignity.

At the same time Meg's story—her shyness and shame and confusion—is achingly familiar. Bad, semiconsensual, drunken sex: so many women I know did this. So many still do. At least one quarter of the 17,592 students surveyed in a 1995 Harvard School of Public Health study on campus drinking said they had suffered an unwanted sexual advance as a result of drinking; that same year, a Columbia University study reported that alcohol plays a role in ninety percent of rapes on college campuses. So Meg is typical. She did it, I did it: we lay there staring at the ceiling and just wanting it to end; we woke up in a haze some morning in some man's bed not really remembering how we got there or what happened next; we found sex compelling and terrifying and foreign, and drank to deal with it, just drank our way through.

I had done that all through adolescence, drinking to numb fear and feelings of inadequacy. The first guy I ever made out with was a big lug of a hockey player from my ninth-grade class named Henry, who had bad skin and long hair and played the drums in a band. We were at a party, drinking a lot of beer, and at some point Henry and I ended up alone in the basement and he started to kiss me. It felt like we were down there for hours. Henry's kisses were wet and foreign-feeling, and I let him put his hand under my shirt and then under my bra because I didn't know what else to do. It felt invasive—an alien hand on something I barely touched myself—but the beer worked: it allowed me to feel a man's hand on my thigh or my breast without feeling afraid.

Drinking continued to work, diluting the discomfort, making things bearable. All through high school I could go to a party or drink at a bar with a group of friends and then I could drive home with whatever hulk of a boy I happened to be seeing—Henry that year, then a football player named Will, then a wrestler named John, all interchangeable more or less because I never quite felt close to or comfortable with any of them—and I could lean back in the car and be kissed and touched, hands groping and probing where I didn't want them, and it wouldn't really matter; I wouldn't really feel a thing. At my senior prom I got blackout drunk, lost a white sandal somewhere on the dance floor at the Hyatt Hotel in Cambridge, and ended up making out in a car by the Charles River with a guy named Mike. I have no memory, no conscious memory, of what that felt like, and I suppose that was precisely the point.

So I can imagine exactly how Meg ended up lying there in a man's bed, staring at the ceiling like that, wanting the failed foray into intimacy to end. It's a classic story, and I can see myself reading from the same script over and over. I can see myself being groped by a boy in high school, feeling that combination of shock and curiosity—and drinking to counter the feelings. I can see myself in college, reeling up the stairs toward Bruce's dorm room, out of control—too drunk to *have* feelings. I can see myself flirting at a party, not knowing how to stop the flirting from escalating, not knowing how to turn off what I've seemed to turn on—and drinking to shut down the confusion this generates, drinking to keep myself going. I can almost *feel* the drink, feel how central it was to such experiences. Deaden the shock; facilitate the exploration. Voilà: *No problem; I can do this.*

Drinking, drinking. Drinking and loving men, drinking and loving men who drink. I never once went out with a man who didn't like to get drunk. Never. Right from the start the idea of going out with a man who didn't like to tie one on was unthinkable to me, and would be for many years.

This seemed perfectly reasonable, to choose drinking men. Alcohol can numb fear, and allow you to fake it, and take you places you literally don't want to go: strange beds. But it can also give you access to romance, a bridge to the positive sides of sexuality. Alcohol felt like the cement in female sexuality, at least it did to me: over the years the two would become so deeply linked that for the longest time I simply couldn't imagine one without the other. A first kiss without drinks? Forget it. Sex without liquor? No way. Drinking was as integral to my sense of sexuality as a body part: no more, no less. And sometimes that form of integration was effective, amazingly so.

A snapshot:

I am nineteen, sitting in a fancy restaurant in Santa Fe, New Mexico, with my boyfriend, David. We are both dressed up. He is wearing a tan suit, I have on a flowered sundress, we are both tan and healthy. We order a round of drinks—margaritas—and, with dinner, a bottle of red wine, a California Cabernet. I am supremely happy in this picture. I feel wonderfully protected, cocooned by the wine and the sense of romance, and together David and I are the perfect image of young love, clinking wineglasses above the pink linen at our table.

Wine and that melting ease; wine and that sense of yielding to sensuality. When I was with men I loved, drinking felt like the most natural ally, the most reliable route to a kind of internal softening. A naturally inhibited person, someone who grew up feeling mystified and insecure about what it meant to feel sexual, I turned to liquor the way a dancer turns toward music: it felt central to the process, central to my ability to shut down the voices of self-criticism in my own head and simply let go, move to a different kind of music. *Pop! Clink! Ahhh.*

David was the first man I'd fallen in love with. He was a friend of a friend who lived in Santa Fe, New Mexico, and I met him there during spring vacation my senior year of high school, and we stayed together through college and for several years after that. Big and uncomplicated and beautiful in a rugged way: that's how he struck me from the start, like the Southwestern landscape, as different from the men I'd known before as Boston was from Santa Fe. He was originally from Montana and he had the chiseled good looks of a mountain boy: dark hair and jade-green eyes and teeth so straight and white my mother said he looked like a model in a toothpaste commercial. I loved him almost immediately.

Alcohol, of course, coursed through our romance like a river, providing the undercurrents. I wasn't aware of this at the time, but one of the things that attracted me so deeply to David was the role liquor occupied in his life. The day we met, we drank tequila sunrises at a bar in Santa Fe, and I remember the particular giddy high you get from tequila, and I remember the way David's hair fell against his forehead, a single dark curl. That was such a powerful combination, the giddy high and the sight of him. I was drunk the first time he kissed me, drunk the first time we slept together, drunk the first time I told him I loved him. I don't think David was an alcoholic—he was one of those people who simply liked to drink and knew how and when to stop when he'd had too much—but he managed to keep a steady supply of drink around him and I grew to depend on its presence: bottles of beer in the refrigerator at the end of the day; bottles of tequila on the shelves to mix with lime and grenadine; cases of beer in the backseat of his car for day trips to the mountains.

It was always there, liquor was, helping us to blur the boundaries and deaden the fear, helping us protect ourselves from one another.

I was by no means a raging alcoholic when I fell in love with David, but I suppose you could say the predilection was there, that I was on the road to becoming one. Part of this was reflected simply in my behavior. I have a lot of *good* drinking memories from those days—drinking Coors beer under the sun by a Santa Fe swimming pool; sipping wine in the back of David's pickup truck at night on a New Mexico mountainside; drinking Champagne under the stars in the high desert—but I also have a lot of unpleasant memories: memories of blackouts; memories of explosive, liquor-laced fights; a particularly embarrassing memory of drinking an entire gallon of cheap white wine during a drive from New Mexico to Colorado, en route to visit my sister at a summer camp where she was working, then staggering out of the car when we arrived, loud and obnoxious and falling-down drunk. I was eighteen then; my sister was appalled.

More to the point, I think my relationship with alcohol began to deepen and shift around that time, my college years, moving from a simple tool of self-transformation—a way to relax and feel less inhibited, a way to be more sexual and open and light—into something more complicated, a more deeply ingrained way of coping with the world. Looking back I can see how certain patterns were beginning to develop, certain classically alcoholic ways of managing feelings and conflicts in relationships that would grow more entrenched and complicated over time.

Almost by definition alcoholics are lousy at relationships. We melt into them in that muddied, liquid way, rather than marching into them with any real sense of strength or self-awareness. We become so accustomed to transforming ourselves into new and improved versions of ourselves that we lose the core version, the version we were born with, the version that might learn to connect with others in a meaningful way. We are uncomfortable, often desperately uncomfortable, with closeness, and alcohol has the insidious dual effect of deadening the discomfort and also preventing us from ever really overcoming it: we become too adept at sidestepping the feelings with drink to address them directly. Feel conflicted? Drink. Insecure? Have a drink. Angry? *Drink*.

In fact, as much as I loved David, my feelings for him confused and scared me. I'd found in David another antidote to my family style—a nice, uncomplicated, loving man, a regular guy unburdened by insight and self-analysis—and I found my own attraction to him disturbing: did it reflect badly on me somehow, this choice of a tall, dark, slightly goofy, nonintellectual boyfriend? Was there something wrong with me, for needing someone so different from the people I'd grown up with? Were my own appetites—for hugs and sexuality and liquor—inappropriate?

Geography protected me from those questions for a long time: the summer after I met David, I went off to college, to Brown, he stayed in Santa Fe, in school, and we conducted the relationship over three thousand miles for the next three years, bingeing on intimacy during periodic reunions, then retreating from it during separations. But that strategy fell apart my senior year of college, when David, who'd graduated by then, moved to Rhode Island to live with me. The dynamic suddenly changed and so, in turn, did my relationship with liquor.

David and I lived in an apartment together off campus and I felt conflicted by his presence almost immediately, as though he wouldn't fit in, as though there was something wrong with me for trying to merge these two lives, my Brown life and my David life. So without really being aware of it I split my life in two that year, going to classes and working obsessively at the library during the day, returning to David, who'd gotten a job with a small marketing firm, in the evening. At night we drank—every night, as I recall—and I spent that year feeling tense, as though I had to work hard to keep the two worlds apart. We didn't go out with my college friends; for the most part we kept to ourselves.

Alcoholics compartmentalize: this was classic behavior, although I wouldn't have known that back then. I've heard the story in AA meetings time after time: alcoholics who end up leading double lives—and sometimes triple and quadruple lives—because they never learned how to lead a single one, a single honest one that's based on a clear sense of who they are and what they really need.

I once heard a woman at a meeting define alcoholism as a fundamental inability to be honest, not so much with other people but with the *self*. She talked about attaching herself to lovers all through college and graduate school as a way of avoiding the messy, fearful business of growing up, as a way of cashing in the chips of her core being by simply handing them over to someone else, letting others define her. Lots of people do this—you don't have to be an alcoholic in order to surrender your sense of self to someone else—but alcoholics do it with particular zeal and precision. We can be ace chameleons, twisting ourselves into two, three, four versions of ourselves and using drink to lubricate the transformations. *You* tell me who to be. And *you*, and now *you*.

When she described this, I flashed immediately onto that year with David, onto the way I split myself into two separate people, playing distinct roles in each life: the David life, which was social and sexual and awash in drink and hidden conflict, and the academic life, which was disciplined and cerebral and restrained.

The academic life, appropriately enough, was also defined by a man. Brown was famous for its lack of distribution requirements and I'd foundered there for my first few years, taking an absurdly random, disconnected collection of courses before settling into a combined major in English and History, and choosing that not because it tapped into some deep reservoir of intellectual interest on my part but because it was a small, new program in which I could stand out. A man named Roger headed that program. He was in his forties, an immensely popular member of the English department, and he had a razor-sharp intellect, and he was the first professor at Brown who made me feel special.

I'd wanted that feeling desperately—it's another classic impulse among alcoholics, to seek validation from the outside in—and I hadn't found it in college. The school was too big: I didn't have an instinctive sense for how to fit in, and I didn't have a clue about what I wanted to study. Academic achievement was something I'd always sought as a form of reward: good grades pleased my parents, good grades pleased my teachers; you got them in order to sew up approval.

Roger, whom I met as a junior, gave me precisely that brand of approval, and I'd found it familiar and reassuring: he gave me a purpose, someone to please. In my senior year I narrowed my major down to eighteenth-century British literature and history because those were his areas of expertise. He became my advisor, and under his direction I wrote a prizewinning thesis, graduating from Brown with honors.

Two days after my graduation I went out to lunch with Roger, a celebratory gesture on his part. He'd suggested this after the graduation ceremony—"Let me take you to lunch!"—and he'd called the next day and arranged to pick me up at my apartment.

We drove to a small, sunny restaurant about ten minutes away from campus, and he ordered us martinis. Then he ordered wine with lunch. We ate lobster salads and talked about writing.

After lunch, in his car, Roger leaned over suddenly and kissed me on the mouth. I was startled and scared and confused when he kissed me, but I was also drunk, so I let him. I let him keep kissing me, and I let him put his hand on my breasts, and when he called me on the phone a few days later and asked me to have lunch with him again, I agreed because I didn't know what else to say.

I must have gotten drunk with Roger six or seven times that

summer. We'd drive to a different restaurant each time and we'd have many drinks—usually martinis, like I'd had with my father —and after lunch, blind drunk in the daylight, we'd sit in his car and I'd let him kiss me again. I'd close my eyes, panicked inside but numb, very numb, and I'd feel his breath on my neck and his tongue in my mouth and I'd just sit there, not knowing how I'd gotten into the situation and not knowing how in the world to get out.

I couldn't have done this without drinking. David would go off to work in the morning and I'd go off to lunch later in the day with Roger, and I'd sit in the car while he kissed me and worry drunkenly about getting home, getting home before David got home and sobering up and trying to keep the anxiety out of my eyes. One day Roger asked me about David, and I told him he was moving to Chicago at the end of the summer to go to graduate school. Roger smiled. "Oh, good," he said. "Then we can become lovers."

Lovers? I'd graduated that spring without a clue about where I was headed. Writing loomed as an ill-defined but daunting possibility; so did medical school, psychiatry. But honestly, I hadn't so much as sent out a résumé; like I said, I didn't have a clue.

"Oh, good. Then we can become lovers." We were at an outdoor restaurant in Newport, Rhode Island, when he said that, and I remember vividly that I picked up my glass and gulped down the rest of my drink. A breeze was blowing, the sun was in my eyes. I thought I was going to throw up.

For the next decade I rarely talked to friends about the relationship with Roger and when I did, I described it the easy way: he was the villain and I was the victim. There's truth in that, but it's also true that I put myself in his path, that I made myself an easy target, and that drinking facilitated that process.

We'd had one lunch before the one where he kissed me, several weeks before my graduation. We'd walked downtown to a tiny basement restaurant called Pot au Feu, a cozy place with brick walls and wooden tables. We drank martinis that time, too, and I could tell that Roger found me attractive.

I also understood, however abstractly, that the martinis allowed me to indulge in that attraction, to flirt with it, to tap in to a feeling of power I was otherwise too self-conscious and fearful to acknowledge. After the second or third drink I know that I was leaning across the table, interest in my eyes, asking questions, drawing him out. I asked him about writing, and about his career and his background. I smiled demurely at all the right moments, maintained the right amount of eye contact, cultivated that particular ego-stroking blend of vulnerability, reverence, and detachment.

I don't remember how I really felt about him at the time—in purely objective terms, was he a nice person? An asshole? I don't know. Nor do I remember feeling physically attracted to him in any genuine way. Feelings of lust—if I'd had any at all—would have seemed shameful and incestuous to me: Roger was a *father* figure to me, and I wanted the kind of adoration and esteem from him that a little girl wants from her dad. But that wish gets complicated when you're a young woman who's had too many drinks. What I remember from that lunch is the drive: to please, to generate approval, and to do that by somehow sexualizing the relationship, because that's the only way I knew how.

This is an instinctive way of responding to someone whose affection and validation you covet—I'd seen women in college do it for years, smiling up coyly at professors or older boys in fraternities; I'd seen it done in movies and on TV all my life; in some barely labeled corner of my soul I, like most women I know, had come to appreciate sexuality as an ill-defined but very real path to female power, and I acted on that appreciation without really knowing it. I could *feel* it.

So when Roger took me out to lunch a few weeks later, and when he kissed me in the car afterward, I felt shocked and confused and appalled but also, oddly, victorious. The feeling was: *I*

got what I wanted; I won. And because I understood I'd partici-
pated in the game, because I knew I'd worked on some semiconscious level to draw him in, I somehow deprived myself of the
ability to get out cleanly. How can you say no when you've
worked to make someone else say yes?

Alcohol puts you in such a box, leaves you with such an impossible equation: you have to sexualize the relationship in order to
feel powerful, and you have to drink in order to feel sexual, and
on some level you understand it's all fake, that the power is chemical, that it doesn't come from within you. So I'd sit there in the
car with Roger, and I'd let him touch me and I'd feel completely
stuck, just the tiniest stirring of inexpressible rage—at him, at
myself—bubbling inside.

The drink of deception: alcohol gives you power and robs you
of it in equal measure.

I never told David about the episodes with Roger, but they in-
serted themselves into our relationship, creating another kind of
distance. He'd come home and ask me about my day. "Oh, it was
fine," I'd say and then I'd fall silent. I felt like I was carrying
around a huge secret (which, of course, I was) and I jumped every
time the phone rang, worried it would be Roger calling to set up
another lunch.

David and I drank that summer, a lot. We took to buying
vodka by the gallon jug, and large bottles of tequila, and we'd
have a drink before dinner, then wine while we ate, then more
after dinner: vodka-and-tonics, or tequila sunrises. On the days I
met Roger, I felt unbearably guilty, partly because I'd seen him,
partly because I knew I was complicit in maintaining the relationship, and partly because I understood that my ambivalence toward
David was a factor in the whole equation too. There in Providence, with my own ill-formed future looming ahead, our differences worried me, gnawed at me. I'd sit there at dinner and look
at him and compare him to the other men in my life, namely, to

Roger and my father: Was David smart enough? Introspective enough? Ambitious enough? Was it enough just to love him, or should I attach myself to someone who seemed farther ahead of me, someone smarter and more ambitious than me, who'd be sure to carry me along into the version of adulthood I thought I should be striving for?

These were tough questions, complicated feelings, but I never addressed them with David, not once. I drank instead and the questions running through the back of my mind faded away, just faded out of consciousness.

Alcoholics are masters at deflecting blame: it's one of the hallmarks of the personality, the way we explain our own feelings by attaching them to someone or something outside ourselves, the way we refuse, without even being aware of it, to take responsibility for our own part in troubled relationships. All that summer I'd sit there at the dinner table and look critically at David, feeling something was missing, something was awry. It never occurred to me, not once, that something might have been wrong with *me*, with my own capacity to accept people's limits, with my own neediness, with my own wish to be validated and defined by other people.

But that sort of honesty—with the self, with others—is impossible when you're drinking. The liquor numbs the real feelings and the real fears and the real doubts; it deprives you of the courage it takes to be honest. You lose your hold on who you really are and you just find yourself in bad situations: sitting in some professor's car, being groped; sitting at dinner with your boyfriend, withholding information. Keeping secrets.

My father kept secrets too.

At the end of that summer, the Roger summer, my mother called me on the phone and said she had something she wanted to talk to me about. It was a weekend morning in late August, and I remember sitting down at the kitchen table, tracing the red-

and-white checks on the tablecloth and thinking, *Someone's died.* My mother never called to talk about anything serious and there was an unfamiliar strain in her voice.

"I'm thinking of leaving your father," she said.

"You *are?*"

She sounded embarrassed and edgy, as though explaining this was going to be exhausting. "Oh, sweetie," she said. "It's such a complicated business." Then she told me that my father had been having an affair. The relationship had been going on for seven years and she couldn't tolerate the betrayal anymore; she was about to go off to Martha's Vineyard for a few days to think things over.

This was stunning news. You never would have known, just never. Thinking about my parents that afternoon, I couldn't re-member one argument, one moment of overt tension, one episode that might have suggested anything so dramatic as an affair, and as I learned more I would be astonished at the lengths my parents had gone to protect us from their problems. My father had actu-ally moved out for a few weeks while I was in college; I came home for a weekend during that time and he moved back in for the two days I was there so I wouldn't know.

I saw my parents as model grown-ups, and their manner, their silence, informed my sense of what adulthood looked and felt like. Grown-ups behaved rationally and calmly. Grown-ups worked during the day and came home at night and sat down for drinks and passed the evening quietly. After dinner my father usually disappeared into his office for a few hours; my mother sat in the living room with her knitting, watching programs on pub-lic television or talking on the phone. I saw them as beyond conflict, way beyond the kind of mess I'd found myself in that summer. Years ago, I believed, in the privacy of their therapists' offices, they'd transcended all that.

My instinctive reaction was to side with my mother, to react with horror and shock, but I also remember breathing a small sigh of relief at the news. It made my father a little less mysterious, helped put some of his remoteness and preoccupation in context. When I sat with him in those strained silences in the family living room, I had thought there was some inadequacy on my part that ground the conversation to a halt. I'd seen him all my life on such an epic scale—lost in his own grand thoughts, above me and my small concerns, possibly even frustrated or bored with me— and the news of his affair shifted the burden for the first time away from me and onto something else. Of course he was preoccupied; he was leading a double life. And of course he relied on that martini every evening: coming home was a painful thing, an exercise in guilt and betrayal that needed easing daily. The information might have been shocking but it also made him human.

A few days after my mother's call I drove up to Cambridge and met my father at the house. He seemed tense and tortured and he tried in the most awkward way to explain. We sat outside on the patio. He made martinis and he gulped his first one down and when he spoke his language was so ambiguous and abstract it was nearly impossible to ask questions. He said, "There have been a lot of troubles," and I can barely recall another word he said.

The evening was clear and quiet, the primary sounds coming from the whisper of trees around our house, and I remember that my father looked old all of a sudden, worried and far away. I know he made a reference to "sexual problems" between my mother and him. I know he made a reference to his "complicated relationship" with his own mother, as well as several references to anger and ambivalence, deep currents of both. But mostly I remember looking at him with a feeling I'd had since childhood: that he held something dark and conflicted and unknowable inside, something I shared but couldn't yet put words to; that he'd remain a mystery to me until he died.

Years later, after my father's death, I had occasion to meet with one of the few people who understood him intimately, a psychologist named Jack, and he filled me in on the source of some of that conflict: apparently my father's own father had had affairs, lots of them, and he'd humiliate his wife, publicly and regularly, by talking about them in front of other people, flaunting them. She would retaliate, not by having affairs of her own, but by acting seductive and flirtatious to anyone who happened to be handy, including my father. Jack told me all this by way of explaining how conflicted my father had become, how the concepts of sexuality and humiliation got welded in his soul from the earliest age, how on the deepest level he couldn't experience sexual love for someone without also feeling shame. My father was kind and empathic and deeply sensitive and as a young man, the model his parents offered put him in a terrible bind: to identify with his mother was to yield to her seduction; to identify with his father was to condone his sadism.

In the end, Jack told me, my father wouldn't humiliate my mother by flaunting his affair as his own father had done, so he'd struggled to keep it secret. The affair had ended after a year or two and then he'd confessed. But some time passed and he'd started it again, then ended it again, then confessed again. From what I gathered, the affair had continued like that—on and off, promises made then broken—and that summer, after the last confession, my mother had had enough.

Although I couldn't quite say how at the time, my father's affair explained things to me, provided some central piece of the quiet puzzle that was our home. Sitting with him on the patio that evening, I thought: *that's* what the silence was about; that's where the veils of sadness and tension came from; that's why I never saw my parents hug, or explode with passion or emotion or rage: all the energy went into hiding things, keeping the lid on feelings. I found the story of my father's affair utterly surprising and utterly validating at the same time, and I remember sipping my drink on the patio and saying, simply, "Oh."

I didn't know what else to say, really. Sexual conflicts? Lust and adultery? My *parents?*

"Oh." It explained things, but I couldn't react past that.

They broke up for about three days. My mother went to the Vineyard, and my father moved in with the other woman, and then, finally, something shifted and he decided he couldn't follow through, couldn't leave my mother. He called her and over the next week they patched things back together.

Years later he told my sister that he drank almost the entire time he was there: drank vodka and drank gin and drank and drank. Drinking was his solution, the medication for sexual conflict.

The amazing thing, of course, is that you do all this—all this drinking, all the keeping of secrets and withholding of information, all the self-medicating—without making the connection between the drink and the outcome. My father drank, and he stayed stuck in the relationship with the other woman, and stuck in the secrecy, and stuck in the feeling of ambivalence, and he didn't understand until it was way too late that all those actions were related, that the drink fostered the secrecy and the secrecy fostered the stuck feeling, that drink and dishonesty and clouded vision were ultimately one and the same, weaving through each other like the threads of a tapestry. That summer with David and Roger I picked up the threads of that same tapestry, drinking and weaving myself into a life that felt woefully overcomplicated, and I couldn't make the connection either. I wouldn't for many years.

The hard things in life, the things you really learn from, happen with a clear mind. About six weeks after that first lunch with Roger, I finally couldn't stand it, couldn't stand sitting in his car and letting him touch me like that anymore, so one day I summoned up all my nerve and went over to his office. I told him, tentatively but very soberly, that I couldn't see him anymore, and that was the end.

I said, "I'm just too uncomfortable with this." He was sitting at his desk and he just stared at me. I stammered, "I hope—I mean, I hope we can still be friends."

Silence.

Finally, he looked at me and said, "Well. If we're not going to be lovers, I don't see the point."

I didn't see him again, or even talk to him again, but from that point on, I could hate him, instead of merely fear him. Years later, I heard he had died, dropped dead of a heart attack while jogging on the East Side of Providence. I didn't feel a thing.

7 Drinking Alone

THAT FALL, AFTER David moved away to Chicago and my parents nearly broke up and I said good-bye to Roger, I learned to drink alone. That's the year my sister started worrying about my drinking—more than a decade before I finally quit. She came to my apartment one day, opened the refrigerator, and saw a large jug of white wine, nearly empty. "Did you drink all this by yourself?" she asked. I looked at her quizzically, not sure what the big deal was. "Sure," I said. "Why not?"

As my drinking progressed, I'd learn to be more discreet. So would most alcoholics I know: we hid what we drank, and when we drank it and how much and under what circumstances. We hid it from our friends and families; often, we took pains to hide it from total strangers.

My friend Max used to tell liquor-store clerks he needed brandy in order to bake Grand Marnier soufflés. He did this several times a week. He'd go up to the rows of nips they keep by the cash register, point to a little brandy bottle, and ask, "Do you think that's two tablespoons? I need some for a soufflé." Then he'd walk out with three or four of them tucked in a bag. I felt an immediate kinship with Max when he told me that, because I did it too. Late in my drinking, when I'd buy nips of Hennessy to hide in my bathrobe pockets, I used to ask for them as an afterthought, as though I'd just remembered I needed a tiny bit for a recipe. "Oh . . ." I'd say. "Um, I also need a couple of those little Cognacs . . . is that Hennessy? Yeah, two of those."

I've heard countless versions of this story, in countless AA meetings. My friend Meg used to pretend she was shopping for a dinner party. She'd walk up to the wine merchant and ask, thoughtfully, "What kind of wine would you recommend with duck?" and then she'd exit with a case, plus bottles of vodka and Scotch and mixers. Lots of us would shop at different stores every day, sometimes going miles out of our way to get to a new liquor store in order to hide the exact levels of our consumption from the salespeople. Two bottles here, two bottles there, a case somewhere else.

Recycling is a problem to the active alcoholic: you have to *see* all those bottles, heaped together in the recycling bin, and that can be a disconcerting image. Luckily, I did most of my solitary, alcoholic drinking in communities that didn't then recycle, so I'd pile the bottles into a heavy plastic garbage bag and lug them out to the curb or heave them into a Dumpster, hoping no one nearby heard all the glass clinking and rattling as I went along. Sometimes I might go two or three weeks without disposing of the evidence. I'd keep the bottles in empty cases in a cabinet under my kitchen sink and then, when the space under there got too crowded, I'd slink out of the apartment at night with a pair of great heavy bags.

Alcoholic drinking is by nature solitary drinking, drinking whose true nature is concealed from the outside world and, in some respects, from the drinker as well. You think you're drinking to have fun, to be sociable or more relaxed. But you're also drinking to shut down, to retreat.

I once heard a young woman at a meeting describe how annoyed and irritable she seemed to get around people on the rare occasions when she didn't drink. She was very newly sober, just a couple of days, and she said when she drank, those irritated feelings just went away and she stopped caring about other people, how they acted around her or what they thought. "If I've got my bottle," she said, "it's like I can slip into a cocoon."

Lots of nodding in the room when she said that. Lots of struck chords. It's not at all unusual in AA to hear people refer to alcohol as a best friend, and to mean that on the most visceral level: when you're drinking, liquor occupies the role of a lover or a constant companion. It sits there on its refrigerator shelves or on the counter or in the cabinet like a real person, as present and reliable as a best friend. At the end, when I started hiding bottles of Scotch around the house, and tucking nips of brandy into my bathrobe pockets, I did so in the manner of a child who's afraid to be without a favorite blanket or a teddy bear. *Protect me. Shield me from being alone in my own head.*

Alcohol is often a multiple partner: you have your true love, which is the drink you're drawn to most often and most reliably, and then you have secondary loves, past loves, acquaintances, even (but not often) an enemy or two. My friend Kenny was strictly a bourbon man, at least by the end: he bought it by the case and drank it, alone at home, while listening to opera. A man I know named Bobby preferred vodka, a love that dated back to the very first time he bought a bottle of booze, in Concord, New Hampshire, when he was seventeen years old. He stopped a man outside a state liquor store and asked if he'd please get him a bottle of "Smire-noff." The man said, "You mean, Smear-noff?" and Bob said, "Um . . . oh, yeah. Isn't that what I said?" There are beer alcoholics and Scotch alcoholics and bourbon alcoholics and alcoholics who drink nothing but expensive red wine. A lot of us changed partners each season, gravitating toward dark, warming liquors in the winter and light, citrus-laced drinks in the summer, gin-and-tonics, or rum on the rocks with a chunk of lime.

I was a white wine junkie. Toward the end I'd slug down just about anything but if I had my choice, I'd drink a crisp, cold, dry white, a French Sauvignon Blanc or a Chardonnay from the valleys of northern California. The look of a bottle of white wine in a refrigerator always reassured me somehow, the way it stood there on the shelf, beads of moisture forming on the exterior, the labels forming sharp rectangles of color against the pale golden liquid. These days, I can go to a restaurant and watch people sipping dark bottles of cold beer or short, squat glasses of vodka or gin, and it really doesn't affect me much. But even now, when a waitress walks by with a tall glass of white wine, six or eight ounces of liquid relief, my pulse still quickens and I find myself watching it wistfully, the way you might look at a photograph of someone you loved deeply and painfully and then lost.

In the summer of 1981, after I'd graduated, I moved into a tiny studio on the East Side of Providence, a sunny space with high ceilings and a working fireplace, and it was there that I fell in love, truly in love, with white wine. I almost felt like an adult in that apartment, living on my own for the first time, but for the most part that was a superficial sensation, the product of simple, physical acts like unlocking the door to my apartment, clicking across the wood floor in my grown-up shoes, setting a bag of groceries on the counter. Or, more to the point, like taking that bottle of Chardonnay from the refrigerator, sliding out the cork, and pouring the liquid into a flute glass. That seemed like such a sophisticated thing to do—pour the wine, light a fire, settle down on the sofa, and leaf through a magazine—and the ritual seemed full of promise and safety, a code of behavior that could lead me straight toward independence.

In truth, I didn't act the part very well at all. I was broke all the time, waitressing at a restaurant in downtown Providence, and I started buying wine in gallon jugs. I unscrewed the cap at the end of the day, rather than easing out the cork with that satisfying, grown-up *pop*. I rarely lit fires and I was too distracted to leaf through magazines with anything like pleasure or concentration. Most evenings I sat on my futon, which I rolled into a sofa until I went to sleep at night, and I listened to the same Kenny Loggins record over and over because it reminded me of David, who'd moved away, and I got drunk and cried.

Recovering alcoholics often talk about drinking "the way they wanted to" when they were alone, drinking without the feeling of social restraint they might have had at a party or in a restaurant. There's something almost childlike about the need, and about the language we use to describe it: wanting our bottles, wanting to crawl into that dark room in our minds and curl up and be alone with our object of security.

Drinking alone is enormously self-protective, at least in theory. The solitude relieves you of human contact, which can feel burdensome to even the most gregarious alcoholic, and the alcohol relieves you of your own thoughts, of the dark pressure of your own company. Drinking alone is what you do when you can't stand the feeling of living in your own skin. Boswell describes this in his *Life of Johnson:* "I drink alone," Johnson explains, "to get rid of myself, to send myself away. Wine makes a man better pleased with himself."

One December afternoon that year in Providence, during a blizzard, I sat in my apartment looking out the window. Snowflakes spiraled down to the ground and I spiraled down along with them, descending gradually into self-pity, until I was blanketed in the feeling. I'd passed the day the way I usually did, struggling without much success to get out of my own way. I'd promised myself I'd go running or swimming every morning, to start the day in some kind of energized way, and I hadn't. I'd worked the lunch shift—eleven to three—and then come home, sat down on the sofa with my list of things to do: *Call X about creative-writing workshop. Call Y about freelancing. Call Brown Career Services and make an appointment for résumé critique.*

These tasks terrified me—I felt so inadequate and small inside, so afraid of failing—and I hadn't checked off anything. I remember sitting there feeling paralyzed and passive and full of self-loathing and by six o'clock or so, telling myself I needed some fresh air, I put on my coat and trudged off in the snow to the liquor store to buy a bottle of wine. I drank most of it that night, sitting on the futon sofa, and before I went to sleep, I picked up my journal and scrawled: *I'm so depressed. Please make this feeling go away.*

I don't know to whom that *please* was addressed: some external force, I suppose, some abstract sense of a fate that loomed in the distance, or an energy with the power to shape circumstances in my favor and *change* me, from the outside in. I kept writing about my need for a "sense of purpose in my life" and I believed—or hoped—that this feeling would simply *arrive*, descend from above in the form of the right career or the right set of friends or the right relationship.

I lived by the words *if only* and I'd continue to do so for a decade. In my twenties the objects of desire were good jobs and thin thighs: if only I could write for a living I'd be happy; if only I were five or ten or fifteen pounds thinner my life would be different. In my thirties the focus would shift to men: if only I had a relationship, I thought. And then, months after meeting my boyfriend Julian, if only the relationship were different, *if only* . . .

There's something about sober living and sober thinking, about facing long afternoons without the numbing distraction of anesthesia, that disabuses you of the belief in externals, shows you that strength and hope come not from circumstances or the acquisition of things but from the simple accumulation of active experience, from gritting the teeth and checking the items off the list, one by one, even though it's painful and you're afraid.

When you drink, you can't do that. You can't make the distinction between getting *through* painful feelings and getting *away* from them. All you can do is just sit there, numb and sipping, numb and drunk.

Another entry from that year is dated September 28, 1981, thirteen years before I quit drinking. The writing is loopy and scrawled; it says: *Spaced-out brain. I'm worried I'm an alcoholic.*

It amazes me now, to see that a part of me recognized the problem so long ago. But I guess that's the way alcoholism works. You know and you don't know. Or, more accurately, you know and the part of you that wants no part of this knowledge immediately slips into gear, sliding the fear into a new category. You wake up in the morning and—presto!—it's reclassified: *a little problem with drinking,* something you'll take care of when you're less depressed.

I was very depressed that year, lost, and I suppose I employed precisely that logic: I'd drink less at some ill-defined point in the future, when I needed less relief. Looking back at that year, I can see that I was angry, too, and fragile as a baby bird: I couldn't find a job; the world seemed unaccommodating and mean; I felt tiny and ill prepared, finally out of the relatively safe and knowable world of academia and exposed in harsher ways than I'd been in college to some of the particular discomforts of being female. My landlord at the time was a big, self-important realtor who lived on the third floor and used to stare at my breasts when he talked to me. A guy named Tony worked at the building as a handyman, and he'd whistle and hoot at me when I went out to my car. I had long hair at the time, almost waist length, and if I passed close enough to him, he'd grab my braid and tug at it as though the mere fact that it was long entitled him to touch it. I took up running that year, and every once in a while, when I was jogging along and some man leaned out the window of his car and whistled, I'd feel a flash of deep rage, a sensation that felt core and true but seemed to vanish as quickly as it hit.

These may sound like small things, nonevents, but over time they accumulate and inform your sense of the landscape: your breasts get stared at enough times and the world begins to feel like an unsafe place. On some level I must have felt furious, but the fury seemed inaccessible and futile, the way it does to so many women who are taught that female rage is taboo. I suppose I drank because I didn't know what else to do, simply didn't know any better way to handle the fear and the anger.

About a year after I quit drinking, I had coffee with a woman named Jeanette at a small café. It was a gray day in early March, about five-thirty, and from our seat by the window we counted as, one by one, four professional-looking women in their thirties walked into the liquor store across the street and then walked out, each clutching a long brown bag.

Recovering alcoholics love to speculate about the drinking habits of other people, especially if their drinking habits look troublesome—it kind of goes with the territory—so as we watched, Jeanette and I sat there and thought: *Hah. There's another one. Hah. Another drunk-in-progress.* But underneath the smug feeling was a sad feeling, and a strong set of memories about what it was like to pick up that bottle every night on the way home, then shut ourselves up in our apartments and drink.

After a while we got to talking about our old and early days of drinking alone. Jeanette, a lawyer now, had a job as a legal assistant in a large, male-dominated law firm in New York, and she told me she usually felt fine as long as she was ensconced in her office, occupied and task oriented and alone.

"The problem," she said, "was having to *deal* with people."

This was the early 1980s and every day Jeanette wore one of those little skirted suits with a bow at the neck and pinstripes, the standard-issue uniform of the working woman, and she said she always had a terrible feeling of cognitive dissonance when she walked down the halls or into a meeting, as though she were an eleven-year-old playing dress-up with her mother's pearls and pumps. At the same time men in the office stared at her like she was on display: at her legs, crossed under the charcoal gray or navy skirt; at her chest, her lips.

As time passed, Jeanette became aware of a growing confusion about the source of her worth: part of it seemed to come from her work, from being efficient and productive and praiseworthy, but an equal part of it seemed to come from being physically attractive to the men in her office, from being, as she put it, "the resident cutie, the fresh young thing in the corner cubicle."

Complicating matters, Jeanette was used to pleasing people, accustomed to generating feelings of self-worth by seeking approval from people like her father and her schoolteachers, and she felt like that whole system had fallen apart, like she was suddenly playing a different game and hadn't yet received the rule book. Instant imposter syndrome: Jeanette was good at her job, but she felt like a fake, a pseudoadult, an incomplete version of a human being incapable on the deepest, most personal level of believing in her own value. This is such a universal female experience, the lack of self-worth and the rage that simmers underneath it, and we both shook our heads.

Jeanette said, "I used to feel so unanchored. So . . ." Her voice trailed off and a hundred different adjectives seemed to linger in front of us: ill formed, inadequate, uncertain, lonely, *angry*.

She smiled. "I never had a security blanket as a kid," she said. "I had this kind of pride, even as a little kid, that I wasn't like my sister, who carried around stuffed animals all the time and slept with them at night. It's so funny that I'd end up with this other kind of security blanket as an adult."

Booze: the liquid security blanket; the substance that muffles emptiness and anger like a cold snow.

Jeanette and I are the same age and listening to her, I imagined the two of us doing exactly the same thing at twenty-one and twenty-two and twenty-three, the two of us and scores of other young women leaving our offices at the end of the day and reaching for something—anything—to medicate the feelings and fill up the sense of void behind them.

After that first year in Providence I started working at a newspaper. Like Jeanette I was able to slide into a persona that felt relatively reassuring and comfortable during the day: working reporter, a young woman at a desk armed with a telephone and a notebook. I did things of measurable value: wrote pieces that were praised by my boss the way essays and exams were praised by teachers in school; made deadlines and treated my co-workers with consideration and generosity; did my job efficiently and well. But whatever success or sense of accomplishment I felt at work didn't seem to extend any farther than the office walls; I'd leave at the end of the day and my sense of professional identity would dissipate or simply stay behind. I'd run into the landlord on my way upstairs to my apartment, or I'd be hooted at on the street, and I'd be scared and confused again, the cosmic questions about self-worth ready to pounce like predators as soon as I left the building.

So I did what Jeanette did, what so many of us did: curled up at home with my bottle; numbed out.

The movie *Clean and Sober* is a somewhat simplistic look at addiction and recovery but there's one very vivid scene, about midway through, when Michael Keaton comes home from rehab and spends his first night alone in his apartment. He scrubs the place until it gleams, light from halogen lamps glinting off the chrome furniture, and then he sits. Sits on one chair for a few minutes, then gets up and sits on another. He's restless and edgy and you can tell from the way he keeps getting up and sitting down that he feels completely at sea, clueless about how to comfort himself, or entertain himself, or just sit there comfortably in his own skin.

I saw the movie in 1989 when it was released, and during that scene I flashed onto the various apartments I'd lived in by myself over the years, and I squirmed. *One of these days that's going to be me*, I thought, *forced to figure out how to live alone, without the armor*.

The armor, of course, is protection from all the things we might actually *feel*, if we allowed ourselves to feel at all. Although he doesn't quite claim that abstinence from alcohol led directly to the depression he documents in his 1990 memoir, *Darkness Visible*, William Styron vividly describes what happens when a drinker is suddenly left without the armor, left without the self-constructed wall that stands between the self and acute self-awareness: "Suddenly vanished," he writes, "the great ally which for so long had kept my demons at bay was no longer there to prevent those demons from beginning to swarm through the subconscious, and I was emotionally naked, vulnerable as I had never been before." Without liquor, which had "turned" on him suddenly, Styron felt numb and enervated and fragile, subject to "dreadful, pounding seizures of anxiety."

Over the course of my last years of drinking, I lived in another studio apartment, this one in Boston's North End, New England's version of Little Italy. On nights when I had no plans, I'd stop on my way home at the Prince Pantry, a convenience store on the corner near my building, and pick up a bottle of white wine. The store had next to no selection—a cheap Italian Soave and a couple of overpriced California Chardonnays—but there was something about buying wine in a convenience store, as opposed to a fully fledged liquor store, that helped me feel like I wasn't really shopping for booze, just picking up a little something on the way home, the way you'd pick up a quart of milk or a box of cereal for breakfast. The wine would be my primary staple for the evening, but during those last few years I began to understand that a single bottle wouldn't quite suffice, wouldn't quite do the trick, so I'd usually pick up two beers while I was there as well. Not a whole six-pack, just two lone bottles of Molson Golden, which always looked perfectly innocent sitting on the counter beside the wine when I went to pay.

As soon as I got home, I'd crack open the first beer and drink it with a deep relief. In ways, I acknowledged that my little stockpile of booze was an ally, just as Styron described it: a defense against my own subconscious, against the demons that threatened to swim up from wherever they hid inside. Sometimes I'd actually think about that scene from Clean and Sober, about the way Michael Keaton just sat there in his apartment, restless and staring. My place was modern and high tech the way his was, with halogen lamps and cool gray carpeting, and I'd understand that the beer, and the one after that and the bottle of wine after that,

served a very specific purpose: it kept me from that piercing consciousness of self, kept me from the task of learning to tolerate my
own company.

Without liquor I'd feel like a trapped animal, which is why I
always had it. Without liquor I didn't know what to do with
myself, and I mean that in the most literal sense, as though my
thoughts and my limbs were foreign to me and I'd missed some
key set of instructions about how to use them. I used to feel that
way on Sunday mornings, when I'd wake up alone in the apartment with nothing before me but unstructured time. *Here I am, in
my apartment. Here I am, puttering through the kitchen. Here I am,
washing a dish and setting it on the rack. Here I am . . . conscious
of being alone, conscious of my own breath and my own skin and my
own thoughts; here I am, waiting waiting waiting and if I keep doing
this, if I don't find some way out of my own head, I'll die of boredom
or go insane or explode at any moment.*

The drink defused that explosive feeling, numbed the self-
awareness. I'd learned that back in Providence and I'd carted the
knowledge along with me ever since, moving it from apartment to
apartment like a piece of furniture I couldn't seem to replace.
Sometimes, the two Molsons and the bottle of wine didn't feel
like enough so after I drank the beers, I'd go across the street to
Pizzeria Regina and order a small pizza with mushrooms and Ca-
nadian bacon, to go. While the pizza baked, I'd sit at the bar and
order a glass of Chianti, which was served in tall Coke glasses,
and I'd drink it while I waited, watching TV or chatting with the
bartender. Sometimes I'd gulp it down fast and have another. I
always left the bartender a big tip and he always kept an eye on
my glass, ready to refill it if I nodded. A tacit agreement: it's
amazing how many companions a drinker can find, even when
she's drinking alone.

My friend Janet, who's sober now, lived about two blocks away
from me during that time, drinking actively, and I wouldn't be

surprised if our paths crossed periodically. She used to drink alone at Regina's, too, and I sometimes wonder if we ever noticed each other there, or if we just sat by ourselves, waiting for our pizzas and staring down at our glasses. Probably the latter. The rituals, the little routines, that alcoholics use to break the drinking into segments and minimize its visibility are very preoccupying. You buy, you edge home with your large brown bag, you lock the door behind you, and only then can you relax. All that planning takes energy.

Late at night we called people. Legions of us did this: almost every alcoholic I know. We'd come in after a long night out drinking, or we'd sit on the sofa for too many hours in a row, finally getting so restless and morose we couldn't stand it anymore, and in a fit of desperation we'd pick up the phone. *Okay. It's one A.M. Someone must be awake in California; reach for that receiver and go!* The phenomenon is so common there's even a name for it: alcoholics I know call it "drink-and-dial."

Several years after she quit drinking, my friend Ginny called up a friend who lived in Seattle and told her she was in recovery.

"Well, I figured *that* was coming," the friend said. When Ginny expressed surprise, she said, "Don't you remember? You used to call me at least once a month and you'd be bombed, talking about how you thought you had a drinking problem."

Ginny was astonished. "I *did?*" She had no memory of the calls, not even one.

Ginny told a group of us that story one night in a restaurant and we all rolled our eyes, cringing with our own memories. Reaching for the address book; seeking out that one person in the right time zone who won't mind being disturbed by a slightly slurred voice at the end of the line; closing one eye so the numbers on the phone pad don't blur when you try to punch them out; waiting for the dial tone, the sober voice on the other end; hearing your own voice as you speak into the telephone, not quite knowing what you're doing, what you're after, why you're even calling—are you depressed? lonely? insane? You just do it. Drink-

and-dial, drink and reach for the phone, drink and search for some kind of human contact.

The paradoxical thing about drinking alone—the insidious thing, really—is that it creates an illusion of emotional authenticity which you can see as false only in retrospect. When I drank by myself, the liquor truly seemed like the one thing that gave me access to my true feelings, a route to real emotion. Drinking and melting down; drinking and weeping; drinking and then sharing that pain with another person across the phone. *I'm depressed. I'm lonely. Help me.* But liquor is deceptive, the feelings it generates illusory: the next day you don't remember the action or the feelings that propelled you toward the phone; when you wake up in the morning, the only real thing you have is a headache.

One night, four or five years before I quit, I went out for drinks with some friends on a Friday night, then went out for dinner and drank more, then ended up at a bar on Newbury Street, a chic stretch of retail in Boston's Back Bay, peppered with restaurants and hair salons and little boutiques. It was a summer night and three of us, me and two men from work, snagged one of the coveted sidewalk tables outside, and we drank Cognac, many glasses. Some nights, you know you're going to get rip-roaring drunk, you set out to get trashed, and this was one of those nights. I don't remember the circumstances behind that impulse, and I don't remember much of the evening, just that I drank and drank and drank and at some point some deep-seated instinct for self-preservation must have kicked in and I knew I had to get home and I ended up in a cab.

I was seeing Michael by then and I took the cab to his house. I have no memory of the drive there, no memory of paying the cabdriver, no idea if I passed out in the backseat or if I rambled at the poor man the whole way from Boston to Cambridge. Michael was out with some friends, and I have the dimmest memory of going into his bedroom, picking up the phone at the foot of his bed, and calling my mother. It must have been one or two in the morning and I recall, but just vaguely, that I heard her voice on the phone and I started to cry.

This was classic behavior for me. Drinking tapped into the side of me that wanted to feel sorry for myself, to get emotionally messy and morose. My mother wasn't like that at all, which may have been why I turned to her: she had a kind of internal reserve, an astonishing capacity for self-comfort, and she handled solitude more effectively than almost anyone I knew. She could spend whole days by herself—painting, knitting, reading; losing herself in art and craft and intellect. By the time I was drinking regularly, in my twenties, I'd visit her at the house sometimes and watch her sit there working on a sweater, needles clicking softly. She seemed so serene, her feet tucked underneath her on the sofa, and I couldn't fathom why she didn't get bored or restless or uncomfortable or lonely. I'd sit and watch and hold my glass of wine in front of me like an amulet. I couldn't do it, be alone without the wine; I didn't know how.

I also didn't know what to say to her on the phone that night. I just burst into tears and I remember her voice on the end of the line: "What's the matter, sweetie?"

I slurred out the words, drunk and weeping: "Mom . . . I think I have a drinking problem."

I don't remember the rest of the conversation, just that I wept into the phone for a long time and finally settled down. At some point we must have finished talking and hung up and I must have passed out. Michael got home sometime after two and found his front door wide open, every light in his apartment on, and me, crashed on the bed with all my clothes on. He got me undressed and under the covers (I don't remember that either) and I woke up the next morning with that horrible, disoriented sense of dread, knowing I'd done something really bad but able to recall only the outlines. When I remembered enough, I got out of bed and called my mother again.

"I'm sorry I woke you last night," I said.

"Do you remember what we talked about?" she asked.

I said I did, and I promised her I'd do something about it, I'd get my drinking under control.

She asked, "Do you think you can?" and I said yes, I'd been really depressed but I'd deal with it, I promised I would. "I promise, Mom. I'll deal with it."

This was three years before I made, and failed to keep, the very same promise during our walk on the beach on Martha's Vineyard. I don't know how much my mother worried about my drinking between that late-night call and our walk at Menemsha Pond, and I don't know if she shared the details about either conversation with my father. He never talked to me about my drinking.

I hung up the phone that morning and thought about my mother, about how alarming it must have been for her to hear me like that, incoherent and sobbing in the middle of the night. I felt intensely guilty for a second, and intensely ashamed, but the feelings didn't last. Like I said, all you're really aware of after a night like that is the hangover. The head pounds. You may feel a twinge of embarrassment, a pang of worry or despair, but most of the pain is physical in the morning, so you choose to focus on that. *Get me the Advil; I feel like shit.* You roll over in bed. *Let me go back to sleep; I'll deal with it later.*

Alcoholics tend to drink alone even when they're drinking with other people. That's a concept I wouldn't fully grasp until I'd quit drinking, but every once in a while I'd catch a glimpse of it, a snippet of the way alcohol isolated me from other people, even when I seemed to be right smack in the middle of them.

That morning, lying in bed with a hangover, it occurred to me that I'd been out with friends all evening and hadn't really made eye contact with any of them, hadn't really had a moment of conversation that felt genuine or connected. The realization was small, a little flash, but it would stick with me, and return to me sometimes, a wave of awareness that made something in my stomach feel heavy, like I'd swallowed a stone. I didn't quite understand how you could spend an evening like that with an intimate group and end up all alone, sitting in a circle around a café table with two other people and no one at the same time.

My friend Jane says that after a while, alcohol becomes a veil, a barely visible shield that stands between the drinker and any chance of real intimacy.

My friend Mary puts it more bluntly: "Emotional bomb shelter," she says. "Just in case."

8 *Addiction*

THE FOLLOWING QUESTIONS, put together by the National Council on Alcoholism and Drug Dependence, are designed to help people decide whether or not they have a drinking problem. This is how I answered them several weeks before I quit.

Yes	No		
x		1)	Do you occasionally drink heavily after a disappointment, a quarrel, or when the boss gives you a hard time?
x		2)	When you have trouble or feel under pressure, do you always drink more heavily than usual?
x		3)	Have you noticed that you are able to handle more liquor than you did when you were first drinking?
x		4)	Did you ever wake up on the morning after and discover that you could not remember part of the evening before, even though your friends tell you that you did not pass out?
x		5)	When drinking with other people, do you try to have a few extra drinks when others will not know it?
x		6)	Are there certain occasions when you feel uncomfortable if alcohol is not available?

Yes	No		
x		7)	Have you recently noticed that when you begin drinking you are in more of a hurry to get the first drink than you used to be?
x		8)	Do you sometimes feel a little guilty about your drinking?
x		9)	Are you secretly irritated when your family or friends discuss your drinking?
x		10)	Have you recently noticed an increase in the frequency of your memory "blackouts"?
x		11)	Do you often find that you wish to continue drinking after your friends say they have had enough?
x		12)	Do you usually have a reason for the occasions when you drink heavily?
x		13)	When you are sober, do you often regret things you have done or said while drinking?
x		14)	Have you tried switching brands or following different plans for controlling your drinking?
x		15)	Have you often failed to keep the promises you have made to yourself about controlling or cutting down on your drinking?
	x	16)	Have you ever tried to control your drinking by making a change of jobs, or moving to a new location?
	x	17)	Do you try to avoid family or close friends while you are drinking?
	x	18)	Are you having an increasing number of financial and work problems?
	x	19)	Do more people seem to be treating you unfairly without good reason?
x		20)	Do you eat very little or irregularly when you are drinking?
x		21)	Do you sometimes have the shakes in the morning and find that it helps to have a little drink?

Yes No

x   22) Have you recently noticed that you cannot drink as much as you once did?

     x   23) Do you sometimes stay drunk for several days at a time?

x   24) Do you sometimes feel very depressed and wonder if life is worth living?

     x   25) Sometimes after periods of drinking, do you see or hear things that aren't there?

     x   26) Do you get terribly frightened after you have been drinking heavily?

The National Council on Alcoholism and Drug Dependence says if you answer yes to any of the above questions, you have some symptoms that may indicate alcoholism. People who answer yes to questions 1 through 8 are said to be in the early stages of alcoholism, which typically last from ten to fifteen years. Yes answers to questions 9 through 21 indicate middle-stage alcoholism, which usually lasts from two to five years. Questions 22 through 26 indicate the beginning of the final stage.

In its last stage, alcoholism can kill: heavy and chronic drinking can harm virtually every organ and system in the body. It is the single most important cause of illness and death from liver disease in the U.S.; it can increase the risk of cancer, cardiovascular disease, and such infectious diseases as pneumonia and tuberculosis; it can also alter brain-cell function, shrink the cerebral cortex, throw the body's hormonal system out of balance, and lead to sexual dysfunction and infertility.

The office of the Secretary of Health and Human Services noted in its 1993 congressional report on alcohol and health that in 1988 15.3 million Americans met the criteria for alcohol abuse (patterns of problem drinking that result in health consequences and social problems or both) or alcohol dependence (alcoholism) as defined by the American Psychiatric Association's Diagnostic and Statistical Manual of Mental Disorders. Alcohol contributes to nearly 100,000 deaths a year, making it the nation's third largest cause of preventable death (tobacco, and poor diet and exercise patterns are the two largest causes). Those afflicted by alcoholism and other illnesses it causes occupy as many as half the hospital beds in the U.S. on any given day; it is estimated that alcohol is a factor in approximately fifty percent of all homicides and thirty percent of all suicides.

I first came across a copy of the National Council on Alcoholism's questions in Nan Robertson's *Getting Better*. At that point I answered yes to the first fifteen questions and I remember thinking I had another five or so years to go. When we're that deeply in love with drink, we have no idea what kind of fire we're playing with.

I get pangs of horror sometimes when I think about what was happening to my brain back then, how all that alcohol was wending its way into my bloodstream and vital organs, how liquor might have been throwing things out of whack from the very start.

Normal drinkers seem to have a kind of built-in alarm system that tells them at a certain point to stop drinking. They ingest alcohol, it passes through the stomach walls and small intestine and into the bloodstream, then moves through cell membranes and mixes in the entire water content of the body: brain, liver, heart, pancreas, lungs, kidneys, and every other organ and tissue system are affected. Alcohol basically depresses the central nervous system, although at low doses it gives the drinker a revved-up, pleasant feeling: at first alcohol increases blood flow, accelerates the heart rate, and stimulates brain cells, all of which makes the drinker feel giddy, talkative, energetic. At higher doses the depressive effects are felt: the drinker gets uncoordinated; vision may be impaired; reflexes are delayed; speech gets slurred. The normal drinker usually calls it quits well before that point: that elusive internal alarm goes off and says, *No more*. Some Asians, who typically have one of the lowest rates of alcoholism in the world, experience what's called the Asian Flush Syndrome: too much liquor makes them warm and queasy, causes the heart rate to rise and the blood pressure to drop. The feeling is unpleasant and the drinker's natural, self-protective tendency is to abstain.

Not mine. No one really knows precisely why some people become alcoholic while others don't, but scientists are closing in on some of the causes. Alcoholism is probably an inherited phenomenon—research over the last thirty years has begun to confirm that alcoholism runs in families, suggesting that although environmental factors may contribute to the development of the disease, most alcoholics probably have a genetic predisposition to it as well.

Addiction to alcohol is also a neurological phenomenon, the result of a complex set of molecular alterations that take place in the brain when it's excessively and repeatedly exposed to the drug. The science of addiction is complicated, but the basic idea is fairly straightforward: alcohol appears to wreak havoc on the brain's natural systems of craving and reward, compromising the functioning of the various neurotransmitters and proteins that create feelings of well-being.

Essentially, drinking artificially "activates" the brain's reward system: you have a martini or two and the alcohol acts on the part of the brain's circuitry that makes you feel good, increasing the release of the neurotransmitter dopamine, which is central to feelings of pleasure and reward. Over time (and given the right combination of vulnerability to alcoholism and actual alcohol abuse), the brain develops what are known as "compensatory adaptations" to all that artificial revving up: in an effort to bring its own chemistry back into its natural equilibrium, it works overtime to *decrease* dopamine release, ultimately leaving those same pleasure/ reward circuits depleted.

A vicious cycle ensues: by drinking too much, you basically diminish your brain's ability to manufacture feelings of well-being and calm on its own and you come to depend increasingly on the artificial stimulus—alcohol—to produce those feelings. This is why an alcoholic may wake up after a night of heavy drinking struggling with two competing motivations. The logical, thinking part of the brain, taking note of the hangover and the feelings of remorse, kicks in with determination and resolve: *Drinking too much is bad; I'm going to cut down; I mean it.* But the far less rational part—this far more mysterious, primitive, and powerful circuitry of pleasure and need—speaks in a more urgent, compelling voice: *No*, it says. *I feel bad. And I need a very specific thing, alcohol, in order to feel good again.*

Seen in this light, alcoholism may be a disease in the purest sense: a physiological state producing a sense of overwhelming *disease*.

The idea that alcoholism is a physical illness was first formally advanced in this country in 1960 with the publication of Elvin Morton Jellinek's *The Disease Concept of Alcoholism.* Today, Jellinek's thinking is standard in medical circles, although the disease theory remains controversial among some doctors and researchers, who believe there isn't sufficient proof of the genetic or biological origin to label it a disease, or who say that the medical model overemphasizes the physiological aspects of alcoholism, thereby ignoring some of its social, cultural, or psychological roots.

Those debates aside, the idea that alcoholism is comparable to other illnesses—diabetes, say—is hard for an active alcoholic to internalize. After all, alcoholism doesn't *feel* like a disease. Tangible, physical symptoms, such as hangovers or tremors in the hands, may appear, but they also pass, they're easy to ignore, and they don't tend to impede the drinker in clear or obvious ways. The morning after that drunken phone call with my mother, for example, I may have woken up with a pounding headache, but I continued to function. As I recall, I went sailing that day, and while I *felt* lousy—a few times the water got choppy and I thought I might actually heave right there over the side of the boat— nobody, least of all me, would have seen me as "diseased." By five o'clock, after a beer and some food, I didn't even feel sick. And for all the advances researchers have made in understanding the disease, I still couldn't have waltzed into a doctor's office that day, taken a blood test, and walked out with a definitive diagnosis: Yes, you are ill, or No, you are not.

Most alcoholics (not all) sooner or later have to grapple with the idea that they have a disease. Some people drink in wildly alcoholic ways the first time they ever taste the stuff: they black out immediately, become violent and out of control, and drinkers like that may have an easier time than some of us understanding that certain powerful physiological forces are at work, that their brains respond to alcohol very differently from those of other drinkers. But those of us who've experienced more gradual and insidious descents into alcoholism have to turn the disease concept over and over in our minds, to learn over long periods of time to believe and accept it.

Back in those years of drinking alone in Providence—and for more than a decade after that—I was nowhere near believing I had an illness, nowhere near even considering it. The body, after all, colludes with the mind, and I was still profoundly affected by the simple matter of physiology, by the simple truth that alcohol made me *feel* better.

Plus, until I got sober, alcoholism seemed more to me like a moral issue than a physical one. This is one of our culture's most basic assumptions about the disease, and one of its most destructive: we figure that drinking too much is a sign of weakness and lack of self-restraint; that it's "bad"; that it can be overcome by will. Child of an analyst that I am, I'd add insight to the list of remedies—and I did, all the way to rehab. Tease out the *reasons* you drink—the hidden rages and fears, the psychological roots— and the problem will resolve itself. *Think* your way to mental health; turn it over to the psychiatric couch.

In fact, that's an enormously self-defeating line of thought. When I finally went to the rehab, I was astonished to hear lectures about alcoholism that suggested my drinking really did have physiological roots, that I lost control and drank as much as I did on certain nights because a set of very powerful physical mechanisms were at work. "Your brain's ability to manufacture the stuff you need to feel good is compromised," one physician told us during my first week, describing some of the current neurological research. "If you abstain, it'll get its balance back." I sat there in awe, thinking, for the first time: *Oh, so it wasn't all me. So it wasn't all a matter of insight and will.*

Neurology may help explain why traditional "talk" therapies have been so ineffective in addressing alcohol addiction: you can load up an alcoholic on a diet of insight but the body tends to speak more directly than the mind; if the brain is screaming for booze, no number of revelations about underlying causes is going to counter that call.

Science may also explain why relapse rates are so high: those neurological reward circuits have extremely long and powerful memories, and once the simple message—*alcohol equals pleasure*—gets imprinted into the drinker's brain, it may stay there indefinitely, perhaps a lifetime. Environmental cues—the sight of a wineglass, the smell of gin, a walk past a favorite bar—can trigger the wish to drink in a heartbeat, and they often do. One of the most commonly cited statistics on recidivism comes from *The Course of Alcoholism: Four Years after Treatment*, a January 1980 report by the Rand Corporation and the most extensive and comprehensive study of its kind to date. The study tracked a group of nine hundred alcoholic men over a period of four years. Of those, only twenty-eight percent remained free of alcohol problems both at eighteen months and at four years after entering treatment; only fifteen percent were in continuous remission for the entire four years. Once you've crossed the line into alcoholism, the percentages are not in your favor: there appears to be no safe way to drink again, no way to return to normal, social, controlled drinking.

A lot of alcoholics use the cucumber-to-pickle analogy to describe that phenomenon: a true alcoholic is someone who's turned from a cucumber into a pickle; you can try to stop a cucumber from turning into a pickle, but there's no way you can turn a pickle back into a cucumber.

So there I was at age twenty, then twenty-one, then twenty-five and older, literally pickling. Whether the process could have been halted at those earlier stages is the subject of some debate these days. In the past few years, a handful of workshops and self-help groups have cropped up to help drinkers moderate their alcohol intake before it gets out of hand. This so-called "moderation movement" suggests that the line between problem drinking and alcoholism is clear, and challenges AA's philosophy of total abstinence. With proper instruction, the thinking goes, one can be taught to drink responsibly. To me, the idea that a budding alcoholic can learn to drink moderately sounds like a contradiction in terms. (I rarely, if ever, drank moderately, even at the beginning.) It also seems to ignore the more deeply-rooted, compulsive pulls a drinker feels toward alcohol; these are needs that don't respond well to the concept of moderation.

More important, the moderation philosophy seems counter to one of the most essential aspects of alcoholic experience—namely, that most of us have already tried, and consistently failed, to moderate our drinking on our own, experimenting time after time with control. One man I know talks in meetings about returning to drinking after three years of continuous sobriety. He decided to "conduct a little experiment with controlled drinking" and bought a bottle of Scotch. He had a drink. Nothing "bad" happened—he didn't die right then and there or fly into a rage or go mad—so he had another. And then another. At the end of the evening, he stood up and announced, to nobody in particular, "The experiment has failed." The bottle of Scotch was empty.

That story is classic. The struggle to control intake—modify it, cut it back, deploy a hundred different drinking strategies in the effort—is one of the most universal hallmarks of alcoholic behavior. We swear off hard liquor and resolve to stick to beer. We develop new rules: we'll never drink alone; we'll never drink in the morning; we'll never drink on the job; we'll only drink on weekends, or after five o'clock; we'll coat our stomachs with milk or olive oil before we go out drinking to keep ourselves from getting too drunk; we'll have a glass of water for every glass of wine; we'll do anything—anything—to show ourselves that we can, in fact, drink responsibly.

In the past, if we got desperate enough, we checked ourselves into asylums, which for decades was the only formal option for the low-bottom drunk. Alcohol rehabilitation centers as we know them today are a relatively recent phenomenon—Smithers, in New York, is one of the best known and most highly respected rehabs in the U.S.; when it opened, in 1973, it was one of only a dozen or so facilities of its kind.

The period prior to that is known today as the "snake pit" era of alcohol treatment: alcoholics were called "ineebs," short for "inebriates," and when hospitalized, they were usually locked up with the mentally ill. When Bill Wilson, who cofounded AA in 1935, was first hospitalized for the disease in 1933, he was admitted to the Charles B. Towns Hospital, in Manhattan. According to Nan Robertson the basic protocol there was known as "purge and puke"—let the guy dry out, load him up with cathartics like belladonna and castor oil, and send him on his way. Wilson was hospitalized there three times without lasting results.

Wilson, of course, ultimately stumbled upon the one remedy that seemed to work: talking with other alcoholics. The reasons this works are varied and elusive—volumes could be, and have been, written about how and why AA succeeds, some critical, some laudatory—but one of the most essential ingredients has to do with the power of group perspective and support. Alcoholics have notoriously selective memories. No matter how sickening the hangover, how humiliating the drunken behavior, how dangerous the blind-drunk drive home, we seem incapable of recalling consistently or clearly how bad things got when we drank.

Drinkers talk about losing the power of choice over alcohol: At certain times, when the need or desire to drink becomes too strong, those memories simply evaporate. Willpower vanishes, resolutions dissolve, defenses crumble.

AA offers a solution. The fellowship—the meetings and stories and friendships formed—help alcoholics counter that flaw of selective memory, help us remember what it was like to drink, what happened to us, and how others like us changed when they stopped. And the twelve steps of recovery outlined in AA literature and meetings help counter the buildup of suffering and humiliation, offering a way of life that has to do with honesty and self-awareness and healing, with addressing directly, rather than anesthetizing, the fears and rages and feelings that compelled us to drink in the first place.

9 *Substitution*

About a year after I quit drinking, three women and I, all sober now, sat in a restaurant and determined that on a single evening in June of 1983, we were, respectively, starving, throwing up, stealing, and popping Valium.

Oh, and drinking.

Janet was the vomiter. For several years, in college, she threw up four or five times a week, not because she had too much to drink (which she had) but because she stuck her finger down her throat and made herself. While Janet was huddled over the toilet bowl, Sarah was stealing a sweatshirt from Kmart, not because she particularly wanted the sweatshirt but because something deep inside her needed to feel shameful and bad and every once in a while—a couple of times a year—she'd find herself creeping into some store like Kmart and stealing something stupid. Amy stole too—Valium, from her cousin's medicine cabinet—and that evening, while Sarah eased the sweatshirt off the rack and stuffed it into her knapsack, Amy reached into the bottle of Tylenol, where she kept her cache of stolen Valium, and took out two pills. Me? I was secreted away in my room, cutting an apple and a one-inch cube of cheese into tiny, symmetrical slices and eating them one by one, a 300-calorie ritual that constituted my dinner every day for nearly three years.

Janet looked around the table at all of us. She said, "Boy, were *we* a fun group," and we all broke up laughing.

In most of the AA meetings I go to, about three quarters of the people introduce themselves as alcoholics (as in "My name is Joe and I'm an alcoholic") and the rest introduce themselves as alcoholics and addicts. Sometimes you'll hear, "I'm an alcoholic and a drug addict," sometimes just "I'm an addict," and sometimes a more specific description, like "I'm an alcoholic and bulimic," or "I'm an alcoholic and coke addict." Some people have trouble with this, believing AA groups should focus specifically on alcohol addiction, but for the most part, at least in the meetings I attend, there's a lot of acceptance for cross-addictions and dual addictions. Many people in AA have at least dabbled in other addictive substances or behaviors and the general feeling is that it's all a question of which one you choose. At heart all addictions are driven by the same impulses and most accomplish the same goals; you just use a different substance, or take a slightly different path, to get there.

For women, that path often winds around alcohol and heads straight through food. You hear about women who became bulimic or anorexic in high school or college, then established some kind of equilibrium around food when or after they started drinking. For men it's usually other drugs, most often pot or cocaine, or it's gambling. Sometimes it's a more obscure behavior, like self-mutilation—you'll hear about people with compulsions to cut themselves with knives, which sounds horrifying and bizarre until you think of self-mutilation as a way to physicalize pain the same way lots of addictions do, the way anorexia creates the physical pain of hunger, the way drinking creates the physical pounding of a hangover. In my experience it's a rare addict who hasn't at least danced around another addiction, or who can't imagine substituting one for another.

The Harvard University Eating Disorders Center estimates that twenty-five percent of women with eating disorders also suffer from substance-abuse problems. Sometimes I think I know all of them, women who traded in one form of pain and obsession for another, or who danced around with both at the same time, women who've spent years struggling not just to live alone with their own thoughts but also to exist with some modicum of peace in their own bodies.

These are women who toss around the phrase *food issues* a lot, as in "I had a lot of food issues back then," or "My food issues are really up these days." Anyone who's struggled with a distorted body image or hyperconsciousness of weight (and that's most women I know) understands what those words mean: they're shorthand for self-hatred and self-sabotage, for loss of control or fear of it, for all the other particularly female rages and fears that, according to *The New York Times*, compel half the population to shell out an estimated $33 billion a year on diet- and weight-loss programs.

And, while they're at it, a few extra bucks on booze.

Janet is thirty-seven. She's tall and striking, with cropped blond hair and red lipstick, and she's one of the most thoughtful women I know—articulate and sensitive, the sort of person who really listens when other people talk, whose eyes well up with tears when she's moved by something you say. When you ask her about her vomiting days, she closes her eyes and literally grimaces, as though the image of herself pinned under the dual wheels of food- and alcohol-obsession is too horrifying to contemplate for longer than about a second.

Janet grew up in a small, insulated town in Vermont, then went off to college when she was seventeen and basically went crazy. I mean that in the bad way, not in the cut-loose, let's-party way you sometimes associate with campus craziness. I mean daily drinking and compulsive overeating and self-induced vomiting, a near total unleashing of addictive impulses. Janet went from one cigarette every week or so to a pack a day by the end of her first semester. She drank hard and she drank to get drunk. Her weight careened up, then plunged down, shot up again, then plunged back down.

Talking about this in my kitchen on a recent spring day, Janet looked at me and said, "You know, it's a miracle I even *graduated*, living like that." We were drinking herb tea, and this time we both shook our heads, not out of pity for the particulars of Janet's experience but out of a more generalized empathy for just about all the women we know, all the women who've struggled like that. "The *pain*," Janet said. "It's just so painful, to live that way."

Painful and extraordinarily typical. All the things that drive you to drink can drive you to do any number of other horrible things to yourself just as easily. For Janet self-destruction came in the form of bulimia, which provides its own brand of mind-numbing obsession: she'd sit in her room at college and she'd consider and plot—what would she eat, how much, how would she get the food, where would she consume it. And then she'd try to talk herself out of another binge, and then she'd talk herself back in ("Just this one time, just one more time and then I'll stop"), and then she'd go out and just *eat*, the same way you go out and just get drunk. She'd load up on cookies and chips and slices of cake, or she'd combine the two obsessions, go out and get rip-roaring drunk, then lose any earlier sense of restraint she may have had about food. And then she'd eat with that particular brand of panicked, frenzied abandon, a sensation that only women who've lost control around food can understand.

Later, when she finished eating and throwing up, or when she woke up in the morning bloated and hung over, she'd hate herself, loathe herself, and the stage would be set for a repetition of the cycle: any sense of herself as competent or worthy would have been drowned away by the liquor, or flushed away down the toilet; any conviction that she could find a better way to manage her fears or her feelings would be undermined by another degree or two; not believing in her soul that she was a capable or valuable human being, a woman who deserved to be fed in a nurturing way, she'd simply, inevitably, repeat the cycle again.

I am consistently amazed to hear women talk about their multiple relationships with addictions, the way they combine two or three, the way they shift from one to another, so naturally and gracefully you might think they were changing partners in a dance. Addictions segue into one another with such ease: a bout of compulsive overeating fills you with shame and sexual inferiority, which fills you with self-loathing and doubt, which leads you to a drink, which temporarily counters the self-hatred and fills you with chemical confidence, which leads you to sleep with a man you don't love, which leads you circling back to shame, and voilà: the dance can begin again. The dance *will* begin again, for the music is always there in women's minds, laced with undertones of fear and anger, urging us on into the same sad circles of restraint and abandon, courtship and flight.

I use the phrase *women's minds* deliberately, as opposed to *female alcoholics' minds*, because I don't think I know a single woman, alcoholic or otherwise, who doesn't engage in that dance to some extent, sporadically or regularly, fueled by varying substances and propelled by varying degrees of self-destruction. Anyone who observes women at cocktail parties knows what I mean, the way a woman will circle the hors d'oeuvres tray, glass of wine in hand, the way she'll hover over a stuffed mushroom or a cube of cheese and say something about it in a voice just one shade too high: "Oh, I think I'll have just one more," or, "Oh, I better not!" Alcoholics and addicts may inhabit the center of the dance floor, but countless others, men and women, stand at the fringes, placing one toe over the line from time to time, then drawing it back to safety.

Michael once came with me to an AA meeting to hear Janet speak. We sat in the back and I pointed out various people I knew. Every other one of them had a second or third addiction: *There's Elizabeth—she was bulimic for about seven years. There's Jamie—alcoholic, but his drug of choice is pot. He hasn't had a drink*

*in a long time but he keeps relapsing on the pot. There's Bobby—
alcoholic, pill addict; he had a shrink in Manhattan who had him on
just about every major tranquilizer there is. There's Amy—she's the
one who used to steal Valium from her cousin. There's John—alcohol
and cocaine. There's Louise—alcohol and heroin.*

He stopped me at that one. "Heroin? *Her?*" We both looked at
Louise, a tiny woman with short, spiky red hair who looks about
twenty-five, maybe thirty. Her right eyebrow is pierced, and she
wears a lot of black, but other than that she looks like somebody's
younger sister, or someone you might see behind the counter in a
trendy café, pouring lattes and listening to jazz.

"Yup," I said. "You'd never know, huh?"

He just shook his head again. "Amazing."

Amazing, yes, at least until you get used to the idea that addictions can touch anybody. When I first started going to AA meetings, when I was fresh out of rehab and really scared and angry
that I couldn't drink anymore, I found myself watching people in
the street in a new way, trying to scope out who had a drinking or
drug problem and who didn't. I'd see some incredibly normal-
looking person, a man dressed in a suit and carrying a briefcase, or
a woman wearing leggings and a sweater and an ordinary haircut,
and I'd think: *Nope. Not her. Not him. No alcoholics there.* But
every once in a while I'd walk into a meeting and see someone I'd
just dismissed like that out on the street sitting there in the front
row and saying, "Hi, I'm an alcoholic and a coke addict." You just
never know. Nobody is immune.

Multiple addictions are both helpful and insidious, helpful because they can propel a lot of people into treatment and recovery
at relatively young ages (a lot of people in AA in their twenties
are there because drugs like cocaine and heroin caused their
drinking to spiral out of control long before it might have otherwise), and insidious because they can mask each other, fueling
denial for longer periods of time. This happened to Janet. She
describes her college years as a period of intense psychic drain,
with the twin addictions of food and drink taking up so much

energy she barely had room for anything else. But then she graduated, settled down in a new city, and slowly the bulimic episodes
grew fewer and farther between, slowly her relationship with food
returned to something approximating normalcy. What she didn't
notice—or, more precisely, what she didn't want to notice—was
that the drinking merely overtook and overshadowed the bulimia,
picking up where the one left off.

But one bad relationship feels better than two bad relationships. As Janet put it, sipping tea in my kitchen, "At the time it
looked like progress."

I traded addictions, too, and felt the same way about the shift.
Starting in the fall of 1982, a year after I graduated from college, I
entered into a dance with anorexia, starving myself with exactly
the same zeal I'd drink with later on and developing an obsession
around the behavior that would pare my weight down from its
normal level, 120 pounds, to a low of 83. Like any addictive
behavior it started slowly at first, building momentum so gradually
I couldn't see the stranglehold it began to develop on my life.
And like drinking, anorexia was a strategy, a way of managing
strong emotion.

I'd moved from my studio in Providence into a new apartment
in the same neighborhood, with two roommates. I'd gotten my
first job as a reporter, working for a small alternative newspaper
called *The Eagle*. On the surface my life appeared to be moving
forward—new friends, a sense of professional direction—but I was
still as scared and shy and angry as I'd been the year before, the
fragile baby bird. So in a sense I built myself a cage, constructed a
set of walls out of my own bones.

The metaphor is apt: anorexia had the feel of a cage, a safe
place where I could feel protected and removed and disciplined
and, above all, in control.

In the summer of 1982 my mother had been diagnosed with
breast cancer. She had a lumpectomy and radiation treatments,

then began a year's worth of chemotherapy. David, who'd gone off to Chicago the year before, came to visit me right around the time she went into the hospital. He'd planned to spend July and August in Providence with me but decided after a few weeks to spend the bulk of the time traveling in Europe with a friend instead. I was deeply disappointed by this, and furious. The little stirring of rage I so often felt and so often quashed rose up in me when he announced his plans, but I didn't say anything. Instead, I walked him to the train station, said good-bye, then headed back toward my office, thinking: *I am not going to eat.* A hunger strike, as willful and deliberate as a carefully crafted political statement.

At the end of the summer David stopped in Providence on his way back to Chicago. In six weeks I'd lost seventeen pounds and chopped off all my hair. I wouldn't make the connection until long after I quit drinking, but I looked like a cancer patient. At the time, though, I had no idea, no idea how angry I was at David, not a clue how worried I was about my mother's health.

The feeling behind that decision—*I am not going to eat*—would take root in me over the next year, mutating from an ill-defined instinct into a mode of self-definition. *I am not going to eat. I am going to master my impulses. I am going to exert power over my appetite and this will make me strong.*

In ways the strategy worked. Starving made me feel special. My office was only a few blocks away from my apartment, but often that summer I'd take a longer route home and walk up Thayer Street, a long stretch of retail near the Brown campus dotted with food shops and funky restaurants. I'd look at pastries in the window of a bakery, and smell the glaze on honey-dipped doughnuts. I'd walk past a café and see a couple sharing a plate of chicken wings at an outdoor table. I'd watch housewives exit grocery stores with bulging brown paper bags, and I'd imagine the women cooking, stealing little nibbles from the pot on the stove. I'd feel above these people, superior, able to restrain where others surrendered. At a time when I felt essentially uncertain and worthless, starving gave me a goal, something to be good at.

I was very, very good at it. In the fall of 1983 I ran a six-mile road race and one of my roommates took a picture of me crossing the finish line. In the photograph my knees are wider than my thighs.

Anorexia was marvelously effective in its own twisted way. I had grown up believing that pain and conflict were to be held like secrets, not to be expressed, and paring myself down to skeletal form gave me a way to literally wear whatever pain I felt, instead of voicing it. I had grown fearful of sexuality, of being physically viewed and pursued by the men around me—Roger; that lewd landlord and handyman from my previous apartment—and starving gave me a way to physically whittle away the parts of me that looked and felt sexual: my breasts and hips, my curves. I stopped menstruating. I became hard and angular, like a twelve-year-old boy.

The parallels between anorexia and alcoholism astonish me today, the way they both served to refract emotion and keep me at a distance from my own feelings, one through food and one through drink. When I was starving, I couldn't think about the deeper motives, couldn't contemplate the fact that I was young and scared and sexually threatened and angry. All I could think about was food: when I'd eat, where I'd eat, how much I'd permit myself to eat, and under what circumstances. I developed elaborate rituals around food, dozens of rules and taboos, and the few things I allowed myself to eat became objects of a kind of reverence to me, in the same way a glass of white wine would later on, or a first shot of Johnnie Walker Black after work.

As happens with most addictions, life took on a blank sameness, each day ritualized and invariable, barely distinguishable from the day before. In the morning I'd get to work before anyone else and eat a plain sesame bagel (150 calories) at my desk, tearing the bagel into tiny bits and eating each bit in a specific order: one bite while I read the front page; one bite while I read the editorials; one bite for Ann Landers. At lunch I'd have a Dannon coffee-flavored yogurt (200 calories), often eating it, spoonful by slow spoonful, while reading restaurant reviews from a stack of alternative weeklies that came in the mail each week. And at night I'd shut myself in my bedroom and eat my most elaborately planned and executed meal, an apple and a cube of cheese (300 calories total), each sliced with surgical precision into thirty-two identical slivers. I'd line the slivers of apple around the rim of a china saucer, then place one sliver of cheese on top of each piece of apple, and then I'd settle down in front of the TV and eat them in tiny, methodical bites, so slowly that the ritual would take me two hours to complete.

When I first quit drinking, I tended to see my anorexic years as essentially abstemious, a period when I drank very little, if at all. In fact, I drank quite a lot. I just compressed the drinking into shorter periods of time, spaced it out into intense, sporadic bursts. Periodically—about once every four to six weeks—I simply couldn't stand the starving anymore, couldn't go on without some kind of release from the absolute rigor and vigilance and self-control, and I'd go out and eat like crazy and drink like crazy. These episodes were usually preceded by some glimmer of insight into my own loneliness, some gnawing sense that my hunger was more than merely physical.

I remember coming home one night and finding my roommates at the kitchen table, smoking cigarettes and drinking bottles of Heineken under a circle of lamplight. They'd ordered Chinese food, and one of the roommates was sitting back in her chair, smiling at something, and pushing a single remaining dumpling back and forth across her plate with a fork, idly back and forth and back and forth. I remember being astonished at that sight, at her lack of reverence for food, and I also remember feeling a shock of wistfulness, a sadness so intense it took me by surprise. I wanted something she had—that ease around food, the conviviality and friendship that seemed to accompany it. I wanted to be able to sit there in the kitchen with my roommates like a normal person, drinking a beer, eating a plate of Chinese food, living my life. But I couldn't. I just couldn't. So when they asked me if I wanted to join them, which they invariably did, I just smiled and demurred. "Oh, no, thanks," I said. "I grabbed a sandwich on the way home from work." Then I excused myself, disappeared into my bedroom, changed my clothes, and went out for a run.

But every once in a while I'd let go. I'd go out drinking with colleagues, get blasted at a bar in downtown Providence, eat a huge bowl of chili and a piece of pie, then stagger back home at the end of the night, drunk and dazed, and eat more, raid my roommates' food from the refrigerator. Or I'd plan a dinner, pull out recipes from *Gourmet*, and cook some huge, elaborate feast: a pasta dish with four kinds of cheese; loaves of buttery garlic bread; a hazelnut torte with buttercream and chocolate icing. Sometimes I did this for my roommates; sometimes I drove home to Cambridge and did it at my parents' house, a semiconscious effort to unite us, just like Mrs. Ramsey in *To the Lighthouse*.

These efforts consistently failed. The technical term for the behavior is bingeing: binge eating and binge drinking, and engaging in it always made me feel awful. I'd drink too much (I *always* drank too much when I ate) and I'd eat too much and I'd be overwhelmed by the sheer force of my own appetites and I'd end up feeling remorseful and depressed, waking up in the morning bloated and full of self-loathing, determined to double my resolve and cut back on eating even more.

I think those dinners also made me furious. Except for my sister no one in my family ever said anything about how thin I'd become, and that quietly enraged me too. I'd stand there in the kitchen, an eighty-pound waif cooking an 8,000-calorie meal, and nobody tried to stop me. I'd show up at family functions—Thanksgiving, Christmas—and sit there picking at my plate of turkey, wondering if anybody even noticed. My hunger strike was not producing the desired effect.

Two and a half years passed. I was twenty-two, twenty-three, twenty-four. I had no real friends to speak of, no sex life, and the only semblance of fun I had came in the form of a bottle, in the rare moment when I'd find myself sitting at a barstool with a

buddy from work and relaxing into a glass of white wine. If anything, drinking felt helpful to me during those years, providing a
periodic push out of the isolation of starving, and compared to the
way I lived most days, that seemed like a good thing, a healthy
thing.

In the fall of 1984 I left Providence for Boston and began the
slow and arduous process of wending my way out of anorexia and
into some more normal relationship with food and the world.
There was nothing clear or simple about that transition: you can't
"abstain" from starving as concretely as you can quit drinking,
and most people who recover from anorexia describe a long, excruciating process of experimentation and risk, of steps forward
and steps back, of learning what functions starving serves and
struggling to accomplish the same goals in better ways.

I don't think you can really get out of anorexia (or any addiction, for that matter) until you simply have no other choice, until
the sense that your back's against the wall grows too strong and
too irrefutable, until you are simply in too much pain—too desperate and deeply bored and unhappy—to go on. I started seeing a
therapist (whom I still see today), and he pressed me to let go of
my rigidity in tiny ways, to learn to tolerate discomfort through
little test-runs with change: small things, like eating two bagels
instead of one in the morning, or introducing cream cheese; bigger things, like going out to dinner with people instead of choosing to stay home with my rituals.

What I couldn't see at that time—what I wouldn't see until
after I'd quit drinking—was how central a role alcohol played in
that process. If you'd plotted my eating and drinking on a graph
in the first few years after I left Providence, you'd see the two lines
creeping up simultaneously: more eating, more drinking. For a
long time the two behaviors overlapped. I started dating again,
usually going out with men who were way too old for me, or
newly divorced, or somehow damaged or inappropriate, and I'd
meet one of them for dinner, eat a relatively normal meal, then
stop at a convenience store on my way home and buy candy. I'd

buy Snickers bars and Cadbury cream-filled chocolate eggs and I'd unwrap them in a frenzy in the car and stuff them down, trying to assuage a feeling of deep hunger, a profound discomfort that I couldn't quite identify and certainly couldn't address in any other way. Sometimes, driven by exactly the same impulse, I'd stop at a liquor store, too, and pick up a nip of brandy, or two or three.

But the drinking felt like progress, the same way it did for Janet. Anorexia had demanded so much privacy and isolation, and at least I could look at my life and see myself climbing out of the cage. The isolation had served me well: as long as I obsessed about food, I hadn't had to obsess about people and the complicated set of needs and fears I'd developed around them; as long as I shut myself up in my room with my rituals, I felt safe. Given how painful it was to surrender that seclusion, it was probably inevitable that any return to the world, any resumption of a social life, would require the resumption of my armor, my protection. I picked up where I left off: drinking.

In retrospect I guess you could say the drinking worked, at least superficially. I gained back the weight I'd lost. I went out to parties and restaurants and bars. But all I'd really done was change substances. Same dance, new shoes.

In 1987, three years after I moved to Boston, I joined a support group for women with eating disorders. There were four of us and shortly after I started attending, one of the members, a tall, thin woman in her late twenties named Dora, was arrested for drunk driving. She'd been bulimic and anorexic for many years, shifting back and forth between the two behaviors, and the group was her first foray into therapy. She didn't like the process at all. You could see a wariness in her eyes, a pang of discomfort flickering across her face anytime one of us said something that struck her as too direct. Soon after her arrest on the drunk-driving charge, she started talking about quitting the group. She sat very stiffly in her chair. "I'm just not getting anything out of it," she said. "It feels like all we do is sit here and complain."

No one said anything.

A minute passed and she continued. "Plus, I mean, things are going really well for me. I don't think I need this anymore."

She had a new job, which she liked, and she talked about that. She'd made a few new friends, and she talked about them. But there was an edginess to her voice, as though she was trying to convince herself of this newfound serenity, not just the rest of us, and finally one of the other members of the group interrupted her and asked, "Well, what about the drunk-driving thing? What about that?"

Dora looked up suddenly, as though she'd been caught at something, then tossed her hair defensively. "It's really no big deal," she said. "So I have to go to these classes for a while. So what?"

More silence.

Then Dora said, "You know that bumper sticker that says SHIT HAPPENS? That pretty much sums it up for me. Shit happens. So what? Why analyze it? I just don't want to analyze it anymore."

She left the group that morning and we never saw her again, but in the years that passed, especially mornings when I woke up after driving home drunk, I'd find myself thinking about her and wondering whatever happened. *She must have had a drinking problem,* I'd think. *She must have turned around and traded in that eating disorder for alcoholism.*

She must have done it. Not me.

10 *Denial*

You OFTEN HEAR in AA meetings that denial *is* the disease
of alcoholism, not just its primary symptom, and it's not hard to
see why. Denial is what keeps you in there, keeps you entrenched,
keeps your feet glued to the floor. Denial can make your drinking
feel as elusive and changeable as the Hydra, many headed, capable of altering form in the blink of an eye. Every time an active
alcoholic looks at his or her drinking, it's shifted into something
else, something that makes it seem acceptable.

Not long ago I heard a young woman talk at a meeting about
drinking a beer in her car on the way home from work. No big
deal, drinking a beer in the car, except that abstaining from alcohol while driving had been one of her rules: if she drank in the
car, it meant she had a problem. "I'd always thought that was a
really bad thing to do," she said, "but then I figured, if *I* was
having a beer in the car, it couldn't be that bad, so I changed the
rule."

Nods all around. We all did it. We all had our version of the
changing rule. Many versions; too many to count.

At the rehab I went to, a group of us sat around the cafeteria
one night and talked about the worst thing we'd done while
drinking, the very worst thing we could think of. Tess, a very
beautiful woman in her late thirties, with fine blond hair and blue

eyes and smooth, lightly freckled skin, went first. She'd gotten really drunk one night in downtown Boston, close to blackout drunk, and she'd picked up some guy in a bar, she couldn't remember which one. They'd gone to a hotel and spent the night together and in the morning, her hands shaking so badly from DTs she could barely hold a cigarette, the man tried to give her money. Tess was appalled and humiliated and she just left the hotel, left him standing there in the room, and walked out into the street. She couldn't find her car because she couldn't remember where she'd parked, and when she finally found it and got in, she realized she was bleeding. Blood was streaming down between her legs and her abdomen was cramping up and she realized: *Oh, my God, I'm having a miscarriage*. She'd been three months pregnant.

The cafeteria was quiet and dim and empty except for us and we all sat and listened. Tess spoke in a soft voice, staring down at her cigarette. She started her car and headed toward Cambridge, thinking she'd get to the Mount Auburn Hospital, where her obstetrician practiced. But then, before she quite knew what she was doing, she pulled into a liquor store: she couldn't handle this situation, she simply couldn't stay in her car and get to the hospital if she didn't have a drink. Her hands were still shaking, shaking terribly, and she remembered pulling her skirt around in front of her, so she could hide the bloodstains between the folds of cloth, and she picked up a six-pack of beer and a fifth of vodka and she got back in her car and drove, opening the first beer and drinking it fast, then opening the next, then opening the vodka.

Tess paused and put out her cigarette. She couldn't quite remember what had happened next: "Something . . ." she said. "I don't know. I was in Cambridge and I was pulled over on the side of the road and there were all these bottles on the floor and I was crying, and then there was a cop there, and . . ." Her voice trailed off and one of the men at the table asked her if that's what got her to the rehab, if that was the end.

Tess looked up. "No," she said, completely blasé. "I felt okay the next day so I kept drinking."

That's how denial works. You keep drinking.

I kept drinking, too, which may be why my mid-twenties—post-anorexic but increasingly liquid—are all muddy to me. I primarily remember the outlines: after I left Providence I moved into an apartment in Newton, just west of Boston, and started hanging around with Elaine, who lived next door. I got a job at a small, business-oriented weekly newspaper. I met my friend Sam (at a cocktail party, aptly enough) and started drinking with him at the Ritz. I even did some healthy things: joined the women's support group; took up sculling on the Charles River, a difficult and demanding sport that gave me something to master besides my own appetite.

Beyond that the details are hazy. I know I trudged into the Mass. General once a week to see the shrink and then sat there on the blue sofa in his office like a lump, stagnant and sad and often mute. Somewhere halfway between anorexia and alcoholism, I couldn't figure out why I was so unhappy, so overcome with inertia. I went through a heavy pot-smoking period around then, my mid-twenties, and I'd shut myself up in my apartment a few nights each week, smoke a joint, then sit there listening to music, my mind flashing with those pot-induced insights that seem deeply profound when you're stoned and utterly banal the next morning. (I once developed an entire theory of personality based on the fact that my mother wore glasses.) Once in a while I'd have a stoned insight about my drug and alcohol use, too, but I never wrote these down, let alone acted on them. For the most part I had the chronic sensation that I was sitting around waiting for my life to begin and I'd sit there in the shrink's office every week and writhe with self-pity, as whiny and self-absorbed as a six-year-old: "I don't know what to *do*." I'm still surprised I didn't bore him to death, right there in his office.

My father and I periodically had lunch together during those years. My office was near his, so every six or eight weeks he'd drive over, pick me up, and take me to a restaurant where we'd have versions of the same strained conversations we'd had when I was a teenager: my father asking me how I was *feeling*, what was *new*; me struggling to hide my self-consciousness behind a relaxed façade. Sometimes we'd each have a glass of wine or two, and that would ease the time together considerably. Our meetings always lasted a precise fifty minutes—shrink time—which secretly amused and quietly angered me. Aside from those lunches and some periodic visits to my parents' house in Cambridge, I kept my distance from the family, and I wasn't sure why. Some instinct for detachment kept me away.

Drinking was the one constant. Drinking and worrying about it, then not worrying. Drinking and questioning and then shutting the questions down.

One summer night in 1986 I ran across a street in Harvard Square and caught a glimpse of myself in the glass of a store window. I didn't recognize the image at first. I'd been at a bar, having a drink with a friend after work, and I was running to my car, on my way to meet Sam, and I saw the reflection out of the corner of my eye: a neatly dressed young woman with a blunt, shoulder-length haircut, a short white skirt and oversized cotton sweater, and fashionable black pumps. I was a little drunk at the time—it was early evening, still light out, but I'd had two glasses of wine so I felt tipsy and disoriented, running across the street feeling lit before dark—and I remember that a question formed in my mind: I thought, *Am I as together as I look or am I going crazy?*

I had the sense of truly not knowing who that was, that twenty-six-year-old woman in the skirt and pumps, and of not knowing if I should worry about her or leave her alone. Did that look like a chic, urbane, young-professional activity, clipping along a street in Harvard Square with a buzz on at five-thirty in the afternoon? Or was it nuts, a sign of trouble?

The question didn't linger. I got to my car, drove to the Back

Bay, parked my car in a hurry, and headed to the Ritz, where I'd sit with Sam and drink expensive white wine for several hours. For the time being, anyway, I'd settled on an answer: urbane and together. Fine. Not to worry.

Sometimes, though, at the end of just such a night like that, I'd stagger into the ladies' room and think: *Something is wrong with this picture*.

To get to the bathroom at the Ritz you had to walk through the lobby and down a set of stairs, and I remember navigating that path one night in a pair of high heels, over soft carpeting. It was late in the evening and I'd probably had seven or eight glasses of wine by then, maybe more, and I reeled across the lobby, bumping into the wall at the top of the staircase. Downstairs, I shut myself in the stall, then leaned over and put my head down on my knees. I was dizzy and drunk and I knew it, and times like that I'd be aware of the two images of myself, competing and increasingly irreconcilable, the way they were that evening in Harvard Square: there was the sophisticated young woman in the bar sipping an expensive Fumé Blanc; and there was the drunken young woman staggering through the lobby of the hotel, wondering if she was going to puke.

Sometimes I'd be so drunk at the end of the night I'd have to drive home with one eye shut, to avoid double vision. Sometimes I'd wake up at Sam's house, in his bed, wearing one of his T-shirts. I don't think we ever had sex but I can't say for sure. I was always too embarrassed to ask him.

So you worry and you deny. You worry and you drink. Jean Rhys describes this in *Good Morning, Midnight*: "In the middle of the night you wake up. You start to cry. What's happening to me? Oh, my life, my youth. . . . There's some wine left in the bottle. You drink it. The clock ticks. Sleep. . . ."

Rhys is describing the line between problem drinking and alcoholism, which appears for the briefest moments and then disappears, renders itself invisible. I've thought of that line in the past as a shifting thing, a fine line, but I've changed my mind: it's invisible, at least to the drinker, who literally cannot see it. A light bulb goes on and then—click!—just like that, it goes off again and you're back in the dark, unable to see.

Click: *Fuck. Something is very wrong. I am in trouble.*

Click: *I'm okay. Fine. Not to worry.*

My friend Gail, who's a professional chef, used to get up at five A.M. and stand in her shower obsessing about what she'd drink that night, and when she'd be able to drink, and how and how much and with whom. She did this daily, obsessing in the shower about booze every morning at five A.M., and every once in a while the light would go on—click!—and she'd realize this was *crazy*, a real problem, a genuine sign of dependence that had spiraled way out of control. But she could always counter that observation, always. *Bad day ahead*—click! *Work. Stress*—click, click! *I'm all right, I have a job, I pay my bills, I can't be an alcoholic*—click, click, click. End of story. I'm fine.

That's the thing about denial around alcohol: if Gail were standing there obsessing about, say, asparagus—how she'd get it, when she'd eat it, how many spears she'd have, whether anyone would smell asparagus on her breath—it might have been easier for her to realize she was losing control. But when it comes to an addictive substance like alcohol, something that alters your mind and shapes your sense of self in the world and becomes central to your ability to cope, the mind's capacity to play with the facts can be limitless. *I have my reasons*, Gail would think. *I know I am obsessing and I know it's crazy but I have my reasons.*

And yes, we all have our reasons. We're bored or we're restless or we're depressed. We're worried or anxious or stressed. We're celebrating, or we're grieving. Tomorrow. We'll deal with it tomorrow. We'll deal with it *when things get better.*

That was my favorite line: *I'll drink less when things get better.*

So I'd do what Gail did, what all of us did: *Stress*, I'd think, sitting there in the stall in the Ritz Hotel ladies' room, my head on my knees. *Tough day at work.* I'd semiconsciously tick through my list of nonalcoholic attributes: *young, female, employed, profes-*

sional. Not a problem. Can't be a problem. Then I'd get up, splash
water on my face, comb my hair, and head back to the bar.
   Click.

A guy I know named William calls himself an alcoholic and periodically says he needs to quit drinking but hasn't yet done it.
   I went for a walk with him in Cambridge one day in the spring
of 1995, about a year after I'd gotten sober. He ambled along next
to me, looking down at his feet, and said, "It's not like I, you
know, wake up in *Cleveland,* in bed with some stranger."
   I said, "I know."
   "And it's not like I get up in the morning and do shots of
vodka. I mean, I *never* drink when I'm working."
   "I know."
   William is thirty-nine, a writer. "I know my work goes better
when I drink less," he said. "I know I have a kind of clarity about
it. I'm *awake,* even when I'm not actually writing. I can *see*
things." He paused. "My logic tells me that I won't get to that
next level with my work unless I stop drinking. I understand that
intellectually. I understand that it's just plain *stupid* not to quit.
So I don't know why I keep procrastinating."
   I said, "Because the expression *One day at a time,* which they
beat into your head in AA, goes both ways."
   He looked at me and asked what I meant, and I told him about
waking up in my apartment one morning and not remembering,
like Tess, where I'd parked my car. No memory at all of where it
might be. This took place in the late 1980s, when I was living
with my boyfriend Julian and feeling hopeless and miserable just
about all the time, anorexia behind me by then but not very far.
   Julian was in New York for the weekend and I'd gone out to
dinner with my friend Paul, a hard-drinking journalist who loved
martinis and always ordered them exactly the same way: as cold as
humanly possible. "A Bombay martini, straight up with a twist,"
he'd say, "and make it as cold as humanly possible." Paul and I

got plastered at dinner—drinks before, a bottle of wine during, brandy after—and in a fit of sloshed generosity I offered to pay for the meal. Then I couldn't figure out the check. I remember sitting there trying to add things up, and the numbers just wouldn't come, and I finally ended up leaving some outrageous tip, like sixty percent, because I was afraid of leaving too little. Classic drunk logic.

After that Paul and I went back to my apartment and I got out a sixty-dollar bottle of port that I'd bought Julian for Christmas. The bottle was nearly full, and Paul and I sat there in the living room and drank the entire thing. He called a cab at one-thirty or two in the morning; I have a dim memory of him getting ready to leave. We were standing on the landing in the apartment and I was in one of those overaffectionate, staggering, syrupy moods you sometimes get in when you drink way too much, and I gave him a hug and told him I loved him. Then Paul left and I reeled off to bed and when I woke up that morning, I couldn't remember driving home or parking the car or walking from the car to the apartment.

William was nodding all through this description, as though he were saying, "Oh, yeah. I know this story; I've done that too," so I continued.

I lay in bed for ten minutes that morning, trying to will my headache into the pillow. My temples were throbbing—what Kingsley Amis describes as a "dusty thudding in the head"—and I had a sharp pain over my right eyeball. Finally I got up, went downstairs to make coffee, and saw the empty port bottle on the kitchen counter. Then I thought about the car. Julian and I lived in the North End of Boston, a small, crowded neighborhood that's crisscrossed with tiny streets; finding a parking space can take twenty minutes on a good day, and Paul and I had been out on a Friday night, when parking can take an hour. We could have left the car miles away for all I knew.

I must have spent the next forty minutes walking around the neighborhood, lugging my headache up Prince Street, across Sa-

lem Street, down Hull Street, up and down Commercial. I finally
found the car on the other side of the neighborhood from mine,
wedged into a tiny space. When I got drunk like that and couldn't
remember driving home, which probably happened every six or
eight weeks, I used to stand there and take inventory, making sure
everything was okay: car lights off; doors locked; no bits of flesh or
blood or clothing on the front grill, nothing that might signify
some horrifying accident.

I got into the car and drove out to the liquor store where I'd
bought the original bottle of port. I bought a replacement bottle,
drove home, poured an inch or so of the new port into a glass (to
drink later, before Julian came home), and put the bottle back in
the cupboard where the old one had been. Later that afternoon I
took the old bottle to a Dumpster down the street, and later that
night, after I'd gone out to dinner with another friend and had a
fair amount to drink, I drank the glass of port I'd saved.

A few weeks later Julian looked at the bottle in the cupboard
and said, "That seems *fuller* than it was before. Did you buy a new
bottle or something?" I looked at him like he was crazy and
changed the subject.

"But you know," I told William, "I'd do things like that and it
amazes me now how I was able to justify them. It was just one
night. One isolated incident. See? One day at a time. You always
think you're just doing it this one time, this one night, and tomorrow will be different."

He nodded. We were quiet for a few minutes and then he said,
"Well, you know, I don't drive."

If I hadn't quit myself, I probably would have loved drinking with
William, a fellow master of comparison and denial.

I don't drive so I can't be as bad as you were. I always had a car
during my drinking days, and often drove drunk, so I couldn't use
that particular line, but I employed plenty of others, most of them
having to do with other drinkers. *Just look at how many other*

people drink the way I do, or drink even more. Just look at Elaine. I said things like that to myself all the time, but I never acknowledged that I'd arranged it that way, surrounded myself with co-conspirators.

Drinkers, after all, find other drinkers. We tend to choose people who speak a certain language:

Let's go get a drink.

Let's have another.

Oh, c'mon. Just one more.

This is so easy to do, so frighteningly simple. For a long time you drink because the drink just seems to be available, and then, at some point way down the line, you drink because you *make* it available. Without being completely aware of it you organize your life in such a way that alcohol is always there: at the table over dinner, in your cupboard and refrigerator, in the cupboards and refrigerators of your closest friends. You hang out with other drinkers, people who find it perfectly desirable and perfectly normal to down six bottles of wine in a single sitting, people who support both the effort and the denial of its consequences.

Drinkers know each other; we can pick each other out of a crowd the way new mothers can, or army veterans, or any other members of a group united by the deepest sort of common cause and experience. We seem to be attuned to a certain kind of music, a chorus of more, and we learn to determine which other people hear it, too, which ones understand our special liquid logic, and which ones don't. The drinker who's in a hurry to get the first drink most definitely hears it, the one who looks up two minutes after you've sat down at a table and snaps, "Where's the damn waitress?" So does the drinker who gulps that first one down, who looks down shortly after the round has arrived and notices the glass is already empty. The chorus plays in the mind, liquid lyrics. The drinker who's always game for another, who'd rather stay and drink than go out and eat, who encourages the rest of the people at the table to keep drinking, who feels secret relief when the nondrinkers in the group pick up their coats and straggle off—

that drinker hears the music. About half the alcohol in the U.S. is consumed by eleven percent of the population: together, we do a lot of singing.

Elaine was a drinker, which in my twisted way is exactly why I liked her. She was a guilt-free drinker, too, no holds barred, the kind of drinker who'd stand up and walk out of a restaurant in a huff if it was determined the place had no liquor license. "Let's go get a drink." Elaine had a gravelly voice from years of smoking and she'd say that in a snarly way, with forcefulness, so you couldn't say no.

A year or so after I met her, Elaine moved to the South Shore of Boston, about twenty-five minutes outside the city, so sometimes I'd drive to her house on a Friday after work and bring an overnight bag, knowing without really admitting to myself that I'd be too drunk to drive home at the end of the night. She lived in a little Colonial house with a big kitchen, and we'd sit at her table and eat cheese and crackers and drink. I drank wine; she drank beer, then switched to wine with me, then switched to vodka. Later, we'd both drink brandy, Armagnac, and finally stagger off to bed. Usually, Elaine would buy a chicken or some pasta which we'd forget to cook.

One morning I woke up at Elaine's house wearing a bra and a sweater but no pants or underwear. I thought: *"Huh?"* Elaine had had a dinner party the night before and four of us had shown up: me, a gay couple named James and Lance, and an old friend of Elaine's named Charlie, who I had a quiet crush on. The five of us drank eleven bottles of Champagne. Then we decided to go out to a bar, and then we got lost and spent two hours just driving, one of those semisurreal outings you try to think of later as an adventure. We all piled into James's Volvo and we drank more Champagne in the car and smoked a couple of joints, which made us all giggle hysterically and then forget what we were giggling about, and I don't remember how or when we got home.

The rest of the night is a blur. I dimly recall drinking more at Elaine's when we got back—bourbon or Scotch, something dark

—and I have an even foggier recollection of sitting on the sofa next to Charlie and kind of leaning on him, leaning my whole body against his arm and shoulder and fighting to keep my eyes open.

I don't remember getting from the living room to the spare bedroom where I slept but I vaguely remember wrestling out of my jeans and socks and climbing into a bed. James and Lance fell asleep in the living room. Charlie called a cab at some point and went home. I woke up in the morning in a half-drunk daze, the kind that makes you feel too uncoordinated to even brush your teeth, and it took me a minute to figure out where I was.

The room was quiet and bright with sun and I remember an odd, hungover feeling of cognitive dissonance, something that would become increasingly familiar over the years: bright sun and a pounding headache; birds chirping outside and a steady throb over my right eye. I lay there for a long time with my eyes closed, curled up in a ball, hoping I hadn't done or said anything I'd regret, hoping I hadn't made a pass at Charlie, hoping I hadn't made an ass of myself. Finally I dozed off.

At eleven or so I went downstairs and found Elaine in the kitchen making coffee. A moment of subversive assessment followed, something that's familiar to anyone the morning after a blackout:

"Morning." I sat down at the table and said this as nonchalantly as I could, then watched Elaine for a reaction. Was she angry at me for any reason? Would she seem disgusted? Would she be laughing at me?

She looked at me and groaned. "Ugh" was all she said.

I ventured a question: "What time did we all go to bed?"

"Oh, God," she said. "You crashed at around three-thirty. I think Charlie left a little while after that and the rest of us stayed up and smoked another joint. I think I'm going to die."

A hangover is like a workout for the muscles of denial, a way to spar with reality and practice telling yourself that you're okay, everything's fine, last night was perfectly ordinary. Elaine didn't seem angry that morning, or disgusted, just preoccupied with her own headache. I was safe.

The worried morning after: every alcoholic I know has had them, lots of them. We'd wake up after a party and spend the morning worrying about what we'd said or done the night before, and finally we'd call the person who threw the party and hunt for clues to our behavior by gauging the response. "I had way too much to drink last night," we'd say, as though this were a rarity, a fluke. "I hope I didn't do anything too stupid." Pause.

Oh, you were fine. Those are the words I was always looking for. *I didn't even notice.* If no one else was worried, I didn't need to be either.

The worst was wondering what I'd said, what confidences I might have broken, what evil tidbit I might have passed along to someone about a mutual friend, what self-aggrandizing comment I might have tossed off. Sometimes when I got drunk I could feel my own sober rules of social conduct just melt away, hear a little voice in my head say, *No: don't start talking about that,* and then go ahead and talk about it anyway. *Did you know that Megan slept with Jim? Back when Jim was seeing Helen? Yeah, and she said he was* . . . Then you wake up in the morning and cringe. That kind of behavior is driven by an information-as-power equation, a wish to see yourself as an insider, a person equipped with Certain Facts.

Ultimately, of course, all you really do is reinforce your sense of yourself as an untrustworthy person. You wake up in the morning and remember bits and pieces; you remember leaning across a table and saying, "Don't repeat this to *anyone* but . . ." You remember knowing you'd regret this in the morning, regret chipping away yet another sliver of your own integrity. And you remember that you went ahead and did it anyway.

Elaine used to call it the "Uh-oh's," that feeling of waking up in a haze after a night of heavy drinking, regretting things you blabbed about, or not being able to account for whole chunks of time, wondering what you'd done. *Uh-oh: did I say something really bad? Have sex with someone? Kill anyone driving home?* I was glad she had a name for it: it happened, I supposed, to everyone.

I did go out with Charlie, one time. A few weeks after Elaine's party I ran into him at a restaurant. He came up to my table to say hello and we had a very brief conversation—just hi, how are you —and I remember feeling about fourteen years old, as self-conscious as if we'd just met.

"I haven't seen you since Elaine's," I said. "Did you have a good time?" Then I felt like a moron, as though I were deliberately evoking an embarrassing set of memories: *Did you have a good time? Do you remember whether I was acting like a drunken fool?*

"Oh," he said. "Sure. Great time."

"Good," I said.

A moment passed in silence, the briefest, strained moment, and Charlie cleared his throat. "Well, I better get back," he said, gesturing to his seat across the room.

"Okay," I said. "Nice to see you."

Late that night, unable to sleep, I thought about my shyness, and I remember wondering, fleetingly, if the drinking created a kind of personality trap: perhaps the shyness, so acute for so many years, persisted because I hid my real self behind the liquor, because I never let anyone get to know me unless I'd flooded my system with several gallons of Champagne. *Charlie probably thinks I'm a real jerk,* I thought. But a few days later he called me up and asked me out to dinner, and the question about being a jerk receded.

We went to a restaurant in Boston and had a lot to drink, and then we went over to see some friends of his, a couple whose name I forget. There was more booze and there was cocaine and I totally blacked out; it's one of the few nights from which I remember literally nothing, not even five minutes, from about eleven o'clock on. I woke up in the morning at the friends' house feeling like someone had taken my brain out in the middle of the night, stomped on it, and put it back in. Charlie was acting distant and weird. He drove me home in his Buick, an old model with a wide, tan vinyl front seat. In the car, dazed and sick, I slid over and put my head on his shoulder and he didn't respond at all, didn't touch me or look at me or smile. I kept my head there for a minute, then kind of sidled back over toward my side. When he dropped me off all he said was "Take care of yourself." I didn't hear from him again and although I felt responsible and humiliated on some core level, I also couldn't absorb the responsibility, couldn't face it. When I talked about Charlie to friends, I used phrases like *one of* those *guys*, and *commitment-phobic*.

So there was always a reason, always a reason to drink and always a reason why things didn't work, life dealing its same old bad hand.

Stupid things happen when you're drunk, things that simply wouldn't happen if you were sober, more careful and attentive. Drunk one night, Ernest Hemingway pulled the wrong chain in the bathroom of his apartment and accidentally brought down an entire glass skylight, leaving him with a permanent scar on his forehead. Throughout my mid-to-late twenties, the Elaine and Sam years, incidents like that happened to me all the time, little episodes that make you look up and say, *Oh, fuck; what now?* I'd leave my car in dangerous places late at night while I drank and then I'd be shocked—shocked!—to find it had been broken into, all my stuff stolen. I lost things: my favorite winter coat at a Christmas party in the Bostonian Hotel; my wallet in a bar; a pair of earrings my sister had given me, while I rambled drunkenly home from a restaurant. I blamed these things on circumstances beyond my control—urban living (the car); thievery (the lost coat, the lost wallet); a very complicated dynamic involving the back of the earring and its relationship to the collar of my coat (my sister's gift). Like I said, there was always a reason.

A lot of us blamed it on hormones, which seemed like a rational enough explanation. My friend Abby remembers this clearly. "Oh, right," she said to me one afternoon, over coffee.

"You'd get really drunk one night, inexplicably drunk, and you'd blame it on the fact that you were about to get your period."

"Right," I said. "Or that you'd just *had* your period."

"Or that you were ovulating."

"Or that you hadn't had enough sleep, or enough to eat."

"Or that the moon was full."

I suppose it's natural to look for reasons; I suppose it's instinctive. Abby didn't get rip-roaring drunk every night, and neither did Gail, and neither did I. We didn't sabotage a relationship on a weekly basis, or humiliate ourselves regularly, or throw up on strangers, or kill anybody driving home. If bad things happened in our lives, they were by and large isolated incidents, or at least they seemed to be, and in many ways, my life—and the lives of many of the alcoholics I know now—plodded along in spite of them. We kept our jobs and our apartments and our checking accounts. We moved from relationship to relationship. We had active social lives. Many of us had therapists. If we drank—well, we deserved to. Life is hard; you need a little release now and then, a little reward. Doesn't everybody?

A lot of alcoholics talk about how they look back and can see that they never knew, never really could predict, when they'd get too drunk, when they'd cross the line from what felt like normal heavy drinking into raging, out-of-control drinking. It was just something that happened, happened *to* us. In AA meetings you often hear the phrase *Bad things didn't happen every time I drank, but every time something bad did happen, drinking was involved.* If you're an active alcoholic, you focus in on the times when bad things *didn't* happen, when you went out drinking and had a good time, got home safely, woke up in your own bed. And when those more destructive or embarrassing episodes occur, when you open your eyes in the morning and can't remember what happened the night before, well, you make excuses, find someone or something else to blame. Pressure, life, hormones.

I hear Tess's words: *I felt okay the next day so I kept drinking.*

I did too.

11 *Giving Over*

LIQUOR CREATES DELUSION. It can make your life feel full of risk and adventure, sparkling and dynamic as a rough sea under sunlight. A single drink can make you feel unstoppable, masterful, capable of solving problems that overwhelmed you just five minutes before. In fact, the opposite is true: drinking brings your life to a standstill, makes it static as rock over time.

For years I could see that truth in other people, but not in myself. I could see it in my friend Elaine, the way her drinking seemed to stand in the way of any real opportunity she had to grow or change or learn from her own experience. *She's too out of it to have a healthy relationship,* I'd think, feeling smug. *She drinks too much. She doesn't know who the hell she is.*

Elaine had been involved with a married man for three years when I met her, and she talked about him constantly, Brian this and Brian that. She adored him, or thought she did, but she also blamed him, relentlessly, for all her unhappiness, for a despair that seemed far more deeply rooted to me, the good, detached child-of-an-analyst observer. You'd sit down with her at a bar and say, "So, how are things with Brian?" and then you'd get a twenty-five-minute blow-by-blow of what happened the last time they were together: the promises he made, the things he said about his marriage, the little seeds of hope he scattered in her path. They broke up at least once every other month and always got back together. Brian drank too.

I knew on some level that the drinking kept Elaine stuck in that relationship and fueled her tendency to blame her unhappiness on the people and things around her, but I didn't quite know how. "Fuck him," I'd say, when they broke up. "You should go out with other people. Get on with your life." Elaine would sit there at her kitchen table and nod, looking down into her drink, but you could tell she had no intention of leaving him. You could tell that leaving wasn't really an option.

Elaine was a defensive woman: hot tempered and not very introspective, the kind of person who just wanted what she wanted when she wanted it and didn't care to understand why. I used to think that was what kept her in the relationship with Brian. No matter how bad things got, no matter how many times he failed to leave his wife and they broke up, there'd always be a moment of unity and reconciliation between them, a moment when all Elaine's fantasies about the relationship seemed about to be realized, and she lived for those: they remedied all the despair of the past in exactly the same way a drink remedies a bad feeling.

I met her for a drink one night, just after one of these reconciliations. They hadn't spoken for a week and then Brian showed up at her house with a bottle of Champagne. He apologized and told her how much he'd missed her, how much he *needed* her, and they spent the night on her living-room floor, drinking the Champagne in front of the fire and making love. Boom: the cure. When Elaine told me about this, she got all lit up, as though all the hurts of the days and weeks and months before had just vanished up the chimney like curls of smoke from the fire. "I just can't say no to him," she said, softly, and she said it with a kind of awe, as though Brian were simply the most powerful, seductive, wonderful man on earth.

I can see now that those are the words of a woman who's lost power over her life, who's given it over entirely. The drinking— not just that one night of drinking, but the years of it, the chronic, daily drinking to counter fear and insecurity and depression—did something to her sense of control, colored her vision over time and made her see herself as a person who didn't have choices.

I met my version of Brian when I was twenty-eight, although I couldn't see it that way at the time. This was Julian, the man I'd been living with the night I got smashed with my friend Paul and lost my car.

When we first met, I thought he was an asshole. For reasons that now escape me, one of our first conversations had to do with pâté. We were standing with a group of people at a party, where we'd been introduced, and he said something about making pâté. I said, "Oh, my mother makes great pâté every Christmas," and he looked at me and said, "Are you sure it isn't *terrine*? Most people don't know the difference," and I thought, *What an asshole*.

Later, I called my mother and told her about that conversation and she said, "Well, technically, he's right: technically, pâté is baked in a crust," and I thought, *Feh. He's still an asshole.*

But then I got a new job and he came into my office with a bottle of Champagne to celebrate—really good Champagne, Taittinger—and a week or so later, when he called me up to ask me to dinner, I thought, *Well, maybe he's not that bad,* and I said okay.

We drank together right from the start. We drank elegant reds and crisp whites, and we drank things I'd never heard of, like Ricard, a French aperitif that Julian would mix in small glasses with water until it turned a soft, cloudy yellow. The first time he cooked me dinner, he grilled lamb with rosemary and we sat on his patio after we ate and drank brandy and listened to Bach violin concertos on his portable tape player. The first time I spent the night at his house he got up in the morning and made waffles from scratch and sprinkled them with Cognac. I thought that was just about the best breakfast treat imaginable.

An alcoholic I know named Louise says she used up her entire twenties looking for "the big improvement," something that would come along and whisk her off toward some new and better version of herself. Always, she used drugs and alcohol toward that end, drinking and snorting her way into an altered state of being, but she did it in other ways too. Most alcoholics I know did. For Louise it would be a new apartment, a new job, a new city. Things would fall apart in one place and she'd pack up and move someplace else. This is known in AA parlance as a "geographic," the constant moving from place to place, and if a new city didn't do it, Louise would turn to something else: another degree at another school, another career change. She's quite eloquent on the subject, on the way she kept twisting the outsides of her life around like a pretzel, hoping that the insides would twist along with it, and the first time I heard her talk about it, I thought: *Waffles, Cognac, Julian.* I walked into his kitchen that morning, and I smelled the waffles and the hot coffee, and I saw him standing there waving the bottle of Cognac over the plates, and a light seemed to go off in my head.

Julian was an art dealer, urbane and cerebral and yet sensual, too, a man who appreciated fine things. He looked like a new solution to an old set of puzzles, a person who could help me learn to feed myself with pleasure instead of anxiety, who could teach me to merge the intellect I'd grown up with and the passion I'd felt lacking. I watched him at the counter and I thought: *Here it is. New life.*

So he was it, the big improvement.

Of course, attaching all your hopes and fantasies to something —or someone—outside yourself almost always has disastrous results. I'd seen it in Elaine, and I'd seen it in myself, the way I'd tried to reshape my own body into something that felt special, the way I'd coveted approval from men in order to feel worthy, and I saw myself doing the same thing with Julian. But it felt so real this time, the new life seemed so accessible, that I ignored the obvious parallels.

Julian seemed like someone who had access to all the things I wanted and felt I lacked in my own life—a worldliness, a confidence—and after a while I found myself clinging to him in the most desperate way, truly believing I could not acquire those traits without him. I remember standing in his living room one day watching him iron a shirt and having the thought that he would change my life, that he was *capable* of changing my life and it would happen, just like that. We would live together in the city, a creative young couple, and we would cook wonderful meals together and drink wonderful wine and all his confidence and sophistication would rub off on me, just ooze into me, a kind of emotional osmosis. The fantasy touched me on the deepest level, and a few months later, when he looked up at me over dinner one night and said, "I've been thinking we ought to get a place together," I felt like I'd won the relationship version of a Nobel Prize, been bestowed a top honor, found my way—found myself—at last.

We celebrated with wine.

And the relationship fell apart almost immediately.

My sister got married in May of 1989, about a year after I met Julian. I cried at the wedding. Actually, I *wept*, not because I was happy for her (I wasn't) and not because weddings make me cry (they don't), but because I got drunk and maudlin and I wanted to lie down on my parents' front lawn and die.

This didn't happen until the very last minutes of the reception. Up until then I pretended I was fine even though I secretly wanted to kill someone, or tear off my dress and run screaming into the street.

Julian and I were miserable together by then and I hated weddings. I hated weddings, and I hated birth announcements, and I hated reading chipper little entries about my peers in the "class notes" section of my college alumni bulletin, and I quietly loathed people who got job promotions or bought new houses or relocated to swell new cities. Events like that were irrefutable pieces of evidence to me, indications that all around me people were getting on with their lives while I seemed to stand still, immobile. My sister's wedding, of course, was a particularly striking indication. She'd graduated from medical school at Boston University, where my father taught, just a week earlier and I'd watched my father stand up on a stage and hand her her diploma, literally passing her the psychiatric mantle. Traditionally, there were two routes to approval in my family: you went to medical school (our clan is riddled with doctors) or you got married. In the course of a week my sister—my *twin*—had done both and I felt like she was sailing across the finish line before I'd even made it out of the gate.

I also hated my dress; *hated* it. All the siblings were in the wedding—five of us all together—and we were told we could wear anything we wanted, so I had a dress made, a pale pink dress that I'd had modeled after something Julian had seen in a magazine. Julian and I had been living together for about eight months by then and we'd gone to see my therapist together shortly before Becca's wedding, far too late, as it turned out. The therapist asked Julian, "What do you love about Caroline? What is it that really keeps you in there?" And Julian sat back and thought for a minute. "Well," he said, "Caroline is like a really good bottle of wine. You can appreciate all the qualities, and all the nuances, but you're just not sure you want to drink it every night."

It took me several years to realize how angry that comment made me because at the time a part of me believed him, believed that I was like a *good* bottle of wine but not a *great* one, and I was expending a whole lot of energy trying to rearrange my packaging, trying to change the label, so to speak, and make us both believe I was worthy. Hence the dress. Julian found the seamstress and he found the dress in an Ungaro ad in *Vogue* and he took me to see the dressmaker one night after work, and on some level I think I truly believed that if I had exactly the right dress and looked exactly the way he imagined, it would be the two of us getting married, not Becca and Andy.

Julian fueled this perception, although perhaps not consciously. He had definite opinions about me, more definite than my own. About three weeks before we moved in together, he sat me down and said, "Okay: there are three things you can do for me." He paused, then said, "One: buy a new winter coat. Two: get your hair highlighted. And three: don't wear any of my clothes unless they look good on you."

I looked down. We'd been watching a movie in his bedroom, where it was cold, and I'd pulled on an old sweater of his that had been lying on the floor, a tattered thing that apparently didn't suit me. We stayed up until two A.M. that night, Julian expressing wagonloads of doubt about me—he thought I wasn't doing enough to keep him attracted to me; he was worried about getting stuck in a rut—and although a part of me was furious at him, a bigger part of me was scared that he was right.

The next day I went into work and banged off a long, articulate letter to him about my own worries (which were mounting). And then the fearful part kicked in. In the end I trashed the letter, went over to his apartment, let myself in with my key, scrubbed the place clean, and left flowers, with a note apologizing for disappointing him. Within the space of a few months I had little streaks of blond in my hair and a brand-new black wool coat that he helped select ("a very classic cut," he said). And I only wore his clothes after very careful deliberation.

As it turned out, the dress I wore to Becca's wedding was all wrong. It was supposed to be off-the-shoulder, but it was cut too low, so it was *way* off-the-shoulder and it kept slipping down, off one shoulder, then off the other. I had to keep hiking it up to keep my breasts from falling out. Plus, it was too tight so I had to suck in my stomach all day, and the seamstress and I had picked the wrong fabric, a lightweight wool that wrinkled terribly, so by the time Julian and I drove from our apartment to my parents' house, where the wedding was, the dress was all crinkled around my waist and hips, like an accordion. I hated it. I stood there during the ceremony with the heels of my pumps sinking into the grass and I felt like an idiot.

I was pretty scared of Julian by then. We fought about our relationship all the time, and big walls of anger and resentment had sprung up between us, and I always felt like we were on the verge of an explosion. Sometimes it was me who exploded and sometimes it was him and we couldn't seem to go a week without some fuse being ignited, setting off a chain reaction of rage. When we saw the therapist together, he talked about my "potential." He always talked about my "potential." "Caroline has a lot of potential," he said to the shrink, "but I honestly don't know how long I can wait around until it's realized." Julian was a brutally honest person, and he meant that in the most factual sense: he loved me but he saw me as a fragile, insecure, and muddled person who needed to grow into a strong person.

He was right, of course—I *was* fragile and insecure and muddled—so I never felt I could argue the point, but I also hated him for saying that, hated him for loving the person he wanted me to become instead of loving just me, and I wanted to shoot him at Becca's wedding. He was better dressed than me, in a really expensive Italian jacket he'd gotten on sale at Filene's Basement, and he seemed more comfortable and chatty with my relatives than I was, moving about from circle to circle, smiling and acting charming with strangers, the way he used to act with me. I chugged Champagne and stood next to him, hoping we looked like a nice, sophisticated couple and knowing that we weren't. I ate salmon with dill sauce and I had too much cake, and at the very end, as we were about to leave, I hugged my sister and burst into tears. I was crying because my mother seemed so proud of her, and I was crying because my father had stood up on a chair and made a speech, and I was crying because I felt like the loser sister beside her, the loser sister who couldn't even pay someone to make a dress that fit right, who couldn't do anything except fight with her boyfriend.

*　*　*

The pale pink dress I wore to the wedding was actually the world's second-worst dress. The world's absolute-worst dress was a scrunchy black minidress made of Lycra that looked like a long tube sock when you held it up in front of you. Julian saw it in a women's clothing store on Newbury Street shortly after we moved in together, and he took me to see it one weekend. "You'd look great in that," he said. I tried it on and came out of the dressing room feeling half naked, like I was wearing a small, slippery black towel.

"I don't know . . ." I said.

"It looks great," he said.

So I bought it. I wore it to a New Year's Eve party a few weeks later and I looked like a cheap imitation of a Victoria's Secret model. The dress had a wide scoop neck and long sleeves and if you stretched it way down it came to about mid-thigh, but it was made of really tight, elastic material so it kept riding up higher than that. I spent the whole night clutching my wineglass and tugging at the hem. Before the party Julian and I had an argument because I'd left some mushrooms in the oven too long and he'd accused me of ruining dinner, so I was feeling alone at the party, as well as self-conscious. I stood there teetering on my black high heels and tugging at the damn hem and feeling exposed and if I hadn't had a lot to drink I probably would have burst into tears or lain down on the carpet and died of shame.

When we got home, we fought some more and Julian told me I should have worn black flats with the dress instead of black heels. "It's the kind of dress you're supposed to wear with flats," he said, and instead of feeling angry I felt like a failure. He was right, you see: flats would have kept the look from spilling across sexy into cheap.

We spent an inordinate amount of time arguing about my wardrobe, which was really a metaphor for arguing about me: who I was, who both of us wanted me to be. Julian would bring home copies of *Vogue* and *Elle* and *Harper's Bazaar* and he'd flip through the pages in the kitchen and point at different outfits. "You should think about this look," he'd say, or "That look would be good for you." This would stir up a million different emotions on my part: I'd feel criticized and belittled, as though my own clothes weren't good enough, and then I'd feel anxious and insecure, as though there was something wrong with my own taste, and I'd flip back and forth between wanting him to tell me how to dress but hating him for doing it too.

Our first Christmas together he bought me a bunch of clothes, a big, indulgent pile that included a black cotton-Lycra miniskirt and a black lace thong teddy, and these confused me more than anything anybody had ever bought me. He was always saying, "You need to *push out*, you need to try new things," and he genuinely thought he was being helpful when he showed me pictures in magazines or bought me things to wear. I sent out signals that I needed and wanted guidance, and although a part of him didn't particularly relish the role of mentor, I was never able to tell him quite clearly how conflicted the guidance made me feel.

So usually I wouldn't say anything. I'd stand there in the kitchen and nod at photos of large-breasted women wearing net shirts and jewelry made of leather and bone, and something deep within me would clench up and freeze. Sometimes I felt like I was carrying around a second version of myself, some tiny person who got angrier and angrier as time went on, but also smaller and smaller and smaller, too small to get out.

At least once a month I'd call my sister in tears. "Julian and I had a fight," I'd sniffle, and then I'd start to sob. It never occurred to me that the drinking and the tears were connected and it took me years to understand that the drinking and the deteriorating relationship with Julian were connected, too, so deeply entangled that I'd never give up one without giving up the other first.

Becca saw that long before I did, saw how connected they were, and once in a while she'd tell me. I'd call her up feeling really sad and stuck, and she'd say, "I don't think you're going to get out of that relationship unless you quit drinking," but I couldn't see that. I thought she was being simplistic and judgmental and besides, most of the time I thought I'd die without either Julian or alcohol, so I hung in there for a very long time: five more years.

As a rule, active alcoholics are powerless people, or at least a lot of us tend to feel that way in our hearts. That's something you usually can't tell from looking, especially when it comes to the high-functioning brand of drinkers, people who manage to hold on to all the trappings of personal power, like jobs and families and intact savings accounts. But you have to step back and look beneath the façades. In fact, very few people who drink alcoholically can learn to feel like powerful players in their own lives; all the strength comes out of a bottle.

I felt powerless with Julian, and so I drank, and the drinking created another feeling of power, a false one, perhaps, but the only one I had access to. By the time we moved in together, I was inhibited in front of Julian nearly all the time, and intimidated by him, and deeply afraid that he'd leave me. We fought about our relationship constantly. He'd complain that I was too passive and insecure. He'd give me that lecture about "pushing out." He'd say, "I need to be with someone who's *strong*," and his words echoed voices I'd heard in my head all my life—I wasn't good enough, I couldn't keep a man attracted to me. When the two of us got home at the end of the workday, I reached for the bottle of wine like it was a lifeline, instinctively and desperately, because it was the only thing that loosened me up enough to relax around him. I had the exact same feeling of voicelessness I'd had with my father all those years ago, and I reached for the same tool to counter it.

We drank every night. Julian, who was a great wine aficionado, would often open two bottles so he could compare and contrast. He'd pour tiny amounts into a glass and swirl it and hold it up to the light. He'd comment on the wine's nose or its legs, and he'd often quiz me on different vintages. "What do you taste?" he'd ask, wanting me to say something specific, like "undertones of blackberry," or "a hint of tarriness." I usually tried to fake my way through these tests but inside I'd be thinking, *Just pour the fucking wine*, and I'd resent him for meting out these stingy little sips. I wouldn't admit it, but after a while I really couldn't care less about the difference between a fine Bordeaux and a mediocre Burgundy, and when he wasn't looking I'd reach for the bottle and fill my glass all the way to the top.

Over the years I have learned to detest the phrase *low self-image*. That and *low self-esteem*. What do these mean, low self-image and self-esteem? Too many women to count—and a good number of men—careen into relationships every day with people who make them feel worthless, with people who help reinforce all their worst fears about themselves: *You're hideous, unlovable, horribly flawed, and if you're lucky for anything, it's that I continue to tolerate you, against my better judgment.* These feelings don't come from anything as banal as "low self-image." They stem from self-loathing, the deepest, most core variety, and in itself that feeling becomes addictive, a way of clinging to a truly hateful image of the self.

I clung to Julian because I thought he saw and acknowledged the real me, the hideous, unlovable, flawed person I really was, and I wanted him to love me in spite of that. I clung to him because I figured that sooner or later he would stop tolerating me and leave, and I clung to him because the alternative was too scary: in order to leave him I would have had to form a vision of myself as worthy and valuable, and I would have had to acknowledge the depth of my own rage, the sparks of fury I felt each time he implied I wasn't good enough. I don't know where that depth of self-loathing really came from; in the end I suppose it doesn't matter. I could (and did) spend hours analyzing the feeling in therapy but I didn't have the resources to act on it, to form that other version of myself. And so I remained paralyzed. That core sense of unworthiness kept me standing there in the kitchen, nodding over Julian's shoulder at half-naked women in *Elle*. It kept me standing at that New Year's Eve party tugging at the hem of that scrunchy black dress, and it kept me reaching for the bottle night after night.

At the time the relationship felt more addictive than the drink: my world got smaller and smaller; Julian occupied more and more space in my head, eliminating room for other concerns. I'd sit at my desk at work and spend whole days writing him letters, long, anguished tomes trying to explain how I felt. My circle of friends diminished: all I could think about was Julian— what he'd said to me, what I'd said back, what this comment or that allusion might have meant—and I found it harder and harder to be with other people. I also found it harder to care about anything else.

The summer after my sister's wedding my mother's doctor discovered tumors on her spine and skull, a recurrence of the cancer for which she'd been treated in 1982. By the time of Becca's wedding my mother had been cancer free for more than five years, which was stastically encouraging: passing the five-year mark appeared to vastly reduce the likelihood of recurrence. But the cancer was back. She was treated with radiation, and started on the drug Tamoxifen, and I went to see her oncologist that summer with my brother and sister to talk about her prognosis. The doctor was both direct and cryptic: he told us the cancer would ultimately kill her but he wouldn't guess when. "It could be two years," he said, "it could be ten." My sister, just out of medical school and far more familiar with cancer statistics than I was, panicked: apparently the two-year prognosis was much more likely than the ten-year one, but I couldn't fathom the possibility. I was too self-absorbed, too entrenched in my own problems, and far too focused on Julian to make room for anything else. I spent appallingly little time that summer thinking about my mother's health.

I did, however, think a great deal about my parents' marriage. My father and I continued to have our intermittent fifty-minute lunches together and every once in a while I'd ask him how things were between him and my mother. They'd gone into couple therapy together after my mother nearly left him and they seemed to have made some sort of peace. My father was never specific—"We're managing," he'd say, or "Things are okay"—but I gathered that they'd learned to live with each other's limits, to tolerate a modicum of dissatisfaction in order to hold on to the things they shared: their intellectual alliance, their love of Martha's Vineyard, us kids.

That didn't seem like enough to me. I'd go over to the house and I'd find them in the living room in the same strained, withholding silence and I'd think, *I want more than this.* Julian and I certainly didn't seem any happier than my parents, but the kind of contact we had, volatile and enmeshed as it was, felt oddly life-sustaining to me. Angry words seemed better than no words; rage seemed somehow more tangible than mere tolerance. Julian gave my life shape, and even if the contours became uglier and more distorted over time, the relationship provided me with a focus, gave my existence an edge that seemed more desirable than the veiled, shadowy unhappiness I still sensed between my parents. Even through the fighting, Julian was always a voice on the phone during the workday, a person to please at home, a goal, a companion.

And, of course, an object of obsession. I often couldn't sleep at night while I was living with him and I took to creeping downstairs at one or two in the morning and sitting in the living room with a bottle of Cognac. I'd stare out the window and worry: What was happening? Why were we so angry at each other all the time? Why was I so scared of him, and so furious and confused? Hours might pass like that. I'd sit and worry and drink until I'd had enough to fall asleep and then I'd get up the next day and repeat the whole scenario: the obsessive letter at work, the obsessive thoughts, the arguments at night, the wine, the Cognac. The shape of addiction is circular.

When you drink to deal with feelings like that, it's impossible to get over them. When you drink to drown out fear and rage, you quite literally disassociate from them, and you stop trusting yourself, stop trusting your own judgment and integrity. At one of the very first AA meetings I went to, the speaker was a man in his late thirties who spent a lot of time talking about how much he and his ex-girlfriend fought when they drank. Alcohol had an "unleashing" effect, he said. They'd drink and all the little hurts and disappointments of the day would get untethered from some deep corner of his heart and then bubble up to the surface. He was a sweet-looking guy with a soft voice, the kind of person I couldn't imagine being violent or mean, but he said he'd go into these rages when he got drunk and then he'd wake up in the morning and barely remember what had happened.

All over the room people were nodding and looking down at their shoes: *Oh, right. That. I remember that.* We all did that: got drunk in a paradoxical way that numbs feelings and gives you access to them at the same time, got drunk and got furious, got drunk and said all the things we were afraid to say sober.

After a while that's how I lived—and drank—with Julian. We'd go along for a few days or a few weeks and we wouldn't fight, but then it would happen again. The anger would simmer until it boiled over and then I'd *drink,* that kind of unleashing drinking that took away the distress of living with him but also put me squarely in its center.

One fall day I took the afternoon off from work and went grocery shopping. Another thing Julian always said when we fought was that I didn't do enough things for him, didn't do enough for the relationship, didn't show him, in tangible ways, that I was actively working to improve things between us. I had an internal war going on about that, afraid on the one hand that he was right and angry on the other hand that he couldn't accept or appreciate the things I *did* do, the ways I struggled to make him happy. But the first hand usually won, and that day I went to four stores and bought all kinds of foods that he liked. I bought arugula and broccoli rabe, and I bought free-range chicken and two kinds of olives, and at the very last store I saw a quart of strawberries that were outrageously expensive but looked good, so I bought those too. When I got home, I set the groceries on the counter and started to unload them. Julian observed. We were so consistently mad at each other by that time we couldn't say anything that wouldn't enrage the other person. He may have thanked me for shopping, but all I remembered was one comment: "Caroline," he said, "you really shouldn't buy strawberries this time of year. They're out of season."

Comments like that would stick with me for days. In a perverse way I almost welcomed them, waited for Julian to say disparaging or critical things that I could file away and mull over and hold against him in the future. I provoked them too. I'd bite my tongue for days at a time, letting the anger fester like an infected sore, and then I'd push just the right button, say something to Julian that would guarantee a fight.

The night after the strawberry comment we went to a cocktail party together, then moved on to a bar in downtown Boston to get a drink and something to eat. Sitting across the table, Julian looked at me suddenly and asked a weird question: "If you could get rid of one piece of my clothing, which one would you choose?"

I didn't know what to say: he had good taste in clothing; everything he wore looked fine. But when I drank, I couldn't just walk away from a dangerous or provocative situation. I always took the bait and I always found a way to fan the fire.

So after I passed on answering his question, I lit a cigarette and said, "So: if you could get rid of one piece of *my* clothing, which would *you* choose?"

I was pissed off that night and I was drunk and I wanted to be more pissed. And I got what I asked for. Julian answered, "That green shirt you wear when you work out." Then he added, "At the very least, you should tuck it in when you wear it."

Add venom and stir, my own personal recipe for rage. I sat there with my cigarette and pictured him criticizing my workout attire, pictured him standing there and actually thinking: *She should tuck in that green shirt.* I was quite drunk by that point and I don't remember all the details; all I know is that the small, angry person I kept inside rose up and took over. I was so angry, I thought I'd burst.

We left the bar almost immediately and had a huge fight on the way home, a major, screaming brawl about our relationship that lasted for hours: whose needs weren't being met, who was disappointing whom, the whole nine yards of accusatory drama. At some point Julian looked at me and said, "I don't think we should live together anymore. I've had it."

Julian was right, of course—we *shouldn't* have been living together, we were making each other miserable—but when I woke up in the morning, everything seemed wrong and surreal: the rage had faded away and all I could recall clearly was the stupid conversation about clothing, the screaming, the feeling of being out of control, the fear of being left. I didn't remember half the things we'd said to each other, and I knew that my own anger had come out in a flood instead of a measured, rational stream, and all I wanted to do was take the night back, take back all the words and start over.

I always felt messed up and confused like that the day after a fight with Julian, as though I'd been transported to some other planet during the night where people went crazy and lost their senses. I'd go out to dinner with Eliza, my main confidante at that point, and I'd spend hours obsessing over every detail of every last fight—what Julian had said to me, what I said back, what it all meant—and she'd be a good girlfriend and say all the reassuring things you'd expect: "You deserve to be happy," and "It's *not* all your fault." I'd stare down at my wineglass and nod, but I really didn't believe her.

When I got drunk and fought with Julian, I felt like a volcano, spewing out all my very worst qualities, anger and insecurity and venom. I felt like a bad person and because Julian was the only person who saw how bad I was, I felt like he was the only person in the world who really knew me, knew the *true* me. The self-loathing would bubble up, and so would the fear that he'd leave me, and I was afraid to tell Eliza the truth: *I'm a terrible girlfriend; I can't even buy strawberries. You have no idea.*

After that fight I started looking for a new apartment. I was miserable, and I drank more. Who wouldn't? I *needed* to drink. If my hangovers were a little worse—well, so was my life. If the dependency felt a little stronger, the need for a drink at the end of the day a little more intense, a little deeper in my bones—well, that was circumstantial: I'd drink less when my life got better, when I had fewer reasons to drink. I knew I would.

"You'd drink, too, if you had my problems." That's the thinking.

"I'm not unhappy because I drink; I drink *because I am unhappy.*"

That is the logic, and every alcoholic on the planet uses it.

And so the pattern becomes more deeply entrenched, and so the drinking continues, increases, spirals onward. Time passes, nothing changes. You wait. And while you're waiting, you drink. And while you drink, you get more stuck.

Almost everyone I know who's quit drinking describes that feeling, the sense that life has turned stale and colorless and slowly ground to a halt. You're someplace you don't want to be—in a bad job, a bad relationship—and you can't fathom a way out of it, simply can't see what steps you could take to change things.

The pain becomes acute. With each day you spend in the bad situation, your dignity erodes just a little bit more, keeping your feet glued more firmly to the floor. You cast around for explanations—whose fault is this? Is it your lover? Your boss? Your family? Are you simply doomed, destined to live an unhappy life? Reality clouds. You wake up after another night of heavy drinking and you can't put the pieces back together, can't figure out what that fight was about or why you ended up in the bed you're in or what happened the night before, and you don't understand—you simply do not understand—why you're so miserable, so fucking depressed and full of hate. And so you drink again; of course you drink again. You can't stand this—it's too much—and drinking is the one sure way, the *only* way, to kill the feeling.

The circle closes in on itself; the cycle is repeated. You are smack in the middle of the dance of addiction and you can't find your way off the floor.

12 *A Glimpse*

JULIAN PRACTICALLY HAD to pry my fingernails out of the furniture and throw me out of our apartment, I was that desperate to hang on. I clung. I wept and railed. I wrote him long apologetic letters, promising I'd change. In the end I did move, just a few days shy of my thirtieth birthday. I found an apartment in a converted warehouse, a smart-looking studio with tall ceilings and a fireplace and a lovely view of the Boston skyline. A very pretty place, but that wasn't really the point. I chose the apartment because it was around the corner from Julian's. Half a block away. Sixty-five steps. I counted.

But sometimes, even when you're that stuck, you can see the way out, a glimmer of truth. A few weeks after I moved, I called my therapist from work and scheduled an emergency appointment.

"Do you have any free time today?" I asked. My voice cracked and he must have sensed the urgency; he agreed to meet me that afternoon at two.

The therapist's office is on the seventh floor of the Mass. General, a small room that overlooks the roof of a Holiday Inn across the street. I sat there and looked out at huge clouds of steam, streaming out from vents on the roof. I was so hung over I thought I'd either die or throw up.

I said, "I think I'm having a real problem with alcohol." I said this in a straightforward manner, without much emotion, but I know I was scared.

He sat back and waited: "What's going on?"

I shook my head. Same old story. Fight with Julian. We were still seeing each other, and we'd had one of those drunken screaming brawls the night before about everything and nothing, and I'd woken up in the morning with foggy memories, little threads of them: screaming in the kitchen; leaving; slamming the door; reeling home in the night toward my apartment; weeping; calling him on the phone when I got home to fight and weep some more, to make him *understand* how hurt I was; hearing the phone just ring and ring because he refused to answer; finally falling into bed.

I looked at the therapist, who'd heard me rage and bitch about Julian for more than a year, and I said, "Alcohol is always involved when we fight. I'm drunk every single time. I lose control."

When I'd woken up in the morning, I was still drunk. My hands were shaking and I felt remorseful, humiliated, as though I'd blown some critical opportunity and not known quite how or why. I'd showered and gotten dressed, then called Julian. Again, he wouldn't answer. I'd gone over to his apartment and rung the bell. He wouldn't come to the door. I'd gone to work, worried all morning, obsessed and blamed myself, then finally had made the appointment with the shrink.

I felt some relief, talking to him about drinking. We'd discussed the subject before—every now and then I'd tell him I was drinking too much, or I'd mention something in which too much wine had played a role, most often a fight with Julian, but I usually skirted my way around the details, justified or minimized the extent to which alcohol was involved. If he brought the subject up again the next week, or asked me how the drinking was going, I'd say, "Oh, it seems to be more under control," and drop the subject. This time, I felt straighter, more honest. Drinking was a real problem in the relationship, not just a leitmotif. I drank and things went haywire.

I paused at one point, then asked him, in a quiet voice, "Do you think I'm going to have to quit drinking?"

My shrink is not the sort of person who makes grand pronouncements or offers direct advice. But he looked at me that afternoon and said, "Yes. I think so."

I went back to my office that afternoon, called Alcoholics Anonymous, and determined that there was a meeting that evening in the Back Bay. The man on the phone said it was a beginner's meeting, and that sounded good. I had an image of lots of young women like me—young professional women who'd be seated comfortably in a room and given literature to read by some kindly, maternal older woman.

The meeting was held in the basement of a church, and it looked nothing like I'd hoped: the room was cavernous and dingy, with rows of metal chairs; cigarette smoke swirled up from every other seat; old men sat and sipped coffee from white foam cups. There were a few women there, even a few professional-looking young ones, but the dominant feeling was gray and male and alien.

An older man at the podium chaired the meeting and the first thing he did was ask us to go around the room in turn and introduce ourselves by first name. People said, "I'm Joe, I'm an alcoholic," and "I'm Hank. Alcoholic." When it was my turn, I just said, "I'm Caroline."

I don't remember the format of the meeting. Thinking back, I guess it was an open discussion meeting, in which people just raise their hands and talk about whatever's on their minds. The only person I remember clearly was a scruffy-looking young man in blue jeans and a T-shirt, maybe twenty-five or thirty, who sat on the far side of the room and talked about being angry. "It's a fucking Friday night," he said. "All my friends are out drinking and I feel like I just don't know what to do with myself, you know? I mean, all my friends drink."

Some people in AA talk about going to a meeting for the first time and identifying right away, hearing someone tell what sounds exactly like their own story, having bells and whistles go off from the start. I heard that young man talk and I looked around at the dingy room with the old men sipping coffee from foam cups and I thought, *No way. No way in hell I'm doing this. This is not me. I do not belong here.*

I left the minute the meeting ended. I think I knew I wouldn't go back but I promised myself—really *promised* myself—that I'd stop drinking so much, that I'd cut down, get it under control. If I didn't, that smoke-filled church basement would be my fate.

I didn't drink that night, not one single drop.

Sometimes you see, but you're not ready to act. As it turned out, that would be the only night for the next five years that I successfully abstained from alcohol.

Or, for that matter, from Julian.

13 *Double Life II*

WHEN PEOPLE TALK about the human costs of alcoholism, they tend to focus on numbers: an annual economic drain of $98.6 billion (that figure combines medical expenditures for alcoholism and alcohol abuse; the cost of lost productivity; and costs associated with alcohol-related crime, car crashes, and fires). About 23,000 lives lost to drunk-driving accidents. An additional 30,000 lives lost to other (nonvehicular) injuries incurred while under the influence. Less tangible, but no less real, are the psychic costs: to oneself and to others.

My sister called me once in tears, the year our father was dying. "I feel like I'm going to lose everyone I love," she said. "Including you. I feel like I'm going to get a phone call in the middle of the night saying you've been killed in a car accident." She didn't say "because you were drunk" but she didn't need to; we both knew. But I brushed it off.

"Don't be ridiculous," I said. "I'm *fine*. Nothing is going to happen." My tone was more defensive than reassuring, though, and she didn't pursue the subject. She just sniffled into the phone and when we hung up a few minutes later, I felt a little guilty but mostly annoyed. *Feh*, I thought, dismissing her fears and her sadness. *Ridiculous*. Then I opened a bottle of wine. Door shut, case closed.

Al-Anon, the twelve-step program for friends and family members of alcoholics, estimates that every alcoholic's drinking affects at least four other people. We worry parents, lovers, co-workers, anyone close who crosses our paths. We lose our tempers with them, we blame them for our troubles, we push them away. We never quite let them in, let them know us too well, because we're afraid that if they got too close they'd be appalled at what they'd find. Accordingly, a great deal of the active alcoholic's energy is spent constructing facades, an effort to present to others a front that looks okay, that seems lovable and worthy and intact. Inside versus outside; version A, version B. The double life grows more sophisticated and more deeply entrenched.

Mostly, we lie. That's a statement of fact, not a judgment. Alcoholics lie about big things, and we lie about small things, and we lie to other people, and (above all) we lie to ourselves. John Cheever wrote about this in his journals, calling dishonesty "the most despicable trait." He wrote, "You take a nap and claim to be tired from work. You hide a whiskey bottle in the cabinet and claim to be a wiser man than your friends who hide whiskey bottles in the closet. You promise to take a child to the circus and have such a bad hangover that you can't move. You promise to send money to your old mother and do not."

Big lies, small lies: it's hard to find an alcoholic who didn't manipulate the truth about *something*, even if it was minor stuff, stuff that really didn't add up to anything at all. My friend Gail used to lie about movies and books. If a group of people at work were talking about something they'd read, she'd chime in instinctively. "Oh, I read that," she'd say, even if she hadn't, or she'd say she *loved* some movie that other people loved, even if she'd never even heard of the movie, let alone seen it. To an outsider this sounds stupid and useless until you consider that people who drink constantly never really get a chance to know how they feel about anything, even things like movies and books. After a while drinkers just fall into the behavior, a way of overcompensating:

we learn to pretend we have opinions because deep in our own hearts, we really don't.

Linnette, a woman I met in my first year of sobriety, lied so much she thought she was going crazy—the conflicting stories she told different people whirled around in the back of her mind like an acid eddy, constantly roiling away, overlapping, melding into one another, making her think she'd lost all hold on reality. She'd tell her mother she needed money to buy protective bars for the windows on her basement apartment and then she'd spend the money on drugs. She'd tell her boss she had to fly home suddenly because her mother had taken ill (she hadn't) and then she'd go on a three-day bender. She'd cheat on her boyfriend, and then she'd cheat on that guy by sleeping with someone else, and after a while her whole life felt like one huge heap of rationalizations and justifications and stories piled on stories. Linnette, who's thirty-four, is a small woman, about five foot three, with wavy brown hair and wide green eyes. She's pretty in a perky, youthful way, with a bright, almost surprised expression that gives her an innocent look and makes her duplicity seem all the more astonishing. *You* lied like that? I must have said that to her fifty times. *You?* She'd eye me sarcastically. "Oh," she'd say. "And you didn't?"

Linnette lied at first to her boyfriend, a Julian-like figure who'd dominated and defined her since she met him, when she was twenty-one. They'd lived together for five years, and over that period Linnette's drinking had escalated along with her private unhappiness. Familiar story: just like me, just like Elaine. She'd lost all sense of power to the boyfriend, whose name was Jason, then quietly seethed, then found herself in one of those wars with the self, too insecure to leave the relationship but too unhappy to stay without the anesthesia.

A few years before she quit drinking, Linnette started flirting heavily with a man in her office, an attentive, adoring guy named Robert, who seemed to fill the deepest needs left by Jason, needs for affection and contact and warmth. One night after work they went out drinking together and Linnette ended up spending the night at his apartment. A week or so later she and Jason had a huge, drunken fight and she stormed out of his house and ran to Robert's. Before long she was caught in one of those impossible cycles: sleeping with both men, covering her tracks, feeling driven by impulses that felt too big to ignore, running to Robert, then running back to Jason, juggling the details and the stories and the rationalizations almost constantly.

"It was such a big fucking *drama*," she told me, one night over coffee, and I nodded and nodded. Oh, yes: the alcoholic drama.

Drink alcoholically for long enough and you start to get the feeling that things in life just *happen* to you, as though you're living in a video, or reading from a script that someone else has written. Life becomes a big, unwieldy set of scenes and all you can do is play your part: enter stage left; exit stage right; read the lines; just pray the critics haven't made it to the show. To an alcoholic, deception is an integral part of the script, the key element.

Linnette wove long, elaborate lies to Jason about where she'd been and what she'd been doing when she was with Robert, because that kept the scenes with Jason intact: as long as she hid the real truth, she didn't have to face the real consequences, leaving him or being left. She wove long, elaborate lies to Robert about her relationship with Jason—minimizing her role in their difficulties, exaggerating her willingness to leave him—because that kept the scenes with *him* moving along, kept him engaged, kept him reading his own lines. Months passed this way. Linnette felt guilty when she was with Jason, needy when she was with Robert, and these emotions fed on each other. The guiltier she felt with Jason, the less powerful she felt—the less able to stand up to him—and the less powerful she felt with him, the needier she felt with Robert, and so it went: one emotion fueling the next.

Her response, of course, was to drink. She drank to drown the guilt and confusion, and she drank to drown the slow erosion of integrity that accompanied the duplicity, and she drank to numb

the psychic shock of running back and forth between relationships, waking up in the morning with one man, going to sleep
that night with another. About a year into this, with both relationships feeling increasingly stressful and tainted and impossible,
Linnette met a third man, Ed, and she started sleeping with *him*.

The first step in AA's twelve steps of recovery states: "We
admitted we were powerless over alcohol, that our lives had become unmanageable."

"This," Linnette said, referring to her own elaborate drama, "is
what they mean."

I met Michael a few months after moving out of Julian's apartment, right around the time I skipped out on that AA meeting.
He was Julian's antithesis. For a long time my friend Eliza called
him the "Anti-Julian" because he was so uncomplicated and
sweet. Michael was unqualified in his affections, a laid-back, regular guy who drank Budweiser beer and didn't know beans about
high fashion.

I met him at work. A freelance illustrator, he came into my
office one day while I was working on a feature story about
women's magazines. I was flipping through a copy of *Glamour* and
he was standing by my desk when I turned to a page that showed
a model wearing a silver net shirt. I heard a shocked voice say,
"Whoa! She looks like she's wearing a fireplace screen!" and I
laughed. That was Michael. He appealed to the part of me that
wanted to be with an easy, comfortable, loving man, and at the
same time he conflicted with the part of me that wanted to be
with a complicated, cerebral, willful man, and so began my own
version of the drunken drama, a four-year jag of insanity that I
could characterize as unmanageable only in retrospect. Two men;
two competing sets of needs; too many drinks.

Michael is just about the kindest man I've ever met. The first
time I spent the night at his house, he woke up and looked at me,
his eyes all earnest, and said, "How did *this* happen? I feel like I

won the lottery." It was snowing outside, hard, but he got up and went to the store and bought eggs and cheese and milk and the newspapers. Then he made omelettes and while he was cooking, he talked to his mother, who'd called on the phone from Connecticut. I remember watching him whisk the eggs and milk in a metal bowl, the phone tucked between his ear and shoulder, and hearing him laugh at something his mother said. He has a great laugh, deep and sincere, and before he got off the phone he told her he loved her. He didn't seem the least bit awkward or embarrassed by that, saying, "I love you, Mom," in front of a woman he'd just spent the night with, and I filed a mental note about that: *Nice man; loves his mother*.

I was like a sponge around him, soaking up that affection as though I'd been starved. But one of the sick things about being drunk and confused all the time is that a good thing can be staring you straight in the face and you really can't see it. So many other things cloud the picture.

After we ate the omelettes that morning, I sat on the sofa and fought with myself about how to spend the day. It was all snowy and gray outside and the idea of hanging out in Michael's living room watching videos all afternoon seemed infinitely appealing, comforting and soft as something cashmere. But the Julian question loomed, scratched at some internal door: *You should get home. What if Julian calls and you're not there? Stay available for Julian.* I had mental wars like that all the time—pulled toward Michael, pulled back toward Julian—and I simply didn't have the guts or the presence of mind to be honest about this with either man.

"I gotta get home," I finally said to Michael. "I have a million things to do this afternoon."

Michael liked to drink but he wasn't the least bit alcoholic—he always knew when to stop—and at first he saw my drinking as fairly social, nothing extraordinary: a girl who likes to get a little tipsy, rather than a girl who needs to get hammered. He had no idea how much I really drank. That was the first big lie, probably the main one. We'd go out to dinner together and I'd drink what seemed like a reasonable amount, three glasses of wine, maybe four. He just wouldn't see the four or five more I drank after he dropped me off at my apartment. I didn't get seriously bombed in front of him for a long time, and the few times I did, he didn't know me well enough to tell.

I hid the relationship with Julian well too. Michael knew I'd been living with him, and he knew we still saw each other sometimes, but I minimized the extent of my involvement. One night, early on, Michael came over to my apartment while I was on the phone with Julian, engaged in a long verbal brawl. He sat on the sofa for about thirty minutes trying not to listen, but after I got off the phone, he looked up from his magazine and said, "That is one sick relationship. Do you know that?" He looked alarmed, more alarmed than he sounded, and after that I started unplugging the phone when he came over. I unplugged the phone when Julian came over too.

Dramas spiral and twist; lies feed on one another. I still coveted Julian's approval, and I still believed that the deterioration of the relationship was my fault, and the more time I spent with Michael, the guiltier I felt around Julian: I felt dishonorable and evil, a person who had no business expecting good things from a relationship, and as that feeling deepened, the harder it got to be straight with either one of them.

I lived this way for longer than I care to admit: a downward spiral, lubricated by drink, made bearable by anesthesia. I lied to both men all the time, and I drank even more because the duplicity made me so uncomfortable. Julian and I would be making plans to get together, and he'd say, "How about Wednesday?" and I'd be seeing Michael that night and I'd say, "Oh. I'm having dinner with Eliza on Wednesday." Or Michael and I would be making plans and I'd say, "I really need a night alone, just to veg out," and then I'd go off to dinner with Julian.

In fact, I wasn't really fooling anybody. As my shrink used to remind me, and not always so gently, I didn't have quite as much power as I seemed to think I had. After I moved out, the relationship with Julian became increasingly ill defined, with both of us struggling in some respects to separate and in other respects to hold on: he saw other women and he knew I was seeing Michael but we developed an unspoken system of withholding the details from each other, a don't-ask-don't-tell policy that provided a measure of distance but also kept the door to the relationship open. So Julian knew I was involved with Michael; he just didn't know how deeply. For his part, Michael knew I still saw Julian, but he didn't know how frequently, or how much brain-space Julian still occupied. Often, I didn't lie so much as I withheld information, or manipulated the facts, and I suppose that helped me rationalize the behavior. I'd drop just enough information about each man to the other to protect myself from being blatantly dishonest, but I limited degrees, never revealed the true extent of either involvement, maintained an illusion of availability and devotion in both relationships that didn't truly exist.

Living like that, you start to feel like you're in the middle of a human chess game: plotting strategy, planning the next move; second-guessing the other players. All brain, no heart. My phone would ring at work. Uh-oh. Julian. I'd panic for a second: I'd spent the last night at Michael's; did Julian suspect? Did he try me that morning and find no answer? What do I say? Strategy deployed: voice gets casual and light. "Did you try to call me this morning? The phone was ringing when I got out of the shower and I didn't get it in time." Hah: whereabouts established; bases covered. He buys it. Sigh of relief.

Or I'd spend a Sunday at Julian's, telling Michael I was going off somewhere with Eliza. The day would pass; Julian would suggest dinner. *Oh, sure*, I'd say. *Sounds great*. But inside, the mind would race. Unanticipated snag; Michael expects me to be at home tonight. How to escape for five or ten minutes to use the phone? What to say? Lies upon lies. To Julian: "Oooops. I'm out of cigarettes. Be back in five minutes." Race back to my apartment. Call Michael: "Hey. I'm still at Eliza's; I think I'll stay for dinner." Chitchat briefly, maintaining a voice that says, Everything is *fine!* Race back. Open package of smokes with a flourish. Phew.

These sound like such stupid little escapades, such unnecessary little falsehoods, but they felt so central, so critical to the maintenance of the fronts. I'd wail about my life in therapy and the shrink would ask, "What would happen if you were just *honest* with Julian, honest with Michael?" and I'd shake my head, unable to answer. I didn't know how to be real, how to tell the truth: that was the heart of the matter. My whole sense of reality was tied into the deception, built into the façades. To be honest would have meant dismantling the whole structure, all the assumptions and impressions about myself I'd worked so hard to create: *I'm together, in control; I'm the person you want me to be.* To tell the truth would have meant disclosing my full self, owning up to flaws and imperfections and depths of confusion I was too ashamed to reveal: *I am not in control at all; I am deeply fucked up.* A whole lot of alcoholics know this state of mind: it's like living in a house of cards, and feeling that if you remove one of them, own up to one lie, the whole thing will crumble down around you.

Underneath the deception was a sense of terrible, unyielding neediness, not unlike the feeling of needing a drink. Linnette once said that in some ways, the drama of these liquor-washed situations is as addictive as a drug, and I think she's right: you get so used to attaching your needs to other people—their responses to you, the feelings they evoke—that you begin to feel you literally can't live without them, as though your deepest desires simply can't be satisfied in any other way. So all your energy goes toward underscoring the drama, reinforcing everybody's role.

For me, it was a play of profound ambivalence. I felt with Julian much the same way I'd felt with my father—slightly inferior, desperate for approval, convinced he held some key to my potential—and those feelings, so deeply familiar, kept me entrenched well beyond reason. And yet I was equally drawn to

Michael, whose kindness and affection tapped a need that felt just as deep, and every bit as alluring.

During this time, I had the sense of being literally at war with myself, one side straining to be proven unlovable, the other side aching for the opposite, one piece of me compelled to reenact an old family drama, another piece yearning for a relationship that felt more sustaining. And so it went, romantic yin and yang. A fight with Julian, a hug from Michael; a criticism from Julian, a compliment from Michael. At heart, I *was* at war: the two men spoke to competing sides of my soul, Julian offering validation, Michael offering survival, and I couldn't, simply couldn't, let go of either one. Linnette felt that way with the men in her life too: driven in the deepest, most compulsive sense toward them, terrified of being without whatever man A or B or C had to give, her whole being tied up in the different ways the relationships defined her. She couldn't let go either.

"Active alcoholics have no tolerance for frustration," she says. "Zippo. We're totally impulse-driven. If we can't get what we think we need, we think we're going to die."

About a year into this Michael-Julian drama, I got pregnant. I didn't know which one was the father. Michael came with me the day I got the pregnancy test (I told Julian I wanted to go by myself) and Julian came with me the day I had the abortion (I told Michael that Eliza was coming with me) and neither one knew beans about the other one's involvement. No one did. I didn't tell a soul except these two men that I'd gone and gotten myself knocked up, which is exactly what I felt I'd done. I blamed it all on diaphragm failure at the time but I'm quite sure it was drunken negligence, pure and simple.

The morning of the abortion I had to have a brief counseling session with a member of the staff, a kind, heavyset black woman whose job was to make sure I knew what I was doing and what my options were. She took me into a little room and closed the door.

"How are you feeling?" she asked.

I hadn't shed a tear up to that point but my eyes welled up just then and I said I felt rotten. I said, "I wish I was at a point in my life where having a baby was an option, but it just isn't right now." And that's when I got choked up. I felt sorry for myself and ashamed and just plain overwhelmed that I'd gotten drunk one night—which night I couldn't even remember—and accidentally created a *life*. I had that sensation of wanting desperately to be some other person, some other *kind* of person, a clean-living, monogamous woman who lived in a farmhouse somewhere and had baby after baby with no doubts or complications.

After that session I was herded into a waiting area where I sat with five or six other women watching *Oprah* until it was my turn. *Oprah* that day was about mothers who steal their daughters' boyfriends and I remember it made me feel a little better, watching how other people fucked up their lives.

Shortly after the abortion Julian and I stopped sleeping together. We never talked about this: our relationship just took an unspoken turn and entered even more ambiguous territory, as though we both silently, and simultaneously, signed an agreement, dismissing sexual intimacy without quite letting go of our attachment. I suppose I was relieved at the change: it eased my guilt a shade, gave me one less thing to be caught at.

My father got sick about a year after the abortion and I started spending more nights at Michael's apartment, partly because he lived near my parents and partly because he was a comfort I needed. Gradually, I took to hiding liquor. I'd stop at a liquor store on my way over to pick up wine for dinner and I'd see those nips of liquor in the rack by the cash register. I'd feel exhausted and depressed, these multiple stresses weighing on me like stone, and I'd think: *Insurance. Just in case I feel I need it.* Nips of Cognac in the purse, nips in the drawer at Michael's where I kept my stuff, nips transferred surreptitiously to my bathrobe pockets so I could sip one or two in the bathroom before I went to bed, to help me to sleep.

At some point—I don't remember when—it got too embarrassing to stand there in the liquor store every other day and ask for
two or three nips of brandy, so I bought a whole bottle and
stashed it on Michael's back porch, behind an old refrigerator. I'd
steal out there at night and take long slugs of it. "I'm going to
smoke a cigarette," I'd say, and then I'd slip through the back hall
and onto the porch. It was nasty out there—cold in the winter,
dusty, cluttered with old furniture and paint cans—but I'd slide
the bottle out of its hiding place and sit there on a small wooden
chair, sipping and smoking, and I'd feel relief.

Michael didn't know about my stash but he did know I was
drinking too much and he felt powerless to do anything about it.
I'd pass out lots of nights, just get into the bed and be out cold
within minutes. I had nightmares when I drank that much, and
I'd toss and turn and moan and grind my teeth. Michael used to
wake up in the morning exhausted and tell me he felt like he was
sleeping with a wolverine. Sometimes he couldn't stand it anymore and he'd get up in the middle of the night and go sleep on
the sofa. I'd wake up in the morning and he'd be gone, and I'd
think, Oh, shit.

I always apologized, with great sincerity. I'd creep into the
living room and crawl on top of him on the sofa and whisper, "I
kept you awake. I'm sorry, Michael." Then I'd kiss him on the
forehead or burrow into his neck and he'd accuse me of trying to
weasel my way back into his good graces. "You're weaseling," he'd
say, and gently push me away. Once in a while he got really
furious and I'd have to slink away and just let him simmer, but
Michael is a very forgiving person who also hates confrontation,
so he never stayed angry at me for longer than a day.

We both blamed these episodes on my father's illness, and then
on my mother's, and I vigorously defended my right to drink in
response. On nights when I didn't visit my family, I'd come home
with a bottle of red wine and a six-pack of beer and I'd place the
goods on Michael's kitchen table with a kind of authority,
squarely, so he'd know I meant business. He calls these my days as

a Wine Terrorist: the gesture said, *No way we're not drinking this wine; no way.*

Michael drank his share defensively, and often reluctantly: if he didn't have half the bottle, he knew I'd drink the whole thing myself. But half a bottle of wine and a few beers rarely did the trick by that point, so I had to supplement and when I was at Michael's, I had to supplement in secret. After a while the behavior started to seem natural, justifiable, and (of course) entirely situational: I was so depressed: my family was falling apart and I was all tangled up with Julian and I was so stressed out, and I figured I'd stop all this at some point down the line, I'd stop it *when things got better.*

One summer morning, a few months after my father died, I went out to the back porch to clear away my stash and got locked out. It was Julian's birthday and I'd promised I'd take the day off and drive up to the beach with him, but I didn't want Michael to know that so I told him I was taking the day off from work to spend some time with my sister.

The stash had grown. I had an empty Cognac bottle behind the refrigerator, plus an empty bottle of Scotch, so when Michael left for work that morning, I took advantage of his absence and went out there to dispose of the evidence. When I reached behind the refrigerator, the door closed behind me, locking from the inside.

The door leading out to the backyard was locked, too, and it was the kind that locks from the outside, so I couldn't get out from there either. I was stuck, standing on the porch like an idiot with my purse over my shoulder and two empty bottles of booze in my hands.

I rattled the doorknob to the apartment. I rattled the doorknob to the backyard. Nothing. I pounded on the backyard door, hoping Michael's landlord, who lived upstairs, might hear me and come downstairs. Nothing. I paced around for about ten minutes, thinking, *Oh, shit. What* now?

A perfect metaphor. There I was, pacing around Michael's back porch with my purse and two empty bottles, trapped in one sense because I couldn't get back into the house and trapped in another sense because I was involved in two relationships and couldn't get fully into, or out of, either one.

I hated myself for living like this, but by that time I felt I'd lost control over the script. The dual existence felt bigger than me, as though it had a life of its own. This is an exhausting way to live, plotting and racing and second-guessing constantly. Sometimes I felt like a fly trapped in a small glass jar, batting about in my own life in a panic, but that only added to the deepening feeling of need around alcohol. Liquor, slowly but surely, becomes the sole source of relief from your own thoughts.

So on it goes. You lie and you deflect blame and you rationalize and the hole you dig yourself gets deeper and deeper. Denial—first of drinking, then of the self—stretches to include more and more bits of reality, and after a while you literally cannot see the truth, cannot see your own role in the disaster you've made of your life, cannot see who you are or what you need or what choices you have. During that period, juggling both relationships, my life took on a deeply fragmented quality, with different personae emerging and becoming more distinct and also more false. At work I was the composed writer and editor, and at Julian's house I was the sophisticated, well-dressed intellectual, and at Michael's house I was the slightly needy girlfriend, and at home I didn't know who the hell I was, which thread led to the real me.

After my father died, the drinking increased. I was aware of this, but I used his death, and my mother's subsequent illness, to justify it. Of *course* I'm drinking: my father's dead and my mother's dying. Of *course* I'm stuck in these two relationships—I can't take on another loss right now. Of *course* I'm a wreck: my life is in shambles.

In reality, though, the drinking merely complicated the sense of fragmentation, contributed to the gradual loss of control. And that's precisely how drinking works. Your life gets ugly and you drink more. You drink more and your life gets uglier still. The cycle goes on and on and on, and in the process you become increasingly isolated and lost, stuck in your own circle of duplicity and rationalization and confusion, the gap between your façades and your inner world growing wider and wider and more complete.

Stress increases; hopelessness mounts. I've always been a somewhat superstitious person, and for years, as a teenager, I'd adhere to little rituals to ensure good luck: holding my breath while driving past a cemetery, picking up my feet when driving across railroad tracks, making wishes at first stars. Usually, I'd wish for really specific things—*please make X call me*, or *please help me get this job*—but in those last years, drinking too much and seeing both Julian and Michael and feeling more and more out of control, I gave up on the specifics and started wishing in the most general way: *Please give me peace of mind; please give me peace of mind.* I had no idea—none—that peace of mind was something I was keeping from myself, that the drinking made it farther and farther out of reach.

Alcoholics drink in order to ease the very pain that drinking helps create. That's another one of the great puzzles behind liquor, the great paradoxes. You hurt, you drink; you hurt some more, you up the intake. In the process, of course, you lose any chance you might have had to heal authentically.

One night Michael invited me and two of his friends over for dinner, John and Andrea, a couple he'd known for years. Andrea is a lawyer, a beautiful light-skinned black woman with green eyes who looks a little like Vanessa Williams, and John is tall and blond, a carpenter and playwright, and they always seemed like the kind of people I'd like to get to know better: kind, intelligent, witty. I'd told them to bring wine, which is what I always told people when they asked if they could contribute something to the meal. "Oh, just bring some wine," I'd say, and if ten people were coming, that would mean up to twenty bottles of wine might come along with them, plus whatever Michael and I bought beforehand, which was always plenty.

We made chicken cacciatore that night and I set out little bowls of olives and tortilla chips and salsa before they got there, and Michael admonished me the way he always did: "Now, just take it easy, okay? Don't get too drunk." And, of course, I didn't pay any attention and I got way too drunk.

I didn't *mean* to; I never meant to. But I'd be feeling edgy before the guests arrived, so I'd have a beer or two while we cooked, and then they'd get there and I'd get a little more anxious —was everything okay? were we timing the food correctly? was anybody bored yet?—and so I'd open the first bottle of wine and pour it around and suddenly my glass would be empty, just like that, and so I'd fill it up again. I never consciously chugged the wine, it just happened, and all of a sudden I'd be bombed.

That night I sat on the sofa before dinner, sipping my wine, and I remember looking at John and Andrea and wondering why I couldn't have a relationship like theirs, a nice, stable relationship where you lived together and didn't tell lies and didn't hang on to your ex-boyfriends and make a huge disaster of everything. But alcoholics are masters at blaming others for the jams they get themselves into, and what I couldn't see, sitting there with John and Andrea, what I *wouldn't* see, is that I was doing exactly that. Linnette did it too: she blamed her boyfriend for the chaos she'd created (he was mean, he made her feel inadequate), and she blamed Robert (Robert didn't understand how hard things were for Linnette, how tangled up she was with Jason), and she blamed her parents for not having loved her right as a kid, and she blamed just about everyone and everything she could find.

So did I. I blamed Julian for being Julian, for being unable to love me the way I wanted to be loved, and I blamed Michael for being too nice to me and too nonconfrontational and not demanding that I make a commitment to him, and I went along like that for years, thinking if only Julian would change, if only Michael would change, if only Julian would move to another city, if only X, Y, and Z would happen, *then* things might work out differently.

It never occurred to me that people like John and Andrea (who are, in fact, a very happily married couple) might have worked very hard to build the relationship they had, that they might have gone through great periods of doubt with one another, and struggled to accept each other's limits, and lived through those moments of profound disappointment when you look into the eyes of someone you love and see that they are unable to meet every single one of your needs. Alcoholics (at least alcoholics like me) can't do that kind of work when we're actively drinking. All our impulses tell us to reach for a bottle at the first stirring of emotional distress, and so those moments are lost, just drowned away with drink.

Ultimately, that summer morning, I got myself off Michael's back porch. The windows were made of slatted glass and finally it occurred to me that I could unscrew the slats and take them out of the little slots that held them in place, one at a time, until I'd opened up enough space to slide through. I removed one, then another, then another. The glass was filthy and my hands were covered with dust. I opened up a space of about two feet, then climbed up on a box, and eased myself through.

I was terrified while this was happening: terrified that Michael would come home and catch me dangling out of his window and I'd have to explain what I'd been doing out on the porch in the first place; terrified that I'd be late to pick up Julian and completely unable to tell him where I'd been, why I was late, why I hadn't called. But I got out of the window, got back into Michael's house, reassembled the slats on the window, grabbed the bottles and tossed them in another neighbor's trash outside, then drove away. The whole thing took about forty-five minutes, and I was a little late picking up Julian, but he didn't seem to notice.

Years later I'd hear people in AA say it over and over—*Unmanageable: my life was unmanageable*—and still I wouldn't quite see how the word applied to me. *Yeah, but that was just one stupid episode. I got trapped out there: an accident.*

In fact, unmanageability was the story of my life: I was living in a state of self-imposed chaos, lying and hiding and keeping secrets and feeling trapped, absolutely trapped, in the whole mess.

14 *Hitting Bottom*

O<small>NE NIGHT IN</small> the rehab I spent some time sitting in the cafeteria with a man named George, who also came from Boston and who had a drinking history somewhat like my own. He'd never gotten himself into too much trouble—he still had a job, working in his family's business, and he still had an apartment, and he still had friends and the trappings of a normal, nonravaged life, and we sat around for a while talking about what it means to hit bottom and whether or not we really had.

"You know," George said, "I never did those things you associate with 'real' alcoholics. I never totaled a car or ended up in jail. I never killed anyone in a blackout. I didn't have those kinds of losses."

I nodded. "Me neither."

"The question," George said, "is how low you have to go before you quit. How bad do things have to get?"

A little while later a man named Chris joined us and we asked him what he thought: How low? How bad before you give it up?

Chris is a heavyset construction worker in his early thirties with bright blue eyes and arms like telephone poles. He looked thoughtful for a minute and said, "Well, I guess really hitting bottom means death. It's a question of getting off the elevator before you get that far down."

The elevator metaphor is common in AA: the alcoholic's ele-

194

vator only goes in one direction—straight down. The good news is you can get off any time you want: after you've truly accepted that you're a member of the crowd, after you've gotten scared or desperate enough to see what direction you're headed, it's a choice you make. Get off or keep going until you end up six feet under.

Hitting bottom is generally preceded by a long, slow fall. This may be a semiconscious process, an almost deliberate decision to leap off the deep end. The invisible line, crossed over and back so many times already, shifts into focus for a moment, a day, a certain defined period, and we look at it, and we jump, holding any prior sense of restraint in our arms, plunging downward.

My friend Abby made the leap after she was raped. Who could blame her? Wouldn't you do the same? The rape was one of those episodes Abby communicated to me over a period of weeks, with her characteristic, small verbal bombshells. One day she told me she'd been raped, just the fact of it. The next time we talked, she told me the rapist was a stranger, who'd broken into her apartment in the night. The next, that she'd been blindfolded the whole time. And the next, that he kept asking her a question: "How do you want to die?"

Abby drank a lot before this happened, and she smoked pot daily, but afterward, something within her shifted. The impulse to control, and to worry, abated. *Fuck it.* It's like the deepest part of your soul just says that—fuck it—and you plunge, justification in hand like a passport to self-destruction. Abby lived in a basement apartment. She started stealing bottles of wine from the landlord's wine cellar, which was adjacent to her front door, and she drank every night until she passed out.

Janet took the leap after her marriage ended. Something clicked the same way, something very deep said, *Nope. Just can't tolerate any more pain,* and her alcohol intake went off the charts. She moved from Vermont to Boston and after a very short time found herself looking up at the clock every night at ten-fifty or ten fifty-five and thinking: *Oh, shit.* Then, no matter what she was doing, she'd race out to the liquor store before it closed to pick up one more bottle, one more bottle to get her through the night, to get her to sleep. Like Abby she was semiconscious of taking this plunge and semiconscious of her determination to keep falling. The fear—in her case, of being alone, of starting a new life, of her own rage and disappointment—was like a monster that took root after her divorce, and began to grow, and then stirred every night around dusk. She'd feel it moving in there, like a mother feels her baby shifting in utero, and she'd stiffen with a sense of powerful panic and move to kill it.

I suppose some alcoholics look for reasons to leap. We maneuver and sidle into position and manipulate events until the one horrible thing happens, the one truly horrible thing that will lead us over the edge. I think of Elaine, the hopelessness with which she was drawn to the married man, the determination with which she drank each time they broke up. Water seeks its own level; a lot of us seek out people who will drown us. In itself, I suppose, the leap is about drowning, about wanting to drown, about needing the perfect excuse to let go of the lifeboat.

"Who could say anything after the rape?" Abby says. "Who was going to call me on my drinking at a time like that?" No one, of course, including herself, the same way Michael (and I) felt unable to acknowledge the extent of my drinking after my parents died. The leap is both generated and perpetuated by loss: loss of hope, loss of faith that life has anything good to offer, loss of self-respect, loss of will. And the insidious thing is, abandoning yourself to drink feels like survival. *Fuck it. The pain is just too big. This is my only recourse, the only thing that will save me.*

Taking the leap, though, isn't the same as hitting bottom. Truly landing, landing with such finality you realize you have to get off the damn elevator or you'll die, requires an elusive combination of despair and grace, something known in AA as "the gift of desperation."

Mary Ellen, a journalist in her early forties, drank for twenty-four years. Two years ago she got a job she'd been coveting for months, an editing position at a magazine in California, and instead of answering the gnawing pangs of anxiety and depression she'd been feeling at her old job, the new position made her fearful and crazy. She worried about screwing it up. She worried about being an imposter, and she worried about being exposed. She already drank daily but she started to drink more. She'd wake up in the morning, dazed and hung over and anxious, and her hands would shake. So she'd put a shot of Kahlua in her coffee, just a little shot to take the edge off. This went on for a period of months. The shots got a little larger. Sometimes she'd pour in a shot of vodka as well as Kahlua. A few times she added so much liquor she could barely taste the coffee.

One bright Friday morning in October at eleven A.M., Mary Ellen found herself driving down a freeway outside Los Angeles and she suddenly saw herself, as though watching from above. She thought: *I am drunk. I am driving down the freeway at eleven o'clock in the morning, late to work, and I am drunk.* That weekend she called a friend who'd gotten sober in AA several years earlier, and met him for coffee. She had her last drink that Sunday and hasn't had another one since.

For Abby it was a much smaller event, much less dramatic in its details. She was at a dinner party in New York, and she got drunk and picked a fight with a woman at the table—a really stupid fight, about whether or not people who claim to recover memories of child abuse can be believed, a subject she knew little about. She was extremely rude to this woman, and she understood on some level that the argument, the wish to *fight*, stemmed from a deeper rage on her part, a rage she'd spent her whole adult life trying to dilute with drink. She woke up the next morning feeling degraded and ashamed. She called her mother, herself a recovering alcoholic, and said, "I need help." That day she boarded a train from New York to Boston. She drank Scotch the entire way, and wept, and that was the last time she got drunk.

Reality sets in at last, chips away at denial. Some of us lose our jobs, or our spouses, or our children. Some of us get into car wrecks, and are ordered by judges to go to AA. For a man I know named Richard, hitting bottom meant reaching a level of self-loathing so deep that all he wanted to do was kill himself, and then hating himself even more because he didn't have the guts to do it. For a man named Troy, hitting bottom meant looking up from his chair one day and realizing that the only two things he had in his life were a twelve-inch black-and-white TV and a bottle of gin, the props of pure isolation. For my friend Ginny it meant losing control in the most literal sense, driving too fast down a winding road in the middle of the night, careening off the road, flying through the windshield of her car, headfirst. She surrendered just before her head hit the glass. "Okay," she whispered, letting go of the wheel, "I give up." These are all people in their thirties, with good jobs and intact families. Richard is an urban planner, Troy is an English professor, Ginny is a lawyer. If you saw them on the street, even while they were drinking, you'd never know a thing. Hitting bottom is usually something that happens internally, where no one else can see it.

My own descent had the feel of a swan dive, a long, slow curving arc, the outlines of which I was able to see only in retrospect.

My father died and I jumped off the deep end. A year later my mother died and I continued to fall, blindly and all too willingly. Ten months after that I landed, in a rehab.

Perhaps my father could see this, could see that his death would have the power to force certain choices in my life. He might not have known that those choices would have to do with alcohol, but he understood that losing him would have to change me. As he put it to me himself, quite bluntly, "Losing a parent is a life-altering event."

He said this in May of 1991, several days after being diagnosed with the tumor. He was lying in bed at the New England Medical

Center, in Boston, and I was perched at the edge, staring down at my hands.

A moment passed in silence and then I looked at him. He *appeared* unaltered: he was seventy-four by then, and still sharp as a tack, energetic and driven, so it was surreal to be sitting with him in a hospital room, trying to wrap my mind around his diagnosis. He hadn't yet had the biopsy to confirm it—that would take place in a day or two—but the doctors knew. The MRI had shown a glioblastoma, a large, particularly aggressive grade of tumor located in the center of his brain, an inoperable site. "He'll lose function in his legs, his arms, and his hands." A young doctor, the chief neurology resident, told us this several days earlier. "Then he'll lose his speech. He'll become disoriented and confused. His thought patterns will become more scattered. He'll get more and more sleepy and more and more apathetic."

And ultimately he'll die.

I don't think the doctor actually used those words, but he didn't have to. Brain tumor; death. The equation was clear, hopeless, and, as my father said, life altering.

My father died on April 7, 1992. One year and eleven days later, on April 18, 1993, my mother died, of metastatic breast cancer. I was thirty-two when I lost my father, thirty-three when I lost my mother. Now I'm thirty-six. In the aftermath of their deaths I finally lost my childhood. Along with it, I suppose, I began to lose my capacity for denial too.

So my father was right. It would just take me several years to figure out exactly how.

In the months after my father's diagnosis I'd leave work most days at five or five-thirty, go across the street to the Aku, and drink two stiff Scotches. Then I'd stop at a liquor store near my parents' house in Cambridge, buy a six-pack of beer, and bring two of the bottles into their house with me. I'd drink one, then wait half an hour or so and drink the other, and I'd sit with my parents, sometimes visiting alone with my father so my mother could get out of the house.

After I'd had both beers, I'd move surreptitiously to the hard liquor. My parents would be in the bedroom, toward the back of the house, and I'd go off to smoke a cigarette, which I always did outside. I don't remember the first time I passed the liquor cabinet on my way to the front door and decided to stop there first. I don't remember taking that first bottle of Old Grand-dad from the cabinet and carrying it with me to the front stoop. I don't remember the rationale, but I must have come up with one: *I should keep this bottle handy. Maybe I should stash it behind the toilet in the front-hall bathroom, or tuck it inside the basket full of old sporting equipment in the closet.* At some point hiding the booze must have seemed like a good idea because I did it, and then the liquor was there for me whenever I needed it, which was often. The logic seemed sound at the time, and I used it, daily, for nearly three years.

Illness, loss; another illness, another loss. Watching me, an outsider could draw a direct line between my parents' deaths and the escalation of drinking that led me to rehab, and in some ways that line would accurately reflect what happened: those losses provided just the excuse I needed to make the jump. My father's illness was long and gruesome, the brain tumor gradually shutting down one system after another, just as the doctor predicted. Over a period of eleven months he lost fine motor control, then mobility in his arms and legs, then cognitive function, then memory, his personality. My mother's illness, following so closely on the heels of his, had the quality of a nightmare: more hospitals, more tests, more anxious phone calls. During both illnesses, and after both deaths, I drank with the no-holds-barred abandon of the truly self-pitying drinker, every night until I passed out.

Yet when I really look back over that period, the two consecutive years of hospitalizations and hospice and horror, what stands out are a few key scenes, ones that had less to do with the facts of illness and loss than with what I was forced to see through those experiences about myself.

*   *   *

About two months after my dad's diagnosis, a morning in July 1991, my sister Becca and I were sitting in our parents' living room and we could hear them arguing in their bedroom. A few minutes passed. Then my mother came down the stairs toward us, looking flushed and angry. She didn't confide in us much about personal matters but we dragged the details out of her.

Apparently, my father had delivered what he called a "death-bed confession," although many months would pass before he actually died. The confession was about the affair that had nearly broken up their marriage ten years earlier. He'd allegedly broken off the relationship at the time, and my mother spent the next decade assuming the affair was over. She'd ask him about it periodically and he would reassure her: still over, no contact with the other woman. He'd been lying. The affair had continued without interruption all that time. *That woman* (my mother always called her *that woman*) had been to visit him in the hospital just weeks earlier.

Becca and I spent the day trying to calm things down, one of us talking to our mother in the living room, the other talking to our father in the bedroom, then switching rooms and parents. My mother was just plain furious, her mouth a sharp line all day long and her eyes burning. My father was more confused. I gathered he'd hoped the confession would relieve him of guilt and lead to forgiveness and he kept saying, "When the chips were down, your mother always came first," as though that somehow explained or excused the betrayal.

Becca and I both left the house early that evening, having eked a promise out of my father that he'd talk to a therapist about all this. We left them both sitting at the dining room table just staring at the walls, a silence so heavy it felt like humidity.

That evening, a few drinks in me, I called my own therapist and told him what had happened. He asked, "How does this situation affect *you*?" and at the time I thought that was kind of an inane question—who cares about me? what about *them*? But later that night I thought about a conversation I'd had with my father several months earlier. I'd been particularly depressed one day and I'd come over to the house to talk to him, wanting support. I talked to him in a general way about Julian and Michael, my ambivalence, my duplicity, my feeling of being stuck in both relationships and incapable of being honest, and I started to cry. "I don't know what to do," I said. "I feel like such a mess."

I was hoping for sympathy, but instead my father got angry at me, surprisingly so. He didn't mention my drinking but he touched, at least indirectly, on its effects. He said, "This is all a giant procrastination. There is a split within you and you *must* deal with it. You *must*."

Until he made the confession to my mother, I didn't know just how intimately he understood that sort of split, how deeply and for how long he'd lived it himself. Although she took care of him until he died, my mother never quite forgave my father for his betrayal, and he never really forgave himself. He died believing in his soul that he'd somehow brought the brain tumor on himself: he told my mother that its location—in the exact center of his brain—was a psychosomatic representation of his own unresolvable conflict.

I thought about that conversation with my father for a long time that night and many more times during and after his illness: in a way, in his own oblique, analytical manner, he'd handed me a gift, a glimpse of foresight. My father's words, and the details of his own confession, hinted at the future. He seemed to be showing me what it meant not just to live in a state of unresolved conflict but to die in it. He seemed to be telling me exactly what that split in me could cost.

One night about six months into my father's illness, I drank my two Scotches at the Aku, then went over to the house to sit with him while my mother went out to spend the evening with some friends. He was heavy with fatigue by this time and more immobilized and confused each week. He was in bed and I sat next to him, drinking a beer. Maybe I drank two beers, I'm not sure, but at some point we both fell asleep and when I stirred thirty or forty minutes later, my father was kind of slumped over against me, his head resting on my upper arm. There was something so touching about this, my poor father asleep and vulnerable like that, that I let him rest there for a while. Then he woke up.

He gave a little start and then started to bluster. He looked at me. "This is *very* inappropriate," he said, through his stutter. "A father and a daughter like this . . ."

I felt like I'd been caught doing something I hadn't known was wrong, and I got up off the bed and went outside to smoke a cigarette. On my way out I retrieved my bottle of Old Grand-dad from its hiding place in the bathroom and took it out to the front stoop. Then I just sat there, taking slugs of it and trying not to think about my father, about that old confusing mix of intimacy and distance.

Drinking and caretaking, drinking and fear; one answering the other. My parents' house felt so loaded with illness and anger and unresolved bits of history it was hard to walk inside without feeling like you had to hold your breath. Details about my father's betrayal would emerge, erupting like volcanoes—he'd given the woman money; he'd taken her on a trip—and they'd fill the house with a bitterness you could practically taste. I'd come in and my mother would be fuming over the stove about something he'd said or something she'd discovered, and my father would be languishing in his bed or moored someplace in his wheelchair, still not understanding why she was so furious. At times it felt like if I lit a match in there, the house might explode.

Privately, my brother and sister and I worried about the potential effect of all that rage simmering within our mother, worried that the stress of caring for my father under those explosive circumstances was going to cause a recurrence of her own cancer. None of us ever gave voice to those feelings. We just buckled down and tried to help, tried to be comforting and empathic and loyal to both parents. But visits were exhausting. By the time I left the house at the end of an evening, I *needed* that Cognac on Michael's back porch, felt I had earned it. I drank myself to sleep nearly every night and I couldn't imagine how a person could get through something like this without liquor. Not drinking seemed inconceivable.

Five months into his illness, a bright October afternoon, I took my father out for a drive. He was confined to a wheelchair by then, so I steered him out to my car, and strained to help him stand up and wobble into the passenger seat. Then I got in the other side and headed west. We drove across familiar territory, the same roads we'd traveled when I was thirteen and he'd drive me out to my friend Nina's house. I'd always wondered what those drives had been like for him, how it must have felt to be sitting there on the vinyl seat beside a thin, mute daughter, what it must have been like to see yourself in someone else and not be able to find any comfortable ground, anyplace to connect.

That day I tried my best to be chatty and conversational, to find that same comfortable ground. I didn't do much better. I'd look over at him in the passenger seat and see him staring out the window, looking sad and vulnerable and so hard to reach. We stopped at one point to get a cup of tea, and I remember wishing we could have a glass of wine together, just one glass to ease the burden of silence, so old and familiar. I felt such a powerful combination of affection and regret that day, grateful I still had my father but unable, even in the face of terminal illness, to fill up that empty space between us. As I recall, I went home that night and got very, very drunk, more drunk than usual.

Memory has a funny way of turning the most painful recollections into blurs. The last months of my father's life are all foggy to me, just random images that rise up like scenes in an old horror movie. Perhaps that's because I was drinking so much, but in retrospect I think the booze was only part of it: the brain gets overwhelmed and just shuts down, leaving you with little flashes, like photos in a scrapbook. I can picture the big hydraulic lift we rented the last few months, which we used to haul him in and out of bed. The lift had a sling attached and we'd shove the sling under him, then hoist him up out of bed and swing him around to

the wheelchair. He'd just hover there in the air like a huge, gro-
tesque version of a baby in the mouth of a stork, all six feet of
him, completely immobilized and helpless, and I find that image
so vivid and appalling, it makes me wish for a drink even now.

I can also picture my father's last day of consciousness. By the
first week in April he'd become so apathetic and incapacitated
that we finally took him off a medication he'd been on since the
diagnosis was made, a steroid that kept the swelling around the
tumor down. This was really the last thing standing between him
and the end and we eased him off the drug over a period of three
or four days, giving him the last dose on a Friday. I went over to
the house after work that evening and went into the bedroom to
see him. His eyes were closed but when I leaned over his bed, he
looked up at me. He still had tiny moments of lucidity, few and
far between, and he had one then. I smiled and said, "Hey, Dad,"
and he choked out the words, "You. Look. Wonderful."

I'd tried so hard to be good to him that last year. I'd tried so
hard all my life, really, coveting his approval for so long, and that
moment, there at the very end, he handed it to me.

He fell into a coma that night. I got drunk.

Most of the images from then on have to do with drinking: the
Cognac I chugged in my old bedroom the evening before he died;
the drunken haze that night when my brother-in-law called me at
Michael's house. The day after he died, I remember drinking a
beer on the front stoop of our house, right around lunchtime. My
brother and sister and mother were inside at the kitchen table,
eating sandwiches, and I sat outside and thought about my alliance with my father, the feeling that he and I had been united on
one side of the family while the other three stood apart, united on
the other. I still don't know if that sense of separateness was
grounded in reality or fantasy, but it didn't seem to matter at the
time. I felt stunned and orphaned and alone, and I nursed that
beer the way a baby might nurse a bottle, as though I were drinking life itself.

Two days later, the morning of his funeral, I remember sneaking a beer in the kitchen. I stood by the sink in my black dress and chugged it down in about two minutes flat, hoping no one would walk in on me. I drank all through the reception following the funeral, and I have a cloudy memory of pounding down glasses of white wine at the dining-room table that evening. Then the memories stop for a while, a grayout, and then I remember sitting on Michael's bed late at night, weeping and weeping, drunk and sloppy and overwhelmed, Michael holding me and letting me cry.

Drinking always helped me cry: that's one thing I still miss about it. After my dad died, I got the feeling I wasn't supposed to grieve for too long, as though my sympathy quotient was limited to about six weeks by some unwritten rule. People at work would come up to me and say, "How are you feeling?" and after a month or so I'd just nod and say, "Better, I guess." Too much mourning makes people uncomfortable and I could tell from their tone that they wanted to hear some improvement. So all that spring and summer I'd keep the grief tucked away in some small compartment all day, and then at night I'd use the drink as the key to that compartment, a tool I could use to reach down inside and open the door and weep. Or I'd drink to numb those tears: drown the feelings, keep the sadness at bay.

Six months after my father died, I was at my desk at work when my mother called to tell me her tests had come out positive— more cancer, tumors in the liver now, more chemotherapy. I just sat there at my desk after we hung up as though I'd been hit in the stomach with something hard. I remember feeling my teeth, the way the two rows clenched down on one another like they were glued.

The fear didn't hit until late that night, after I'd been to see my mother and talked worriedly on the phone with my sister and finally had a few glasses of wine. Then I was able to let go and just feel it. I sometimes thought if I didn't have that wine, if I didn't have that bridge to my own emotions, my insides would turn to granite.

More blurs. The beginnings of chemotherapy and my mother feeling so sick: sores in her mouth and throat, her hair starting to fall out. Anxious visits, perched on the end of her bed, watching her closely as though I might be able to read the future in her gestures. Drinking. Drinking and drinking. I was good about limiting my consumption when I was at the house—since our talk on the beach on Martha's Vineyard I'd been careful about maintaining control when I was with her, and during that whole last year of her life, I don't think I had more than two beers in front of her at one time. But I let loose when I got back to my own apartment or over at Michael's.

I was still engaged in the whole drama with Julian and Michael at this time, too, still running around and spreading misinformation all over the place, and even now, even when I look back on that time and see how out of control my drinking was, I still believe the liquor was a genuine support, a crutch I simply couldn't have managed without. A bottle of Scotch had the quality of a rock to me by then, something that kept me from falling into that sea of chaos and drowning even as it weighed me down.

On April 7, 1993, exactly one year after my father's death, I called my mother and asked her how she was feeling about him. She paused thoughtfully and said, "You know, it was a *strange* marriage. There were good things about it and there were bad things about it." There was surprising simplicity to her language, an acceptance in her tone, and I thought about how hard she'd worked in the past year, how mightily she struggled not only to understand and forgive my father, to reorient her life without him, but also to fight her own illness. Much of this effort had been reflected in her work: the summer after he died, she painted a collage called "Atlantis," about a false world under the sea. A second, which she called "False Map," was about attempting to navigate the world with erroneous information.

At some point during that conversation it hit me that she did all that without a drink, that she faced a great deal of pain directly and got through it without a drop of alcohol. I thought about that a lot after she died. I don't know if I was quite able to see her as a model, but I know I admired her tremendously, and I'd taken careful note of her growth during that last year. On the phone that night she sounded self-assured. She sounded solid and good. And very sober.

One week after that conversation, my mother woke up with pain in her ribs and stomach so intense she couldn't lean over to tie her shoes. We took her to the hospital in an ambulance because she didn't think she could make it from the house to the car. The cancer had gone haywire within the course of those seven days: liver failure, disease everywhere.

She spent three days in the hospital. On the third day the oncologist came in and talked to her about how sick her liver was, about what measures she'd want the doctors to take if, say, her heart failed. She told him she didn't want repeated attempts but that she'd want them to try once to revive her. My mother was sixty-five. She said, "I'm not so old that I'm ready to give up." When he left the room, she turned to me and said, "I don't want to die in the hospital. I want to die at home, with comfort care."

The next day we took her home. Two men came to deliver a hospital bed, from the same rental company we'd used when my father was dying. One of them stopped in the middle of the living room and said, "Weren't we just here?" That's how it felt to me too: *Didn't we just do this?*

On my way home from the hospital I stopped at a liquor store, bought a fifth of Dewar's, and stashed it in my purse. I got quite drunk that night. The next day I woke up to the sound of her moaning. She was in so much pain she literally couldn't speak. The hospice nurse administered morphine, a great deal of it. By midmorning she was in a coma. The house was full of people by then—my brother and sister, aunts and uncles, Michael—and around noon Michael and my half-sister Penny went out to get us all sandwiches. An uncle had brought over a case of wine and the refrigerator was full of beer.

Halfway through lunch I took my wineglass and went into the bedroom to check on my mother. Her breathing had shifted, grown more rapid and shallow. Minutes later we were all there in the room with her, gathered around, my sister and me holding her hands. She died at about one P.M. My glass of wine was on the night table beside her bed. I picked it up as soon as I let go of her hand.

All the images from that day on are clouded by alcohol. I cried, I drank. I can picture myself sitting in the living room several hours after my mother's funeral, after all the guests had left the reception, so loaded I could barely keep my eyes open; I can picture my sister looking at me with an expression of deeply sad resignation, cooled by the slightest trace of disgust. "Maybe you better go take a nap," she said. "You're drunk." I argued with her for about two seconds but I also knew she was right so I went upstairs and passed out for an hour.

I can also remember one night in Michael's apartment a few weeks later, getting bombed while he was out, and slipping into drink-and-dial mode, flipping through my address book, looking up phone numbers of my mother's friends. I was in an oozy, drunk, weepy state and I must have drunkenly punched out the numbers of four or five women. None of them were home, but I did get a phone call from my mother's friend Janet the next day. Apparently, I'd left a message on her machine. She said, "Are you *all right*? You sounded like some kind of a cat, all howly."

I can see now that I was grieving without really grieving, holding myself together during the days and then yielding to the unrestrained, liquid version of strong emotion after dark. But I couldn't come close to seeing it then; I wouldn't. The summer after my mother died, I passed out at Michael's house at nine-thirty one night and woke up around midnight to the sound of him yelling at me. He was pulling on my arm and saying, "Get in here. What the fuck are you doing?"

I staggered up off the bed and followed him into the kitchen. On the counter was half a bottle of Cognac and about three quarters of a bottle of rum—a bottle of his rum, actually, that I'd stolen from a cabinet in his kitchen and hidden on the back porch. My stash. Michael was livid. "I can't fucking believe this," he said, pouring both bottles down the kitchen sink. "What the fuck are you *doing?*"

I started to cry. "I can't help it, Michael," I said. "I have a drinking problem. I can't help it."

I still called it a "drinking problem"; I couldn't make the leap to alcoholism because that was too great an admission, far too final. So I just stood there in the kitchen and wept and appealed to his pity. "I can't help it. I really can't help it."

Michael was furious, but he put his arms around me and held me while I cried and in the morning, over coffee, he pulled me onto his lap and said, "You really scare me. You have to do something about this."

I promised I would but I think I knew I wouldn't. Not yet.

Not yet. There was still a long list of not-yets. I hadn't killed anyone yet, or lost my job yet, or ended up in jail yet. I hadn't wrapped my car around a telephone pole, or grabbed a gun and shot someone in a bar, or gotten drunk and ended up raped by a stranger. Not yet.

That's what they're called in AA: "yets," all the things you didn't do when you drank but could have if you'd kept on going. Those things could have happened so easily—one wrong turn, one false move, a little girl's skull absorbing the shock of a fall instead of my knee. But they hadn't happened. Not yet.

YET. Some people in AA say it stands for You're Eligible Too.

I continued to drink.

By that point I don't even think the alcohol worked anymore.

Certainly drinking was no longer fun. It had long ago ceased to be fun. A few glasses of wine with a friend after work could still feel reassuring and familiar, but drinking was so need driven by the end, so visceral and compulsive, that the pleasure was almost accidental. Pleasure just wasn't the point. At the end I didn't even feel like myself until I had a drink or two, and I remember that scared me a little: alcohol had become something I felt I needed in order to return to a sense of normalcy, in order to think straight. After one or two drinks I'd feel like I'd come back into my own skin—more clearheaded, more relaxed—but the feeling would last for only half an hour or so. Another few drinks and I'd be gone again, headed toward oblivion.

Active alcoholism is such a demeaning state. Some part of you, the part that resists denial, acts as the observer, quietly aware. I'd look at myself in the mirror some nights and I'd sense that observer staring back, loathing what she saw: a depressed, anxious, self-sabotaging thirty-four-year-old woman who could not seem to get out of her own way. Dark circles beneath her eyes, creases of worry across her forehead, those little burst blood vessels flecked across her skin. Sick and tired. A sick and tired woman.

My mother's last words to me were "Stop smoking." The night before she died, I'd smoked a cigarette outside and then gone into her bedroom to kiss her good-night. She might well have smelled liquor on my breath—I'd been drinking wine and Scotch since five o'clock—but she chose to focus on the smoke. She smelled it on my breath and as I turned to leave the room, she called out, "Stop smoking."

Stop smoking. Two months after she died, I enrolled in a smoking-cessation program at a local hospital, aware on some level that I was tackling the wrong substance. I dropped out within three weeks and continued to smoke, but the words stuck with me. Stop smoking. I think she meant: Stop suffering. Stop being so self-destructive. Stop killing yourself.

The gift of desperation has a spiritual quality. At some point, if you're very very lucky, it dawns on you that you really *might* kill yourself if you keep living the way you're living. It's just a matter of time, just a matter of time before you drive home drunk one night and run someone down or end up in jail or lose your job. You can be so lucky for only so long, and at some point it dawns on you that you are the only one capable of orchestrating your own future, of ensuring that you live a different sort of life.

I gradually began to feel more and more alone in the world, a sensation that seeps into the heart slowly after a major loss. I was on my own, my parents dead. If I truly fell—ended up jobless, homeless, suicidally depressed—there was no one to run to, no one to pick up the pieces. Not my brother or sister. They had their own lives, their own problems. Not even Michael. I didn't think he'd stick by me much longer if I kept drinking the way I was drinking.

This was by no means an overnight revelation. I drank my way to it, and as they tend to say in AA, I needed every single drink it took to get there, every drink and every attendant moment of degradation and despair.

One morning, a few months after my mother died, Becca called me at work. After about five minutes it became clear to both of us that we'd spoken on the phone the night before and I'd been too drunk to remember the conversation. Becca started to cry, realizing that, and she said, "I know you can't help it. But I just can't call you after seven o'clock at night anymore. I never know if you'll be there or not."

There was something resigned in her tone, and unspeakably sad. I thought: *She's right, I am really not there.* After that I just sat at my desk clutching the phone, not knowing what to say, wanting to apologize, wanting to explain away my unavailability somehow but knowing I couldn't.

A few months later, drunk one night and driving home from a restaurant in my mother's car, I ran over a curb and blew out the front right tire. I drove for another three blocks before I realized what I'd done, and then I pulled into the driveway of a total stranger and pounded crazily on the door. The stranger helped me call Triple-A and then I passed out in the car waiting for the road guy to show up.

Then Thanksgiving weekend rolled around, and I fell down while carrying my friend's two children. I spent the day after that on Michael's sofa, thirteen stitches in my knee and my whole leg throbbing. We had one bottle of wine in the house and it was Sunday, liquor stores were closed. That one bottle wouldn't do it, just wouldn't do it, so at about five-thirty that evening, on the pretense that I was going stir crazy from being shut up in the house all day, I talked Michael into going out for a drink. "Let's go have a beer," I said. "I really need to get out." I swore up and down that my knee felt better (it didn't), and I got up from the sofa and said, "C'mon, I'm going nuts in here," and Michael finally shrugged and said okay.

Michael drives a Jeep and it was excruciating trying to hobble out of his apartment, down the steps to the curb, then up and into the front seat of the car. Excruciating, also, to hobble across the street and into the bar, and excruciating to sit there on a barstool, unable to find a comfortable position for my knee and drink the damn beer. But I drank it. I drank two beers, and although what I really wanted to do was stay and drink shots of tequila, stay and numb the pain in my knee the best way I knew how, it hurt too much, so we finally went home.

On December 19, eight months after my mother died, I went to a Christmas party with Julian. He and I had such a strange relationship by then: we seemed to have some huge blowout every six months or so—one right after my father died, one a few months after my mother's death—and we'd stop speaking for weeks at a time, sometimes months. Sometimes these took place because I'd have a fit of conscience and I'd get drunk and make a confession about the extent of my involvement with Michael, just like my father had done with my mother, and sometimes they happened because a particular fight had escalated out of control. It was always Julian who called things off, telling me he couldn't take it anymore, telling me I was too confused and angry to deal with, and it was always me who came scratching at his door as soon as I sensed he'd cooled off enough to speak to me.

That December night the relationship was at a characteristically tense point, not quite patched together but not hostile, either, and I remember driving to the party with him and thinking about the extent to which I seemed, against my will, to be recreating both my parents' lives. My mother had lived this way, unable to leave a man who never quite left her feeling appreciated or fully loved, and my father had lived this way, torn between two relationships, saddled with chronic ambivalence, unable to wrench himself free of the complicated, duplicitous patterns he'd established. I also remember feeling weighted down with guilt about Michael, who knew I was going to a party but didn't know with whom. I had a heavy, exhausted feeling, as though so many thoughts were tangled up in my head my whole brain might shut down at any minute. But I didn't pay too much heed to the feeling; confusion had become such a normal state I was used to it.

I promised myself I wouldn't get too drunk that night. The party was full of people from the book world, writers and agents and editors, and I knew I'd feel somewhat intimidated and shy but I also knew I didn't want to make an ass of myself, so I vowed I'd hold back, impose some limits.

Several hours into the party I found myself staring into a little plastic cup of white wine and realizing it was half empty. Half a glass is not enough to a drinker—it's only a few swallows away from empty—so I wound my way through the crowd toward the bar. When I got there, the white wine was gone; they appeared to have run out. I didn't leave the bar and I didn't wait for the hostess to replenish the stock of Chardonnay. Instead, I grabbed for the bottle of red and topped off my glass with that. Instant rosé.

Toward the end of the night I caught a glimpse of myself standing in the dining room talking to a tall, attractive man who looked a little like Harrison Ford. I didn't physically see myself—I didn't catch my reflection in the window, or glance across the room at a mirror. I was drunk and that small observer, the part of me that still had some integrity and remained conscious and aware, kicked in with a whisper: *You're drunk. You're slurring your words and you're unsteady on your feet and you look like a real asshole.* In the morning I wouldn't remember the conversation I'd had with the man, but I would remember that moment, that glimpse of myself as a drunk young woman at a party. Not a pretty young woman, not a sophisticated young woman. A drunk, out of control.

Julian and I left the party shortly after that. I drove; the car was weaving all over the road. He asked, "Are you all right? Do you want me to drive?" I said, "I'm fine. I only had two glasses of wine."

I was always saying that: "I only had two glasses of wine." Michael laughs about that now, the way I'd stagger into his living room at nine or ten o'clock at night and I'd say, "I am *so* tired. I can't believe how tired I am. I only had two glasses of wine." Usually he wouldn't say anything, but inside he'd be thinking, *Yeah, right.* I don't know if Julian bought the line that night or not, but I used it twice on the way to his apartment: "I'm fine. Only two glasses."

The drive to Julian's took ten minutes. I pulled up in front of his apartment and he started to get out without saying much of a good-bye. He seemed angry at me and I didn't know why. I wanted him to invite me up for a drink. I wanted to talk to him. I wanted what I always wanted: to know we were still connected and that he still loved me, to know I still had him hooked in the relationship, that he wouldn't abandon me. He didn't give me any such feedback; he just got out of the car, and I drove away.

I drove down the street, then drove around the block. Then I parked in front of his building again, got out of the car, and rang the doorbell. I honestly don't remember too much of what happened next. He let me in and I entered one of my drunken rage states and the scene was so damn familiar by then, it could have been any one of hundreds: me, standing in the kitchen frustrated and yelling about our relationship; him, standing there frustrated and yelling back. At some point I left and drove home in tears, driving with one eye shut to stop the double vision, driving and weeping.

I went to my mother's house, which we hadn't yet sold. I'd technically moved in there after she died, to keep the place occupied, but I never stayed there, sleeping at Michael's house almost every night instead because my mom's house felt haunted. But I went there that night and sat on my mother's bed and called my sister. It must have been one-thirty in the morning and I called her, drunk and weeping, and said, "I don't know what to do. I don't feel like I'm ever going to feel normal."

I remember her voice so distinctly. She said, as quietly and patiently as my mother might have, "You know what I think you need to do."

My sister had dropped hints about my drinking for years. She was in training as a psychiatrist, and she'd seen scores of alcoholics in hospitals, some in emergency-room settings, some as patients. Every once in a while, when I confided in her about being depressed, she'd say, "Well, I really don't think you're going to get out of it unless you quit drinking." Or she'd tell me about some patient she'd seen, a young woman who'd given up drinking and found her life had turned around within six months, found a level of clarity she hadn't thought possible before. She was patient, and quietly persistent, and she tried to be nonjudgmental, even though she was getting more and more worried about my drinking, more and more convinced she was losing me to it.

"You know what I think you need to do."

I was silent for a minute, perched on my mother's bed in the dark. I said, "Quit drinking?"

She said, "Yes."

And I nodded. I knew.

I slept that night in my sister's old bedroom, a room she and I had shared as children. In the morning I woke up filled with those same drinker's feelings: self-loathing and remorse. I lay in bed and stared at the ceiling and I remember thinking that somewhere along the line, I'd begun to identify myself as a victim of circumstance, as someone who'd simply *become* confused and angst ridden and chronically depressed, as if by accident. I remember thinking I didn't have much choice in the matter, that perhaps this was simply my lot in life: too much drinking, fucked-up relationships, depression. Grist for the writer's mill; the price of admission. But that price seemed increasingly high, dangerously so. I still had productive days at work, but I also had dismal ones, days when I felt so depressed or hungover I couldn't focus, couldn't write anything more ambitious than a headline or a photo caption.

That understanding terrified me. My professional identity was the only part of my life that still seemed intact, and words felt like my one solid link to the world, my sole route to a kind of contact that had integrity. I thought about Ernest Hemingway, who'd killed himself with a twelve-gauge shotgun, and about James Agee, who died of alcoholism at the age of forty-five. I had a dark, heavy sense of resignation, inevitability, as though I were in a box and simply couldn't get out.

Later that morning I called Julian and apologized. He wasn't angry, just weary sounding. "You don't know what you want," he said. I didn't have it in me to argue so I didn't. He said, "You don't trust me. You don't trust me because you don't trust *yourself.*"

I nodded into the phone. He was right. I had long ago stopped trusting myself, stopped trusting my instincts and my own behavior. I never knew anymore, never knew when I'd get too drunk and what I'd do when I got too drunk, what kinds of things I'd say, how I'd end up feeling in the morning.

Around noon, hungover and miserable, I went back to Michael's and spent a long time sitting at his kitchen table reading *Esquire* magazine. The issue contained an excerpt from Pete Hamill's book *A Drinking Life*, and I read every word. In it he quoted Shirley MacLaine, who disapproved of drinkers. "If she saw a scene in a movie, or read a script where a character succumbs to another because of drunkenness," Hamill wrote, "she'd shake her head. 'It's a cheat,' she'd say. 'It's using the drink instead of forcing the painful choice.'"

Click: one of those little lights went on in my head and I thought, *Right: that's what happens when I drink with Julian.* Instead of making the painful choice, instead of walking away, or standing up for myself, or figuring out what I really needed, I'd drink, and the drink would make me succumb to the dynamic, succumb to the relationship and the anger, keep my fingernails dug in. I thought: *That's me.*

I think my pride kicked in at that moment. My life was so woefully embarrassing: the drinking, the fighting, the running from man to man. It was embarrassing and tedious and *exhausting* and in the end, what was the point? Where was all this leading? You drink to avoid those painful choices and you wake up in the morning and all those choices are still with you, still unfaced; all those unresolved problems are hanging around your neck like pieces of lead, weighing you down, keeping you from moving forward. Humiliating. And terrifying, because I couldn't see an end to it: Michael, Julian, depression, anxiety, lies, drink, drink, drink. My life could go on and on and on like that, just as my father's had.

I thought about my father that morning. I thought about the sense of sorrow that had seemed to bind us for so long, that sense of deep dissatisfaction, of being slightly *off* so often. I thought about how he'd lived his whole life with that feeling—trying to address it in therapy, trying to excise it with understanding, only to realize while he was dying that he'd never really found the level of peace he'd wanted, never tasted freedom from his own depression. I thought about the work he'd never finished. He'd started writing a book about emotion before he got sick, an effort to sum up a career's worth of thinking on the subject, and he never really got past the first chapter. I remembered an afternoon I spent with my mother the summer after he died, clearing out his office. She stopped in front of his bookshelves at one point, her hands on her hips, and she sighed, a heavy sigh of frustration and sadness. She was looking at published works by other psychiatrists, men she felt had half his insight. "He talked about writing that book for ten years," she said. "He just couldn't focus." Then she shook her head. "What a tragedy."

Sitting in Michael's kitchen that morning, I felt unspeakably sad, thinking about my father, sad and horrified because I could see myself so clearly following in his footsteps, heading down that same path, losing my own focus.

I thought about his words to me: *This is all a giant procrastination and you must deal with it. You must.*

My father said something else in the first weeks after his diagnosis that had stuck with me, one of his pronouncements that seemed to come out of the blue. He was still in the hospital at that point, sitting in a chair, and I was visiting him alone. The room was silent and he looked up, pensive and still. "Insight," he said, "is almost always a rearrangement of fact."

As I sat in Michael's kitchen that morning, reading *Esquire* and feeling so paralyzed, I remembered those words. A *rearrangement of fact.*

Fact One: I drank too much.

Fact Two: I was desperately unhappy.

I had always thought: *I drink because I'm unhappy.* Just then, I shifted the equation, rearranged the words: *Maybe, just maybe, I'm unhappy because I drink.*

This was not a hopeful sensation, a moment of optimism. I felt desperate, and all I had to cling to for that instant was a mere seed of faith: *maybe* things would change if I quit drinking; *maybe* drinking was, in fact, the problem, and not the solution.

I saw my sister that afternoon and asked her to find me a rehab program. Two months later, on February 19, I had my last drink.

15 *Help*

B ETWEEN THE DAY I knew I had to stop drinking and the day I finally did, I cried almost every night. I'd sit in a little room at Michael's house where he keeps his stereo and CD player, and I'd listen to the same sad Dwight Yoakam song over and over, "You're the One," and I'd weep. I felt like I was giving up the one link I had to peace and solace, my truest friend, my lover. I felt like I was trading in one form of misery for another, like I was about to leap into a void, like my life was ending.

The sense of panic and impending doom are familiar to anyone who's quit drinking. Wilfrid Sheed, author of *In Love with Daylight: A Memoir of Recovery*, writes that "giving up booze felt at first like nothing so much as sitting in a great art gallery and watching the paintings being removed one by one until there was nothing left up there but white walls." Norman Mailer put it a little more bluntly, stating darkly that sobriety kills off all the little "capillaries of bonhomie."

I spent weeks thinking in short, declarative sentences:

I'll never have fun at a party again.

I'll never have an intimate conversation again.

I'll never be able to get married. How can you get married without Champagne?

I drank every night, of course, and I drank every drink with the acute consciousness of an inmate on death row eating a final meal. My sister recommended a rehab center in New Hampshire called Beech Hill and I'd settled on February 20, so two months loomed ahead of me in chunks. My last month of drinking. My last week of drinking. My last Scotch at the Aku. My last beer in Michael's kitchen. My last glass of white wine.

I had my last drink in Michael's living room, a little before midnight. My friend Sandy, one of the few people I'd told, had come up for the weekend from Philadelphia and she and I went out to dinner together the night before I left. I had beer and wine before dinner and wine with dinner and Cognac at the bar after dinner, and when Sandy excused herself to go to the ladies' room, I stole a few slugs off her glass of brandy too. When we went back to Michael's, I opened another bottle of red. I don't remember this, but according to Michael, I stood up, announced, "I'm going to bed," then chugged a full glass of red wine and staggered out of the room.

I drove myself to the rehab: threw two suitcases in the back of my car and drove away from Michael's house. I was hung over. I smoked cigarettes the whole way and gagged a couple of times on the smoke: I was vaguely nauseated from the night before and jittery inside. I thought about one morning years earlier—I must have been in my early twenties—when my mother looked at me across the breakfast table and said, "Honey, your *head* is shaking." It was true: sometimes when I was really hung over my whole head would develop a slight but constant tremor, like my brains were shaking in a fry pan, and that was happening on the way to rehab. But aside from that I think I looked okay. And just in case, I stopped on the side of the road outside Dublin, New Hampshire, where Beech Hill was, and reapplied my lipstick. Appearances: I maintained them until the end. When I got there, the intake nurse took a Polaroid of me for my file. I look pale and thin and frightened, but my lipstick looks fabulous.

Beech Hill is located on top of a mountain, which sounds picturesque and serene but isn't, at least not in late February. Most of the time I was there the weather was frigid, the sky blank with fog, and when you looked out the picture windows in the cafeteria at the hills and countryside stretching out below, all you could see was a monochromatic winter blur: endless shades of brown and gray.

Inside, the building looked like a hospital, only slightly less obvious. A main entranceway led into a lounge, where people sat in chairs and watched TV or read or played board games; to the right of the entrance, through a set of double doors, was the cafeteria; to the left, past the lounge, two long corridors. Our rooms were in those corridors, simple, Motel 6–style rooms, with single beds and basic furniture: a desk, a dresser. I had two room-mates, both in their mid-thirties, a large black woman from New Jersey with a crack problem whose name I forget, and a small blonde from Connecticut named Alison, an alcoholic like me, also in rehab for the first time.

Technically, this was my second visit to Beech Hill. I'd driven up there once before, in late January, for a "tour." This turned out to be unheard of, and would be a subject of great amusement among the people I met there, but it seemed perfectly appropriate to me: a visit, like touring a college campus before you decide to apply. I'd driven there during an ice storm, met with the director of admissions for about fifteen minutes, made sure the place didn't look like an insane asylum, then driven back, teary eyed the whole way. I'd told her I'd check in on the twentieth; she looked at me and said, "That gives you a lot of time to change your mind, you know," and I waved away the concern. I had no idea how many people decided to go to rehab then backed out at the last minute. Plenty, apparently.

Having made a *reservation*, as it were, I suppose I expected a welcoming committee when I finally arrived, some kindly nurse or receptionist to take my hand and lead me to my room and assure me that everything would be okay. *Oh! You're Miss Knapp! Welcome!*

That didn't happen. People arrive at rehab unannounced all the time, often dropped off roaring drunk by friends or relatives, and the staff takes you as you come. I checked in on a Sunday afternoon and that's how they took me. There was only a skeleton crew on hand, so I lingered for a while by the nurse's station, waiting for someone to deal with me.

A tall, thin man, a nurse's aide, finally led me to an intake area, took my vital signs, then helped me get my bags out of my car. They search your bags at rehab—standard practice, to make sure you haven't snuck in any drugs or alcohol—so he wandered off with my luggage. Someone else suggested I take a seat in the lounge or the smoking room and wait for a nurse who'd do a more complete intake exam.

The smoking room was built off the main entranceway, a dingy, glass-enclosed area equipped with what looked like retired lawn furniture, the glass stained yellow. They called it The Lung. I sat out there for half an hour, thinking: *What the fuck am I doing here?* An older man with a sad face named Ray sat at a nearby table, along with a slightly hysterical woman in her forties named Pat (inexplicably, she'd change her name to Penny halfway through my stay), and some wasted shell of a man whose name I forget, a heroin addict who'd also just arrived.

I never considered the possibility of quitting drinking without going to rehab, never considered just buckling down and joining AA at home. In fact, I never thought I'd end up in AA at all. I still associated AA with old men in smoke-filled rooms, images from that meeting I'd gone to five years earlier; I'd also developed a semiconscious bias against the whole concept of twelve-step programs. They sounded New Age and cultlike, all that talk of a Higher Power, and every time I turned around some new, bizarre-sounding group seemed to have cropped up for another group of victims. Shoplifters Anonymous. Emotions Anonymous. Maxed-Out Visa Card–Holders Anonymous. Twelve-step programs seemed like a fad, and a mode of victimized self-definition, and I wanted no part of them. I suppose I figured I'd just go away for two weeks, dry out, then grit my teeth and get through.

But the rehab was a good place for me, providing equal doses of hope and fear.

The hope came that first afternoon, a sheer and simple feeling of surrender that came from telling the nurse who did my intake exam exactly how much I drank and not feeling I had to lie about it. The hope came from the sheer and simple act of seeing that I could get through twenty-four hours, and then seventy-two and then ninety-six hours, without a drink, something I hadn't done for more than five years. It came from one of the first sober conversations I had that first night, with a beautiful young woman named Elena, a speed freak from Manhattan who came up to me after dinner, saw how scared I was, and said, "You look like you could use a cigarette."

We sat in a corner and talked for a little while and although I don't remember a word of the conversation I do remember the sense of relief: the feeling that my problems weren't nearly as unique as I'd thought they were; the sense that it might be possible to make connections without alcohol.

Some people in early sobriety experience the classic pink cloud, a euphoria that comes from feeling like you're *doing* something at last, taking charge of your life for the first time. I sailed along on that cloud for most of my time at Beech Hill, floated on a wave of relief. Finally, I'd identified the problem. Finally, I'd sought help.

The analogy is ridiculous, but rehab almost felt like camp to me, the way we were shuttled from activity to activity and meal to meal, the way we formed alliances, the sense of shared history and experience. Rehab sparked the good student in me, the good camper. During the day we went to lectures and therapy sessions; at night we went out to AA meetings in nearby towns in New

Hampshire, or we sat around the cafeteria, or both. I listened intently to people—counselors, lecturers, other alcoholics. I surrendered easily to the routine, relieved to have nothing to do but focus on the problem at hand: why I drank, how I drank, how my experience compared to that of others. I felt like I'd made the right choice, at long last.

My third or fourth night there, I wrote a glowing note to my therapist, telling him I was fine, better than fine, telling him I'd never felt so much *love* from people in my life. I meant it. The place emanated a sense of survival, as though we'd all been through a horrible war and had landed, alive, in a safe place. Which, in many ways, was exactly right. I felt something I hadn't felt in many years: gratitude.

Small things reinforced that. I woke up without a hangover my first day, and then the next and the next. I didn't obsess about drinking—where, when, with whom, how much—because the possibility didn't exist, and that felt like liberation to me. I laughed. At night, shuttling off to an AA meeting on an old yellow school bus, we stopped at a traffic light and a young guy named Wayne leaned out the window. "Excuse me!" he yelled to the car stopped beside us. "Do you have any Grey Poupon?" I howled at that, a deep, genuine laughter that felt so much more real than drunken laughter, and I remember shaking my head, aware all of a sudden how rarely I'd really laughed in the last few years, and amazed, awed, that I could actually feel that good without a drink.

Rehab was by no means all fun and games. Beech Hill was a scary place, too, and the fear came from what I learned about the disease and what I saw. We'd hear horrible statistics at lectures: someone would stand in front of the room and say, "Look to the person on your right and the person on your left. Of the three of you, only one is going to make it." There are usually thirty or forty patients at the hospital at any given time and I had a hard time believing that only a handful of us were going to succeed. I'd figured everyone there would be more or less like me—young people who drank too much and came there, for the first and only time, to stop—but the client population was all over the map: young and old, male and female; people like me, facing their alcoholism for the first time; people with longtime sobriety who'd relapsed; people who'd been in and out of rehabs and detoxes for years—years and years.

Those were the ones who really scared me, the chronic relapsers. Tess, the woman who'd ended up that night in a hotel with some guy and miscarried the next morning, was one of them. She'd been in and out of rehab programs, in and out of AA for fourteen years and I couldn't understand how that happened, why she couldn't just stick with it. We became good friends, she and I and a group of four other people, and we'd spend our evenings together sneaking cigarettes in the cafeteria and drinking decaf and fruit juice from foam cups. One night my friend Chris tore the bottom off a paper cup, then jammed the paper circle onto a coffee stirrer and stuck it in my juice, an umbrella drink, Beech Hill–style.

Little things like that gave me hope for us: our humor was intact, at any rate, and I was sure the members of our clan would come through okay. We were all determined and motivated: Chris and Tess were heading back to the Boston area, as was George, the friend I'd spent that one evening with, talking about the business of hitting bottom. Sean, a tall, skinny marketing executive, was hoping to end up in a halfway house somewhere in eastern Massachusetts, and Tommy, a lovely, intelligent painter from a suburb of Hartford, Connecticut, promised he'd join us all in Boston for reunions. So we had plans to stay together, to go to meetings together, to support each other. I couldn't see how we wouldn't, we all had so much hope.

I felt that way in particular about Tess. "You're going to be a really important part of my sobriety," she'd say to me, and I'd say, "Oh, you too. I can't imagine doing this without you." She was so young and so pretty, so smart. If I could quit drinking, she could.

I saw Tess a handful of times after we both got back. She

moved into a halfway house in Medford, Massachusetts, I was staying at Michael's, and we went to three or four meetings together. Then I heard from her less. I'd call her at the halfway house and she wouldn't call back, or she'd tell me she'd see me at a meeting and then she wouldn't show up.

I got a call from her about a month after we both left Beech Hill and she was back at the rehab, having slipped. Then I got another call, two months after that: back in again. Last I heard, she'd been kicked out of a sober house somewhere in southern New Hampshire because she'd slipped again. She was going to meetings, but it didn't sound like she was doing too well. I don't know where she is now, or if she's sober.

George relapsed shortly after Tess did, checked himself back into the rehab, then relapsed again. He called me from Beech Hill after the first relapse, promising he'd come to a meeting with me when he got back, but he never did. I haven't seen or heard from him since.

Sean relapsed next. He was one of my favorites, a whip-smart guy who'd been in and out of treatment for a long time. He'd stayed sober at one point for three years, but then decided to try an experiment in controlled drinking. He really wanted to prove to himself that he could find a way to drink, really believed he could do it this time if he just set the right limits. So he went out into the woods one day with a fifth of Scotch and a six-pack of beer and drank it all. One little spree; that would be it for a while. Then he drank on a Saturday, and the next few Saturdays after that. He'd buy a supply of liquor, an exact amount, and lock himself in his house, drink the liquor and blast old rock-and-roll music on his stereo. He truly believed he could continue to do this, but a few months later he was back to daily drinking, daily blackout drinking, and when he finally woke up one day and discovered that he'd gone to work in a complete blackout and wildly offended nearly every person in his company, he decided to check himself into rehab.

I saw Sean about a month later. He'd ended up in a halfway

house in Connecticut, stayed for three weeks, then left and spent three weeks out drinking. He called me from New Hampshire, saying he wanted to check back into the halfway house and asking if he could come down to Cambridge and spend the night at my house before he went back. I called Chris and asked him to join us, thinking we'd have a nice rehab reunion.

Sean showed up reeking of booze, drunk and hostile. He sat at the kitchen table and lectured Chris and me, told us he drank because he loved to drink and because he needed to drink, told us we were fooling ourselves if we didn't think we loved and needed to drink too. He'd stashed beer outside, and when he went out to get it, I told Chris, "I can't deal with this."

In the end, after a long altercation, we finally drove him out to the halfway house he planned to check back into and left him there, under a tree with his bag of beer, at eleven-thirty at night.

I heard from Sean one more time, about six months later. He was sober again, living in another halfway house outside of Boston, but I've been wary about seeing him. Watching someone up close like that in the middle of a relapse scared me too much, so I've kept my distance.

Finally, there was Tommy, the painter, whose alcoholism seemed as improbable as mine. I saw him once, about five months after we'd both left New Hampshire. He'd relapsed twice since then, and he stopped through Boston on his way back from a bender in Provincetown. He said he really wanted to get sober this time, really wanted to start going to more meetings, but he sounded halfhearted about it.

We went out to dinner that night, and he told me a story about getting incredibly drunk a week or two earlier and throwing a pot of broccoli soup out the window, straight off the deck of his second-floor condo. He laughed at that, as though it had been a truly hilarious episode, just one of those silly things you do when you drink too much. I had a hard time laughing back.

When Tommy left that night, he said, "It gives me hope to see you. You look so healthy," but something about the words sounded empty, something about his expression looked blank, and I had the feeling I'd never see him again. I haven't yet.

Tess, George, Sean, Tommy: watching them was like seeing dominoes fall, one after the other. Only two of us, me and Chris, have stayed sober continuously since leaving New Hampshire and every time I think about the others, I get a shiver of nerves, a reminder of exactly how precarious sobriety can be.

The rehab was like an AA boot camp: the people who ran it and worked there as doctors and nurses and counselors pushed AA and used AA language and communicated, directly and indirectly, their belief that joining AA was the single most reliable way to stay sober, if not the only way.

Some people find the absolutism of this approach oppressive at best. Wilfrid Sheed describes his own thirty-day stay at a rehab as damn tedious, a full month of AA browbeating and brainwashing and dogma, and although he subsequently came to appreciate AA meetings—the drama, the camaraderie—he initially felt, he writes, "like a recruit who's been stuffed into the same-size uniform as all the other recruits, because it's the only size they have. 'One disease fits all.' "

I can see his point—the language of twelve-step programs is nothing if not repetitive, and right from the start you hear the same clichés and catchphrases and slogans over and over and over. *Don't drink, go to meetings, ask for help*: the AA mantras. *Keep it simple. One day at a time. Let go and let God.* But I welcomed the sense of brainwashing. I felt like my brain could use a good scouring out by then and I was both frightened and desperate enough to set aside whatever biases I'd brought and just listen, to absorb. I believed what I was told and I believed I belonged there, and every time I heard someone tell his or her story at an AA meeting, I connected with some part of it, saw a piece of myself. The people I heard at meetings also had a confidence, a calm self-acceptance, I'd coveted all my life, and I wanted what they had: serenity.

Rehab, in the form of AA's twelve steps, also seemed to provide a blueprint for living, something I'd always felt I needed and lacked, as though I'd missed some crucial handout years ago in personal-conduct class. If you'd asked me, prerehab, what the twelve steps were, I'd have shrugged: something about powerlessness; something else about finding a power greater than yourself. I was astonished to discover that only one of the twelve steps, the first one, mentions the word *alcohol* (specifically, the admission of powerlessness over drink). The other eleven all have to do with getting by, with learning to be honest and responsible and humble, to own up to your mistakes when you make them, to ask for help when you need it. I remember sitting in on one of many lectures that described the twelve steps and thinking, *Oh! So that's how you're supposed to live.* The serenity I heard at meetings seemed not only available at that moment, but attainable.

When I got home two weeks later, I did everything I'd been told, followed every last suggestion. I went to ninety meetings in ninety days, one each night. I forced myself to raise my hand during meetings and tell people I was new. I asked people for their phone numbers and I called them up, feeling as timid and self-conscious as a teenage boy calling up a girl for a date. I felt like an alien in my own life and I don't think I've ever been so scared.

My first day home, at Michael's house, I opened up the refrigerator and froze, unable to quite believe there was no beer in there, nothing substantial to reach for. That night we sat on his sofa and watched a movie. It was the first time since I'd known him, the first time ever, that we'd passed an evening together without a drink and I felt exactly like Michael Keaton in *Clean and Sober*, anxious and restless and disoriented, as though I was trying to adjust to an amputation.

Which, of course, I was. You take away the drink and you take away the single most important method of coping you have. How to talk to people without a drink. How to sit on the sofa and watch TV and not crawl right out of your own skin. How to experience a real emotion—pain or anxiety or sadness—without an escape route, a quick way to anesthetize it. How to sleep at night.

The answer in AA is both simple and complex: you just do it, a day at a time. You practice. You ask for help. For a long time you panic and squirm and you live through the discomfort until it eases. And it does ease.

I got back from rehab on a Saturday and went back to work two days later. That first day I asked my friend Beth, the only person in my office who knew I'd quit drinking, to go out for coffee with me after work. I was so accustomed to going out for drinks with her, to sipping that first glass and sliding gently into that more relaxed and sociable version of myself, I thought I might wither away, right there at the coffee shop. We went to a café in Harvard Square, and I remember feeling acutely self-conscious, groping for things to talk about, verbally clumsy, *stupid*.

You do everything for the first time. Here I am, going to a restaurant for the first time and not drinking. Here I am, at a work-related function, not drinking. Here I am, celebrating my birthday without a drink. Liquor stores loom out at you on every street corner, people holding glasses of wine or tumblers of Scotch jump out at you from TV and movie screens, and you realize how pervasive alcohol is in our culture, how it's absolutely *everywhere*, how completely foreign it is to abstain.

Can I get you something from the bar? Here's the wine list. Anything to drink?

You can't go a week without hearing phrases like that, and sometimes, especially early on, they infuriate you, constant reminders that everyone in the world can have a drink, a single simple drink at the end of the day to take off the edge, and you can't. One drink. Just one drink.

A few weeks after I quit drinking, I walked into Michael's house at the end of the day and sat down on the sofa. I wanted a drink, a single glass of white wine, so badly I thought I'd cry. I just sat there with my teeth clenched. I thought about pouring the wine into the glass, walking with the glass from the kitchen to the living room, curling up on the sofa and taking the first sip. I wanted that wine so badly I could taste it, and the only thing that kept me from rushing out to the liquor store to buy a bottle was the understanding that as soon as I drank the first glass, I'd be obsessing about the next one, and the next and the next and the next. I would not drink one glass; I would drink—and obsess about—one bottle, possibly more. That's the only option at times like that, to think past the first glass, to think it through. You've never had "just one drink" in your life.

I held on to the things people in meetings told me. *One day at a time. You don't have to tell yourself you're never going to drink again. Just today. Just do it today.* I clung to stories about people whose lives got better. I heard the phrase, "If you're new, keep coming," and I kept coming. Just as when I drank, I didn't know what else to do.

People do get and stay sober without AA. Pete Hamill did, and hasn't had a drink for more than twenty years. Wilfrid Sheed went to meetings for a few years, stopped when he realized he was going for the entertainment alone, and has stayed sober without them. But I'm sure I couldn't stay away from alcohol without AA, without the support and the sense of camaraderie and the knowledge that it's out there, a place where you can constantly be reminded of what you are, where you came from, what you need to do in order to change.

After a month or so I began to realize that the meeting at the end of the day provided relief the same way the drink used to, that it gave me the same sense of easing into a kind of comfort. AA is like a daily shot of hope: you see people around you grow and change and flower. You hear people struggling, out loud, to get through the days. Meetings keep things in perspective.

During my first year a woman at a meeting raised her hand and said that her brother had died very suddenly of a brain aneurysm several days earlier. The woman was still shell shocked and disbelieving but she talked for about five minutes about what it was like to get through this experience without a drink, about how painful it was but also how grateful she felt to be *present*, available to her family, capable of feeling the full range of emotions that accompany such experiences.

When people talk like that about their deepest pain, a stillness often falls over the room, a hush that's so deep and so deeply shared it feels like reverence. That stillness keeps me coming, and it helps keep me sober, reminding me what it means to be alive to emotion, what it means to be human.

16 *Healing*

Early sobriety has the quality of vigorous exercise, as though each repetition of a painful moment, gone through without a drink, serves to build up emotional muscle.

About a year after I quit drinking, I arranged to meet with Jack, the psychologist who knew my parents well and who'd filled me in on some of the details of my father's family history. Driving to his office, I thought about my father: how similar our patterns of ambivalence and duplicity had been, how alike we were, how much I missed him.

When I sat down with Jack, I talked generally about some of the ways my life had changed, how I felt less depressed and stuck than I used to, and then I asked what I'd come to find out: "Do you think my father was an alcoholic?"

Jack looked surprised, as though the answer was obvious. "Oh, *yes*," he said. "*He* thought so. He knew it."

I suppose I'd begun to think so too, once I understood my own relationship with alcohol more clearly. But hearing it articulated so blankly, a simple statement of fact delivered by someone who knew, made it real for the first time, and I felt a sharp stab of pain and horror for my father. It was the pain of understanding just how deeply our alliance ran, and the pain of grave disloyalty, as though I'd been caught breaking a profound family pattern, a code of behavior.

Jack said it had taken my father a long time to admit to his alcoholism and even longer to say it out loud—until he was dying.

That's where the feeling of horror came from. I pictured my father in the last eleven months of his life, the only time I knew him when he didn't drink, and I wondered about what it must have been like for him, to see the patterns of his life that clearly, to understand how deeply liquor had shaped and constricted his relationships, to do all this while he was dying and he couldn't, just couldn't, change the outcome. I felt so sad, imagining that, and of course the first thing I thought was: *God, I want a drink.*

Early in my father's illness, one night when we were alone together at the dining-room table, my father had looked at me and mused aloud, "I wonder if my death will be liberating for you."

At the time I didn't say a word—the comment seemed ghoulish to me—but I thought about it on the way back to my car after seeing Jack. I remember walking along the sidewalk, aware of an odd sensation that did, in fact, seem like a kind of freedom. I felt like I was on the verge of something, a way of seeing myself or living my life that no longer required such entanglement with my father, a capacity for choice I'd never felt before. The clarity that comes with sobriety may have had more to do with that feeling than my father's death did, but I wondered that night if the two were related, if I would have been able to let go of alcohol without letting go of my father first. Perhaps, perhaps not, but heading along toward my car I had the sense that I was letting go of something, some need to define myself first and foremost as my father's daughter, with all the dark complexity that entailed.

I drove to Michael's feeling oddly wistful. I wondered if my father would have been proud of me, to see me acknowledge my own alcoholism, or if he would have seen my sobriety as an act of abandonment somehow, a willful separation from our alliance.

A minute later, stopped at a traffic light, I closed my eyes and thought, *Please be proud of me.* Perhaps I willed the feeling, or perhaps I imagined it, but I sensed just then that he *would* feel pride, an aching kind of pride, as though if he'd looked down at me that moment, he would have seen me as somehow picking up where he left off.

I cried that night for the first time in a long while: cried over my father's life and death; cried for the regrets he'd died with; cried with a mixture of sadness and wonder and guilt, understanding for the first time that in getting sober, I was holding on to the pieces of him I cherished—his insight, his wisdom, his charm—but also leaving him behind in some way, giving myself the chance to move past our ancient pact and toward something better.

Better. The word seems thin, even a little deceptive. Sobriety is less about "getting better" in a clear, linear sense than it is about subjecting yourself to change, to the inevitable ups and downs, fears and feelings, victories and failures, that accompany growth. You *do* get better—or at least you *can*—but that happens almost by default, by the simple fact of being present in your own life, of being aware and able, finally, to act on the connections you make.

About a year after he got sober, my friend Mitch noticed a spigot on the side of his house. He'd lived in the house for eleven years, drinking in it for ten, and he'd noticed that spigot many times, always wondering, *Gee, I wonder where you turn that thing on.*

That day he went into the basement, looked up at the network of pipes on the ceiling, and then followed them until he found the one that led to the spigot. And there it was: a small handle that, if turned counterclockwise, allowed water to flow through the pipe and out to the tap on the side of his house. A minor revelation, of limited consequence, but it meant that Mitch could now take a hose, attach it to the spigot, turn on the water, and wash his car.

He tells this story metaphorically, by way of describing a quality of deliberateness that creeps into life when you put down the drink. When you're actively alcoholic, you don't bother to solve problems, even petty ones, in part because you have no faith in your ability to make changes and in part because even the smallest changes seem improbable and risky. You begin to feel like you're trapped in quicksand: any move you make threatens to drag you down farther so after a while you just stop, resign yourself to the most complete form of inertia. Mitch used to sit there on that porch, glancing at the spigot, and thinking: *What's the point?* You get so used to being a passive participant in your own life, so used to being entrenched in the same gray rituals and patterns, that even the most trivial action—turning on a spigot, finding the damn source of water—seems useless and overwhelming.

The first time I heard Mitch tell that story at a meeting, I looked around and saw a dozen heads bobbing up and down in recognition. A lot of people laughed, but the laughter was em-pathic, the kind that comes from knowing exactly what it's like to be stuck there on the porch feeling so utterly inert.

People in AA meetings often talk about struggling with the littlest things: getting their laundry done, or flossing their teeth, or dragging themselves out for a walk or a jog. These can sound silly and beside the point until you realize that the struggle is really with passivity and self-loathing, with the mundane activi-ties and daily decisions that can determine how you see yourself from moment to moment. *Do you sit there entrenched in the inertia? Do you yield to the fear of motion, yield to the vision of yourself as lazy and unworthy and bad? Or do you get up off the damn porch and do something? Do you show yourself that you're competent and capable and decent?* Passivity is corrosive to the soul; it feeds on feelings of integrity and pride, and it can be as tempting as a drug.

Early on, I heard a woman at a meeting say that with each decision in sobriety, you are faced with two possible choices: the alcoholic choice or the healthy choice. The alcoholic choice is the self-sabotaging one, the one that makes you feel self-pitying or resentful or somehow defeated. The healthy choice is the one that reinforces your vision of yourself as a better person, more in charge of your life, equipped with options. A few months later I heard someone else describe this equation another way. He said, "If it feels warm and fuzzy and comfortable and protective, it's probably the alcoholic choice. If it feels dangerous and scary and threatening and painful, it's probably healthy."

Nods all around. Getting up off the porch can be all of those things. When you've been sitting still for so long that all your bones and joints have stiffened into one position, even the smallest motion can hurt.

Big motions hurt more. I remember standing in my aunt's living room during my first sober Thanksgiving, after nine months without a drink. A pile of relatives from my mother's family were there—aunts, uncles, cousins—and the atmosphere was characteristically restrained and genteel, the way it had been at those Sunday dinners at my grandmother's house when I was a kid. The men wore neckties and polished shoes; the women crossed their legs and nibbled hors d'oeuvres, blotting their lips with cocktail napkins.

Sitting there, I listened to the soft hush of conversation, the gentle clink of wineglasses, and I felt the stirring of an ancient set of feelings: an old anger, a deep disquiet, a sudden wish to stand up in the middle of that room and *yell* something, shatter all that restraint. I felt as though an old, rebellious part of me was straining to get out: the part that resisted and resented our calm, orderly family style; the part that grew up longing and yet fearing to be different; the part that wanted to call attention to whatever pains and rages lurked beneath the surface, instead of relinquishing them to the quiet.

Self-pity triggers my craving for alcohol more than any other emotion. I felt invisible in that room. I'd been there for more than an hour, and in characteristic deference to privacy and decorum no one had said a word about what felt like my triple losses: my second Thanksgiving without my father; my first without my mother and without alcohol. I felt exactly the way I'd felt in my anorexic twenties, an eighty-pound ghost of a girl huddled over a plate of turkey, and exactly the way I'd felt at age six, shy at the table and unable to crawl into my mother's lap.

I had a fantasy of myself drinking just then, not drinking in the sophisticated, martini-glass sense but in the raging, obliterating sense, drinking to get drunk, drinking in order to yield to that rebellious urge and show everyone in the room just how angry I was, just how out of place I felt, just how self-destructive I could be in response.

I thought: *This is why I drank: to medicate these very feelings.* And then I tried to carry that idea a step farther. I thought: *This is why I got sober, to deal with this anger, this sense of disappointment.* At *last.* I wanted a drink just then, badly, but I didn't have one.

Not drinking is a choice one makes every day, sometimes many times a day. The immediate decision is clear: either you pick up the glass or you don't. But in instances like the one at Thanksgiving, a larger set of choices can be at work too. Not drinking that day meant acknowledging certain truths: that self-destruction would have served no one, least of all me; that medicating those emotions wouldn't resolve or alter them; that, ultimately, the drink provided a futile, self-defeating solution. Alcohol is what shielded me all those years from the messy business of standing in that room with my own emotions, coming to terms with my own quiet, restrained, complicated heritage, finding ways to tend to my own needs, instead of waiting for others to jump in and tend to them for me. In a word, alcohol is what protected me from growing up.

That seems like such an obvious insight, so simple it borders on the banal, but until that moment I'd never really grasped the idea that growth was something you could *choose,* that adulthood might be less a chronological state than an emotional one which you decide, through painful acts, to both enter and maintain. Like a lot of people I know (alcoholics and not), I'd spent most of my life waiting for maturity to hit me from the outside, as though I'd just wake up one morning and be done, like a roast in the oven.

Men—my father, Julian—might flavor the process, provide me with a dash of sophistication here and a pinch of self-assurance there, but by and large I saw growing up as something that happened *to* you. In some ways giving up an addiction involves reversing that equation, understanding finally that growth comes from the inside out, from trying and failing and trying again. When you quit drinking you stop waiting. You begin to let go of the wish, age old and profound and essentially human, that someone will swoop down and do all that hard work, growing up, for you. You start living your own life.

Circumstances—in particular, my parents' deaths—had been chipping away at my childhood for some time, but most of these had been out of my control. Choosing to get sober may have been the first truly adult decision I'd ever made, a step toward growth taken on my own behalf.

A few weeks after Thanksgiving I went out to dinner with an old drinking pal named Edward, a man in his forties I knew from back in the Elaine days. Edward is well known in book- and magazine-publishing circles and he's arrogant in the name-dropping sense, full of self-conscious bravado. He's also somewhat lecherous, the kind of guy who touches you a little too much, and stares at different body parts—your mouth, your breasts—when he talks to you. This didn't really bother me much in the past. Edward had been one of a series of casual friends I'd targeted as different from my family, representing a more brash and boisterous style, so I'd always liked hanging out with him, or thought I did. We'd go out to dinner a couple of times a year, and he'd always take me to fancy restaurants, and I'd sit and sip my expensive wine and listen to him tell stories and numb away any discomfort his ogling generated with the drink.

This time, with me sober, he took me to Biba, an elegant restaurant in the Back Bay, and he sat right next to me in a banquette, instead of across the table, and every time his leg brushed against me, every time he touched my hair or my arm, I had to resist the urge to take up my fork and plunge it straight into his hand. I didn't have the nerve to move, or to ask him to move, and I certainly didn't have the courage to plunge my fork into his hand, or to tell him he was being an odious, leering creep, so I just sat there, ate my food, watched him drink his wine, and felt genuinely ill at ease for ninety-three full minutes. I clocked it: *Here I am, forty-seven minutes of discomfort; here I am, fifty-three minutes; here I am, ninety-three minutes.*

On his fourth glass of wine Edward looked at me and said, "You are an incredible woman." He was staring at my chest and I could smell the wine on his breath and for an instant I had a feeling of concentrated rage, as though every moment I'd ever sat in a restaurant feeling objectified and powerless and leered at had coalesced into that one minute. I thought: *This is no fun without a drink. No fun at all.* I managed to edge away from him and we left shortly afterward, but that evening would stay with me for a long time.

I drove home thinking about the trade-offs you make when you drink: about how many times I'd chosen drunken company over sustaining company in the past; about how hollow that is, opting for the trappings of intimacy—the restaurant, the candles, the wine—but shielding yourself from its warmth. That evening left me with a creepy feeling, as though I'd stepped back into old clothes and found them rubbing against me all wrong. I got home and took a shower. I haven't seen Edward again.

I'd love to say I woke up on my first day without a drink and simply found myself plucked out of my old life and plopped down in a new one, a clean, clear, self-reliant new one full of flowers and light, but I doubt that happens very often, if at all. For the first few weeks I felt sporadic surges of confidence and relief, a sense of possibilities that stemmed from understanding that I'd finally *done* something to improve my life.

That feeling has stayed with me, but it's tempered, regularly, by moments like the one in the restaurant with Edward. Anxiety looms and you think: *This is why I drank.* Sadness and shame wash up. *This is why I drank.* Feelings of rage surface. *This is why I drank.* The drink may have become the main obstacle between you and any hope of change, but a hundred other obstacles lie behind it and most of those have to do with emotions, the very beasts you never learned to contend with in any other way.

Sometimes I think I am literally phobic about feelings. A few nights before the two-year anniversary of my mother's death, I found myself at home, alone, with an unplanned evening ahead. I stood there in my living room at one point and I could sense it, an edge of emptiness and grief tugging at me, and I wanted to *run*, flee, eradicate it. *This is why I drank. This is why I drank.* The feeling is immediate and laced with panic, and so is the response: *Anesthetize me. Fuck it.*

In the end I lit a cigarette, another great antidote to strong emotion, and I made myself a cup of tea. The feeling abated, as it always does despite your unshakable conviction that it won't, and then the feeling passed. Another moment, gotten through without a drink. Another emotional muscle flexed.

Like vigorous exercise sobriety can also be tiring, wearying. A lot of people say the problems in their lives that were directly related to alcohol cleared up immediately after they stopped drinking, or nearly so: if you went on terrific spending binges every time you drank, you'll probably stop when you put down the liquor; if you got drunk and drove recklessly, you'll no doubt begin driving more carefully. Those are fairly predictable outcomes.

What some people call the "ism" problems of alcoholism take more time. You don't wake up on Day One of sobriety with fabulous new money-management skills. The rage and self-destructiveness that compelled you to get in that car and career down highways don't vanish overnight. You drank to drown out fear, to dilute anxiety and doubt and self-loathing and painful memories, and when you stop drinking, all those emotions come to the fore, sometimes in a torrent that feels overwhelming. Putting down the drink may give you an opportunity to solve problems, but abstinence won't solve them on its own. Depending on your mood, that realization can seem either burdensome or hopeful. Or both.

The simple admission of alcoholism can have that dual quality, as well, by turns feeling like a great burden and a great source of hope. Some days, bad days, I'm just plain sick of it, sick of *being* an alcoholic, sick of thinking like an alcoholic, sick of having to maintain the vigilance of sobriety: *Don't drink, go to meetings, ask for help. Don't do the things that trigger the wish to drink; don't get too hungry, angry, lonely, or tired* (the acronym in recovery for those four states is HALT).

I find myself carping on days like that: *I'm sick of myself, I'm getting on my own nerves. In my next life I want to be happy-go-lucky and nonaddictive and dumb.* I fall into self-pity, dangerous waters, and I feel angry that I can't do things that "normal" people can: have a beer, one simple fucking beer. At times like that all I can do is exercise that same set of mental muscles, do what I've been told. I collect myself. I take a deep breath. I try to remember that one simple beer never solved anything, that the way to the other side of a bad feeling is through it, not around it.

I still think about drinking, and not drinking, many many times each day, and sometimes I think I always will. We live in an alcohol-saturated world; it's simply impossible to avoid the stuff. When I read the papers now, I find myself scanning the pages for items about drink-related disasters, things that will reinforce my sense that I've made the right choice: what celebrity got pulled over for drunk driving; what college kid got drunk and plunged out of a five-story window; what alcohol-fueled argument between a couple fired up into a case of domestic violence. Evidence of the havoc liquor can wreak is in there in black and white, almost every day, but it's not nearly as prevalent as the other messages: the liquor ads, the images of gaiety and romance, phrases like CHAMPAGNE BRUNCH: $19.95. At times I've grumbled to friends about longing for a return to Prohibition, a gripe that stems from the feeling, familiar among many alcoholics, that if *I* can't drink, no one should. But alcohol occupies a large role in the social world and it's important for me to remember that I have to come to terms with it, that I still have a relationship with liquor, even if the relationship now has the quality of a divorce rather than an active involvement.

Yes, a divorce. I am currently divorced from white wine and beer and Scotch and Cognac, and for the entire first year after the initial separation, I took out my own version of a restraining order, avoiding alcohol the way you'd avoid running into an ex-lover at a restaurant, steering clear of places I might see liquor, people I might see it with. I felt particularly afraid of wine and terribly vulnerable, worried about what dark pangs of longing the mere sight of it might evoke, the mere smell. That's abated somewhat, but not entirely.

I once heard a woman say that as an alcoholic, a part of her will always be deeply attracted to alcohol, which seemed a very simple way of putting it, and very true. The attraction—the pull, the hunger, the yearning—doesn't die when you say good-bye to the drink, any more than the pull toward a bad lover dies when you finally walk out the door. Alcoholism is a disease of relapse and I understand that no single force—not meetings, not will-power, not prayer or guidance or simple wanting—can guarantee that I won't slide back into the relationship, in exactly the same way one slides back into a destructive romance.

Acceptance—*I am an alcoholic; I cannot drink*—ebbs and flows like the sea, washing up one moment, receding the next. I can look back at the *way* I drank in those final years, I can find countless pieces of evidence to suggest that when I put alcohol into my system I experienced a set of physiological responses—a compulsiveness and loss of control—that other people don't. But I still have trouble connecting that to the concept of permanent, progressive *illness*. What about the times when I drank and didn't lose control? What about the times when alcohol still seemed to work, when it seemed such a pleasant social lubricant and path to relaxation? Couldn't I have just one? Those questions evoke a deep set of fears and worries, shared by many alcoholics: *Maybe I was just weak; maybe my drinking testified not to a physiological condition but to a profound character flaw, a moral failure.*

Those are difficult fears to live with, in part because they receive such widespread social support. The idea that alcoholism is a disease—dangerous and fatal if untreated—can be deeply threatening to a culture that not only harbors a profound distaste for illness of any kind but that also uses and glamorizes alcohol to the degree it does. If you like your daily six-pack or your gin-and-tonic at the end of the day, if you see drinking as part of your right as an adult member of society, you're not apt to look kindly on those of us who can't tolerate it. *Something must be wrong with her,* you may think. Or *I'm glad it's her and not me.*

The stigma surrounding alcoholism has abated a great deal in the past few decades, but it's still present, sometimes powerfully so. In my first year of sobriety I told only my closest friends and relatives that I'd quit drinking, and my reticence with others stemmed directly from a fear of being judged: *She must be a weak person.* I know, objectively, that the opposite is true; I know it takes strength to give up so insidious an addiction, but I find it difficult to fully internalize or appreciate that fact. Apparently, others do too. About a year after I quit drinking, a friend of the family took my sister aside and said, "Given the tremendous rate of relapse among alcoholics, and given that Caroline has stayed sober for this long, do you think that maybe she's not *really* an alcoholic?"

Would that it were so. Unfortunately, it's not. In the end it's up to me to understand that my alcoholism is a part of me, a reality I'm learning to live with, not a moral failing.

That's not always easy to see, and like most alcoholics I know, I still find myself playing mind games with definitions and acceptance. I sit in a meeting and hear someone talk about doing something drunk that I never did—going to jail, killing someone in a car wreck—and I think: *Well, maybe I wasn't that bad; maybe*

. . . I find myself staring at the ceiling at two-thirty in the morning asking questions: Did I ever *really try* to control my drinking? Couldn't I do it differently? Couldn't I give it one more shot? Or the wish for a drink just washes over me, hits from out of the blue, and it feels far bigger than me, too big, and the idea of total abstinence seems unthinkable. *Never?* I can't *ever* yield to this feeling? I can't *ever* seek that form of relief? Those are the worst moments, the scariest ones, and all you can really do is ride them out, wait for the feelings to pass, or share them with another alcoholic, who knows exactly—*exactly*—what those moments are like.

My friend Abby came over to Michael's house for dinner one night in her third month of sobriety. I opened the door and she stormed in, clutching two bottles of seltzer water, and she started yelling.

"This sucks!" she said. "It's a fucking Saturday night and I just want to sit at the table and drink red wine. It *sucks* that I can't do that!"

She was angry and frenzied and at that moment she couldn't believe that her rage would abate, that she'd be able to get through the evening and reach any sort of peace or optimism.

I stood there and said, "I know. It *does* suck," and I tried to tell her all the things people told me early on, when I felt that same way. I said, "Don't think about forever; it's too big. You only have to decide not to drink this one day." I said, "Break it up into small goals. Maybe decide not to drink for a year, or six months. If your life still sucks after that, you can always go back to drinking. It's always an option." And I waited for her storm to pass, which it did.

You wait. You get through. You mull over little bits of acquired wisdom. When you question your alcoholism, you say to yourself: *If I am an alcoholic, I shouldn't drink and if I'm not an alcoholic, I don't need to.* That's a nice piece of logic. You say: *People who aren't alcoholics do not lie in bed at two-thirty in the morning wondering if they're alcoholics.* A good reality check.

You say: *Help*. And the amazing thing is, you find it.

*   *   *

My terror that I'd be bored and lonely in sobriety abated almost immediately. In fact, as time goes on, I become more aware of how bored and lonely I was *while* I was drinking, and how much more textured and varied life seems without it. Abby once asked me to describe a typical evening in my drinking days, and I rolled my eyes and said, "Blah. Exactly the same thing, every night. I'd leave work, get drunk, watch TV, and go to bed."

She asked, "And how about now?"

I thought for a minute, then smiled and said, "Well, now I leave work, go to a meeting, watch TV, and go to bed."

She said, *"Excuse me?"*

But she also understood. The differences are internal, as though a kaleidoscope has shifted, yielding shapes in color instead of black-and-white. I work hard during the day and the work seems purer, as though it belongs to me in a new way. I leave my office each evening with a sense of calm I didn't know before, something that resembles dignity. Most nights I end up in a church basement instead of a bar, and even if I don't say a word during a meeting, I have the sense of being in the midst of a human place, where people are actively struggling with their lives, and I almost always leave meetings with a feeling of hope that was foreign in the past. I watch TV at night, or read or talk on the phone, and I retain what I have seen or read or said. I don't pass out on the sofa, or sit there with my eyes drooping, struggling to stay awake. I sleep at night, deeply and peacefully, and I wake up in the morning without a headache, and I don't worry when I run into people: *Did I say something stupid the last time I saw him? Did I make an ass of myself at her party?*

These may sound like minor differences—watching TV sober versus watching TV drunk, getting into bed versus falling into bed—but there are qualitative gulfs between the two. Not long ago I heard a woman in her ninth month of sobriety say that before she quit drinking, she had only two emotions, anxiety and despair. "Now I have, like, too many to count," she said, "and some of them suck, but some of them are really, really good."

Almost everyone in the room knew what she meant. Life becomes so insular and blank in the last stages of active alcoholism; the drinking at that point is much less a search for pleasure than it is a search for the absence of pain. Joy gets drowned out along with every other emotion, and to rediscover it in sobriety is an amazing thing, the emotional equivalent of realizing that your shoes are painfully tight and then sighing with relief when you finally take them off.

I find joy these days in the oddest places, the smallest ways. I set out my recycling bin every Tuesday night with an odd, quiet delight. Nothing in there these days but plastic milk cartons and empty water bottles. I go out to dinner with a friend and I take note of the fact that we are communicating without booze, that at last I am the chemically unaltered version of myself, and that, in fact, I can almost say I like that person. I relish the understanding that I'll drive home safely, and wake up remembering where my car is, how I got from the driveway to my bed.

Laughter is still new to me, or feels that way. Sometimes a pack of us women go out to dinner on Tuesday nights after a meeting, and we sit in a booth and howl. Sitting there, I sometimes realize how little laughing I did those last few years of drinking, how the drink seemed to drain my world of pleasure, slowly but surely, the way life drains out of a cut flower. If anybody had told me I'd laugh in sobriety as much as I do, I never would have believed it. But my life has acquired a quality of lightness, and a sense of possibilities I didn't even know I'd lost. The days seem simple and clean, so much simpler and cleaner than they did before. Half-consciously, I seem to have been following a suggestion I heard early on, a variation on the AA admonishment to "keep it simple": *Less drama, more laundry.*

I worry a little about the phenomenon of substitution, about whether I'll stumble into some new-and-improved method of fending off growth and strong emotion. At the moment I appear to be developing an abnormal attachment to my vacuum cleaner, having channeled my drive for control into a compulsion for cleanliness and order so strong I practically wander around my house with a ruler and protractor, making sure everything is lined up just so, at perfect angles. I've always been like that to an extent, but it's worse these days ("What's next?" Michael asks. "Plastic on the furniture? *Velvet ropes?*") and I'm particularly compulsive during periods of stress. I spent my first sober Mother's Day on my hands and knees, scrubbing the kitchen floor with so much vigor you would have thought I was trying to scour away grief itself.

But I've faced some grief more directly too. In my third month of sobriety my family buried my mother's ashes, underneath a cherry tree by our house in Martha's Vineyard. We dug a hole, poured the ashes in, then filled the hole and covered the spot with things she would have liked: a ring of white stones from the beach, a circle of dark, smooth stones inside that, some feathers and bits of beach glass. Later, after we'd all gone indoors, I slipped back outside by myself. Many AA groups give out chips to people in their first year, a way of marking different lengths of sobriety. They look like poker chips—a pale blue one to mark one month, a lavender one to mark two months, a dark blue one for three months, and so on. I had my two-month chip in my pocket, and I took it out and slid it under one of the rocks on the gravesite. I felt tremendous sorrow in that act, in the accompanying acknowledgment that she'd never get to see me in sobriety, that we'd never experience a different, richer sort of relationship. But I wanted to send her a message of some kind, to tell her I was okay, and standing there alone, I had the feeling she knew.

During the same period, in my third month, I began to find it too painful and too embarrassing to lie to Michael and Julian anymore and I began to tell the truth. This seems to be a phenomenon of sobriety, and a key one. You're still entrenched in all the same problems you had before you quit drinking, but you react differently, because reacting in the same old ways becomes intolerable; it just hurts too much without anesthesia.

One night, Julian and I had dinner and then went out for coffee. He asked me about work, if I thought I might leave my job within the next year and go on to something else.

I said, "No way. There've been enough big changes for one year." Then I added, quite deliberately, "My job for the next year is to stay sober and to figure out where my relationship with Michael is going."

He looked at me and nodded and didn't pursue it, but later that night, as I was driving him home, I asked him how he was feeling about our relationship and we started to talk. He told me all kinds of things I'd heard before, how I had let him down, how I had hurt him, how I'd disappointed him, and I realized, driving along, that I had a choice. I could respond in my usual defensive manner and get embroiled in a big fight about who did what to whom and which one of us hurt more. Or I could let him have his say, let him have his feelings, and let the matter go.

I let it go.

When you're drinking, you're too cloudy and too angry to step back like that. You can't see clearly and you certainly can't see that you have choices in how to deal with people, how to negotiate relationships. That night marked a turning point with Julian, as though I finally loosened my grip on him, and although we're still friendly to one another, we no longer harbor hopes or fantasies about what might happen, or so much rage about what did.

In my fourth month I bought a small house with some money I inherited from my parents and moved in there, alone. Michael and I still see each other most nights, but I am taking time to be alone, trying to understand myself as a person a little better before I make any choices about myself as part of a couple.

Choice is the key word here, and it's still a relatively foreign one for me. For the first time the relationship with Michael isn't washed over by waves of alcohol or haunted by Julian; for the first time I feel I'm with him because I've decided to be, not just because I've been buffeted in his direction by circumstances or pain or need. There's great relief in that: I often look at Michael

these days with the sense that I'm finally seeing the relationship
through glasses that have the right lenses. Sobriety has helped me
appreciate his kindness with greater purity and depth, as though it
exists in its own right now and not merely as a measure of comparison to Julian. I can't imagine a more steadfast or supportive
partner: Michael hasn't had a drink in front of me since I went off
to rehab, and he's as bolstering about my sobriety as anyone in
AA. These days he does a great imitation of me in the kitchen
before a dinner party, compulsively trying to drink a glass of wine
and smoke a cigarette and stir a sauce all at the same time, and I
appreciate his ability to capture the frenzied insanity of those days
and to help me laugh at it too. If I've been through a war, he's
been in charge of triage through most of it, and sometimes the
gratitude I feel toward him wells up so powerfully I think I'm
going to burst.

I wish I could say that sobriety resolves ambivalence of its own
accord; unfortunately, it doesn't, and I still find it difficult to face
a relationship without all my old sources of distraction and relief,
all my old exit ramps from the Big Questions: Who the hell am I
without those addictive crutches? What do I really want and
need? How do people learn to manage feelings of conflict or disappointment or doubt?

These, of course, are familiar questions: I'd asked them of my
old boyfriend David back in college; I'd asked them of myself as I
struggled to give up anorexia in my twenties; I'd asked them in
therapy for more than a decade; I'd asked them of Julian. But I'd
never really given myself a chance, a sober chance, to reach any
conclusions. Today, even bigger questions loom, more urgent
ones. Do I want to be married? Do I want a child? I don't know. I
can only sense the shadowy outlines of my own hopes, as though
the haze from all that alcohol still needs time to burn off.

Michael is patient, more tolerant of my ambivalence than I
am, and that, oddly enough, generates another sort of confusion.
I'm still not used to being with someone so accepting and
nonjudgmental, and I sometimes find myself feeling lost without

the chaos and drama of a more volatile relationship. At heart I'm not sure how comfortable I am with comfort, a phenomenon that seems to be familiar to lots of alcoholics and that raises unsettling questions: do I need to feel pain in order to feel passion? Is there some middle ground between conflict and comfort that I've failed to reach?

And so the pendulum swings back and forth, back and forth, with such predictability it would be laughable if it didn't cause me so much anxiety. I think about marrying Michael one day, leaving him the next, having children together one minute, packing up and hightailing it to Alaska another. I feel almost embarrassed about this sometimes, ashamed of my own confusion and ambivalence, as though a woman my age should be farther along this process, equipped with a clearer sense of her own needs and expectations, a greater tolerance for other people's limits.

Not long ago my brother-in-law commented to me that most women in their mid-thirties hold a sharklike view of relationships: either the romance is moving forward (toward marriage) or it's dead and they want out.

I just shrugged and said, "Not me. I'm just floating along. Or stagnating, depending on your point of view."

But then I have to remember that, in fact, I'm not really stagnating at all, just muddling along, trying to make up, in the psychic sense, for lost time, for lessons lost to all that liquor.

At meetings recently I've listened to a man I've come to respect a lot talk about leaving a long-term relationship, about the pain and healing that's accompanied it. He laughs at himself in the process, jokes about the volume of bad videos he's rented since he moved out and the irrational thoughts he's harbored about being alone. But I also sense a great deal of dignity in his struggle, and a great deal of courage.

He says, "I have to remember that there's not one aspect of this —not *one*—that would be improved by a drink or a drug."

I hold on to that thought every time I feel uneasy about the relationship with Michael, every time my instincts tell me to address the discomfort with alcohol. Faith is a new concept to me, too, but I seem to have acquired a bit of it: as long as I don't drink, as long as I expose my doubts and fears to the clear light and refuse to drown them in liquor, I believe I'll find my way, as a person, as part of a couple.

After I moved, maybe six months into sobriety, my friend Jane came over and we performed the Ritualistic Snipping of the Black Lycra Dress. This was a joyous occasion and we planned for it several days in advance.

Jane is one of my closest AA friends, a wise and thoughtful woman of forty-three with a delightful sense of the absurd, and when she got to my house that afternoon, you could see the zeal in her eyes.

"Okay," she said, "where is it?"

I ran upstairs and retrieved the dress and together we held it up in my kitchen by the light. Off the rack and without a body to stretch it out, the dress was about five inches wide, a long scrunchy tube of a thing with long scrunchy arms dangling from either side.

We both shuddered, standing before that symbol of such an unhappy, insecure, alcohol-soaked time, and when Jane reached for the scissors and performed the first ritualistic *snip*, I felt something in my heart lighten, as though a piece of me had turned toward the sun.

We snipped that dress into a dozen pieces and decided to give one piece to each of my closest friends, to dispose of in my honor as they saw fit (my sister flung hers out her car window on the Massachusetts Turnpike). Then we moved outside and performed the Ritualistic Burning of the Black Thong Teddy. We rolled the little lace thing up into a ball, doused it with lighter fluid, and set it on fire in the barbecue.

"Hah!" Jane said. "The end of an era!"

I smiled and smiled, and as the smoke from the flaming teddy circled up into the sky, I wondered if any of it reached my parents, if their spirits could see me somehow, and know that I was on the right road.

These days I go to four or five meetings a week, and they help keep me grounded and stable and sure of myself. Sometimes I still can't believe I'm sitting in church basements after work instead of elegant bars, sipping coffee from a foam cup instead of wine from a lovely glass. The act seems so contrary to the image I cultivated for so long, ridiculous almost: Me? In AA? But the meetings make me remember, and they keep me scared. I hear people tell their stories and the details stick with me for hours—how someone got rip-roaring drunk and drove home, how someone hid liquor in a closet, how someone lost all self-respect and pride and hope. The details bring me right back, and they help me feel grateful that I've found a different way to live.

So do the people who struggle, and the people who don't make it the first time around. You see people in their very first weeks of sobriety, people who are frightened and despairing and not at all sure that meetings are going to help them, and you breathe a sigh of relief, relief that you've gotten past the worst of that stage, relief that you've figured out what it means to be hopeful. Or you see people who relapse, who go out and drink and then come back looking beaten and broken and whipped, and you close your eyes and pray they make it, pray that sobriety will stick this time. You say to yourself: That's the alternative. That could be me. You say: That *was* me.

A few months after my one-year anniversary I went to the meeting I usually go to on Wednesday nights, on the ground floor of a church outside of Boston. It's a big meeting—about fifty people each week—and it's oriented toward alcoholics in their first year of sobriety. One person tells his or her story for the first half hour, and then the meeting opens up, first to those in their first month of sobriety, then to those with three months or less, then six months or less, and so on.

A dozen people must have spoken that night. I heard a woman named Megan, sober for about six months, talk about being in incredible pain—losing both her job and custody of her son—but getting through it, managing to get through it without a drink. I heard a guy named Bill talk about living with fear—he'd lost his job, too, and he was terrified of looking for another, and he had to keep reminding himself that there's a big difference between walking through fears, which you do in sobriety, and escaping them, which you do through drink. I heard people talk about being angry and hopeless, and about being grateful and relieved, and about just getting through the day.

At the end of the meeting there was a presentation for a young guy named John, who was celebrating one year without a drink. He's a model AA citizen, the kind of guy who goes to tons of meetings and sits in the front row at every one and always raises his hand, and I'd watched him work all year, work really hard to live with his own feelings one day after the next and just keep coming. He was so happy that evening, so grateful to get that one-year medallion, and so moved by the amount of support he'd gotten over the year, that his eyes welled up and his voice kept cracking.

"I can't thank you all enough," he said, and his face was the picture of hope.

I sat near the back and looked out over the room. Familiar faces, unfamiliar faces, all of us more or less like John, pulling in the same direction. Then I had an image of every person in that room climbing into bed that night, all fifty of us getting into our beds clean and sober, another day without a drink behind us. It was a simple image but it filled me with a range of complicated feelings: appreciation for the simple presence of all those people; admiration for their courage and strength; a tinge of melancholy for the amount of pain it must have taken each and every one of them to put down the drink; affection for their humanity.

I didn't realize until hours later that there was a name for that feeling. It's called love.

Appendix A

Source Notes

CHAPTER 2: DOUBLE LIFE I

page
13   The skid-row bum represents three to five percent of the alcoholic population: Robert O'Brien and Morris Chafetz, M.D., *The Encyclopedia of Alcoholism* (Second Edition), edited by Glen Evans (New York: Facts on File, 1982), p. 186.

CHAPTER 5: *IN VODKA VERITAS*

page
61   The wine, beer, and liquor industries spend more than $1 billion each year in advertising: O'Brien and Chafetz, op. cit., p. 7.

CHAPTER 6: SEX

page
77   The role of alcohol in unwanted sexual advances on college campuses: Henry Wechsler, Andrea Davenport, George Dowdall, Barbara Moeykens, and Sonia Castillo, *Health and Behavioral Consequences of Binge Drinking in College: A National Survey of Students at 140 Campuses*, *Journal of the American Medical Association* (December 1994).

77   The role of alcohol in rapes on college campuses: CASA Commission on Substance Abuse at Colleges and Universities, *Rethinking Rites of Passage: Substance Abuse on America's Campuses* (New York: Columbia University, June 1994).

CHAPTER 8: ADDICTION

page
113   15.3 million Americans in 1988 met the criteria for alcohol abuse or alcohol dependence: Secretary of Health and Human Services, *Eighth Special Report to the U.S. Congress on Alcohol and Health* (1993), p. xxi.

114   Alcohol contributes to nearly 100,000 deaths annually: J. McGinnis and W. Folge, *Actual Causes of Death in the United States*, *Journal of the American Medical Association* (November 1993).

114   Those afflicted by the disease and other illnesses it causes occupy as many as half the hospital beds in the U.S. on any given day: Nan Robertson, *Getting Better: Inside Alcoholics Anonymous* (New York: William Morrow & Co., Inc., 1988), p. 184.

Getting Better: Inside Alcoholics Anonymous (New York: William Morrow & Co., Inc., 1988), p. 184.

114   Alcohol is a factor in approximately fifty percent of all homicides: Secretary of Health and Human Services, op. cit., p. 246.

114   Alcohol is a factor in approximately thirty percent of all suicides: National Institute on Alcohol Abuse and Alcoholism, *Alcohol Research: Promise for the Decade* (August 1991), p. 3.

115   Asian Flush Syndrome: O'Brien and Chafetz, op. cit., p. 39.

115   Alcohol addiction as a neurological phenomenon: "Clinical Crossroads: Conferences with Patients and Doctors at Boston's Beth Israel Hospital," produced and edited by Thomas L. Delbanco, M.D., and Jennifer Daley, M.D., *Journal of the American Medical Association* (September 1995). The author also wishes to thank Dr. Steven E. Hyman, associate professor of psychiatry at Harvard Medical School and director of psychiatric research at Massachusetts General Hospital, for clarifying the material in this section.

116   Controversy about Jellinek's disease concept of alcoholism: O'Brien and Chafetz, op. cit., p. 89.

118   Rand Corporation statistics on relapse: *The Course of Alcoholism: Four Years after Treatment* (January 1980).

CHAPTER 9: SUBSTITUTION

page
124   The $33 billion diet- and weight-loss industry: Molly O'Neill, "Congress Looking into the Diet Business," *The New York Times* (March 28, 1990).

CHAPTER 10: DENIAL

page
146   About half the alcohol in the U.S. is consumed by eleven percent of the population: O'Brien and Chafetz, op. cit., p. 73.

CHAPTER 13: DOUBLE LIFE II

page
175   $98.6 billion economic drain: National Institute on Alcohol Abuse and Alcoholism, *Alcohol Health? Research World*, Vol. 18, No. 3, 1994.

175   About 23,000 lives lost to drunk-driving accidents: National Institute on Alcohol Abuse and Alcoholism, op. cit., p. 3.

175   An additional 30,000 lives lost to other (nonvehicular) injuries incurred while under the influence: O'Brien and Chafetz, op. cit., p. 2.

Appendix B

Where to get help

The only requirement for membership in Alcoholics Anonymous is a desire to stop drinking. Accordingly, most AA meetings are open to anyone who needs or wants help. No matter how fearful, tentative, or skeptical you may be, you can walk into most AA meetings, take a seat, and just listen. There are no fees either – AA is financed entirely by volunteer contributions from members – so the only thing you need is willingness.

Most AA meetings are open to the general public as well as to recovering alcoholics, although a small proportion of meetings are open to alcoholics only; others are organized around specific concerns or groups – in some cities, for example, there are meetings for gay men or lesbians and meetings just for women or men. The best way to find your first meeting is to call Alcoholics Anonymous, which is listed below. Local AA offices are staffed by volunteers, themselves recovering alcoholics, who can help you find a nearby meeting, steer you toward a specific group, or direct you to a beginner's meeting, oriented toward newcomers to AA. For further information or literature on AA or Al-Anon, contact the following:

Alcoholics Anonymous – General Service Office
P O Box 1
Stonebow House
Stonebow
York YO1 2NJ

01904 644026

Al–Anon Family Groups (UK & Eire)
61 Great Dover Street
London
SE1 4YF

0171 403 0888 – 24hr confidential helpline for families and friends

Drinkline
National Alcohol Helpline

0345 320202

About the Author

Caroline Knapp graduated magna cum laude from Brown University in 1981. She is currently a contributing editor for *New Woman* magazine and British *Cosmopolitan*, and a columnist for the *Boston Phoenix*, where she worked as lifestyle editor for four years. Her work has appeared in *Mademoiselle* and *The Utne Reader*, among others. Her previous book, *Alice K.'s Guide to Life*, was published in 1994. She lives in Cambridge, Massachusetts.